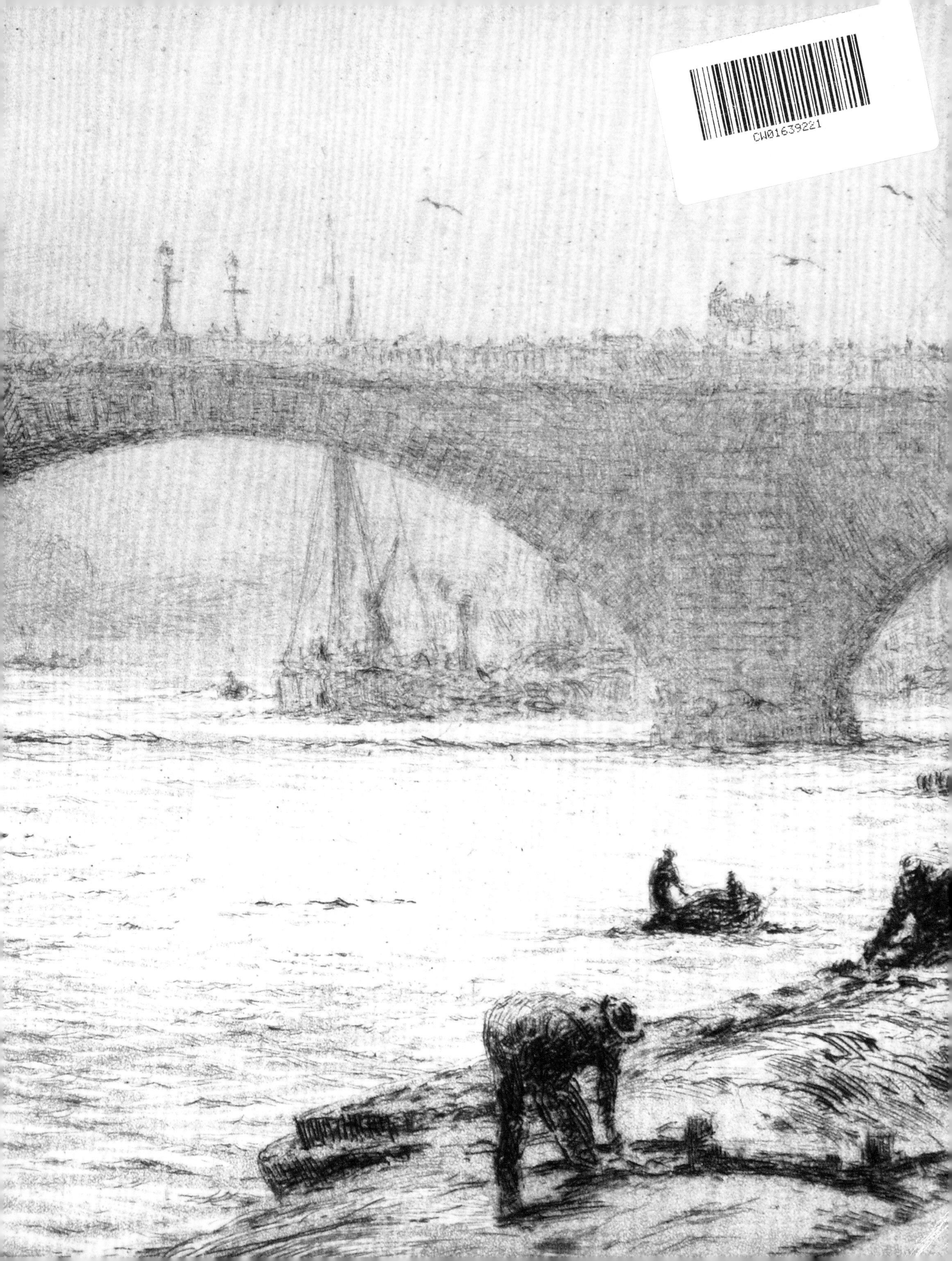

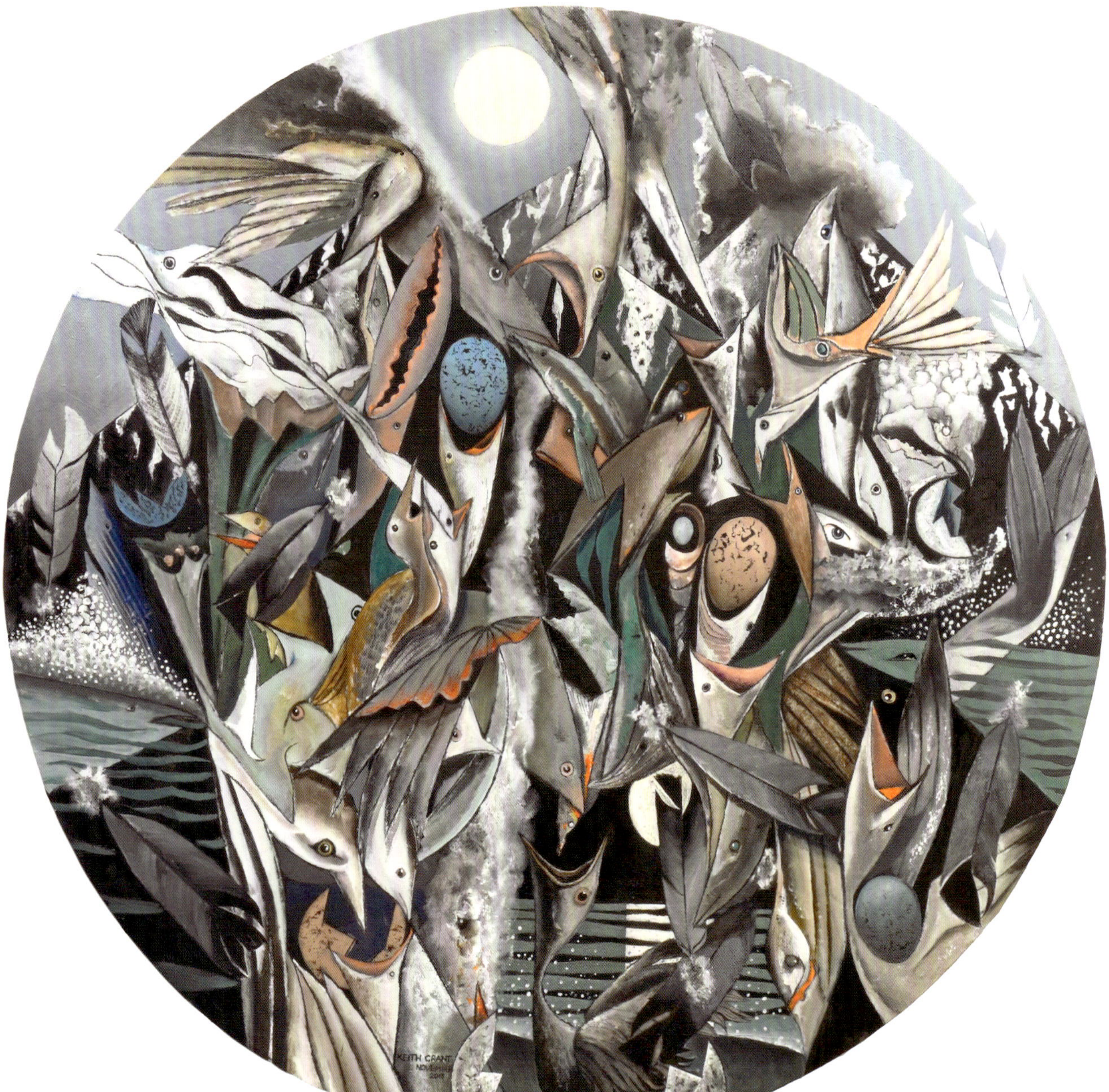
KEITH GRANT

Chris Beetles Summer Show 2014

CHRIS BEETLES GALLERY

8 & 10 Ryder Street
St James's
London
SW1Y 6QB
020 7839 7551
gallery@chrisbeetles.com
www.chrisbeetles.com

IBSN 978-1-905738-64-9

Catalogue in publication data is available from the British Library

Written and researched by David Wootton
Edited by Catherine Andrews and David Wootton
Design by Jeremy Brook of Graphic Ideas
Photography by Julian Huxley-Parlour
Reproduction by www.cast2create.com
Colour separation and printing by Geoff Neal Litho Limited

Front cover: William Walcot, *The Air Show* [57]
Front endpaper: William Lionel Wyllie, *London Bridge* [36]
Frontispiece: Keith Grant, *Tondo* [122]
Back endpaper: Edmund Blampied, *Charity Concert* [114]

EDWARD LEAR

Edward Lear (1812-1888)

Though now best known for his nonsense poems and drawings for children, Edward Lear made his initial reputation as an ornithological illustrator, and then earned his living as a landscape painter. During extensive travels in Europe, the Middle East and Asia, he made frequent, evocative sketches that acted as the basis for astonishing oils and watercolours.

Edward Lear was born at Bowman's Lodge, Upper Holloway, London on 12 May 1812, the second youngest of the 21 children of Jeremiah Lear, a stockbroker and member of the Fruiterers' Company. Educated by his eldest sisters, Ann and Sarah, he learned to paint in the family's own art room, and began to earn his living as a painter at the age of 15. He was employed as an ornithological draughtsman from the age of 17, and made his name in the next few years with books of coloured plates, beginning with *Illustrations of the Family of Psittacidae, or Parrots* (published in parts between 1830 and 1832). The President of the Zoological Society, Lord Stanley (later the Earl of Derby), invited Lear to stay at Knowsley in order to produce an accurate record of his collection of living specimens and skins, and this later resulted in the private printing of *Gleanings from the Menagerie and Aviary at Knowsley Hall* (1846; compiled by John E Gray, lithographed by J W Moore and coloured by Gabriel Bayfield). The stay would also lead to the publication of his best-known volume, *The Book of Nonsense* (1846), an elaboration of drawings done for the Earl's children.

In 1837, the Earl enabled Lear to make his first journey to Italy, the artist then settling in Rome for a decade, and establishing himself as a topographical painter. Having suffered from asthma and bronchitis from infancy, he found the Mediterranean climate kind to his health, and returned to England only for short visits. However, he was known in his home country – initially through albums of lithographs, and later through the paintings that he exhibited at the Royal Academy, the British Institution and the Society of British Artists. Impressed by the lithographs of his landscapes, Queen Victoria invited him to give her some drawing lessons. When in England, he also attempted to expand his own technical expertise by studying at the Royal Academy Schools (1850) and working with William Holman Hunt *en plein air* (1852).

From 1853, Lear spent long winters abroad – in Egypt and the Middle East (1853, 1857), in Corfu and other parts of Greece (1854, 1861-62), and on the French Riviera (1864-65, 1867-68). His last major sketching tour would be to India in the years 1873-75. By then, he had settled into Villa Emily, a house that he built for himself in San Remo. It was named after the second wife of Lord Tennyson, Lear having met and befriended the couple in 1871. When he built a second house for himself in San Remo, in 1881, he called it Villa Tennyson. He died there on 29 January 1888. A year later, a selection of his landscape drawings based on Tennyson's poems were published in a limited edition. However, by that time his fame as a nonsense writer and illustrator had eclipsed his achievement as a topographer.

His work is represented in numerous public collections, including the British Museum, The Courtauld Gallery, the Government Art Collection, the V&A and the Tate; the Ashmolean Museum (Oxford), The Fitzwilliam Museum (Cambridge), Liverpool Public Library, the Walker Art Gallery (Liverpool) and The Whitworth Art Gallery (Manchester); and Blacker-Wood Library, McGill University (Montreal), Houghton Library, Harvard University (Cambridge MA), the Museum of Fine Arts (Boston) and Paul Mellon Center for British Art at New Haven.

Further reading

Peter Levi, *Edward Lear: A Life*, London: Tauris Parke Paperbacks, 2013 (revised ed); Briony Llewellyn, 'Lear, Edward (*b* Holloway, London, 12 May 1812; *d* San Remo, Italy, 29 Jan 1888)', Jane Turner (ed), *The Dictionary of Art*, London: Macmillan, 1996, vol 18, pages 904-906; Vivien Noakes, *Edward Lear 1812-1888*, London: Royal Academy of Arts, 1985; Vivien Noakes, 'Lear Edward (1812-1888)', H C G Matthew and Brian Harrison (eds), *Oxford Dictionary of National Biography*, Oxford University Press, 2004, vol 32, pages 994-1000; Vivien Noakes, *The Painter Edward Lear*, Newton Abbot: David & Charles, 1991

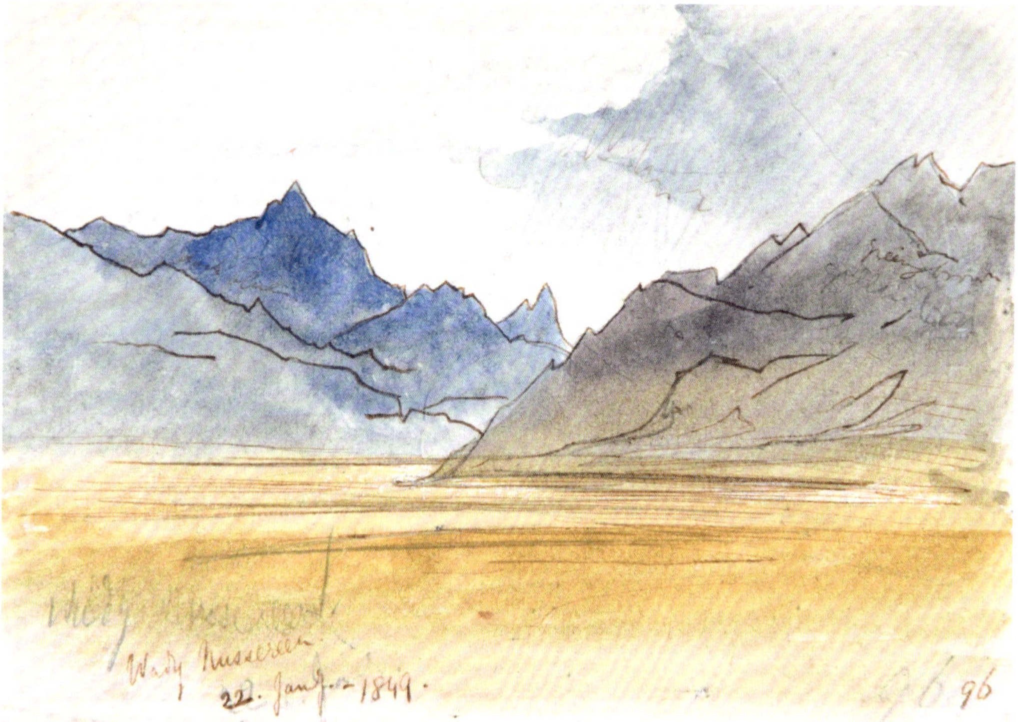

01 Wadi Musallam
Inscribed 'Wady Mussereer' and 96, and dated '22 Jany 1849'
Pen ink and watercolour with pencil
3 ½ x 5 inches

Wadi Musallam

Having been thinking about a trip to Egypt from early in 1848, Edward Lear arrived in Cairo in January 1849. There he met his old friend, the Reverend John E Cross, who had offered to finance an expedition to Sinai and Palestine. They set out together by camel on 13 January, and travelled along a route that can be charted through the many drawings that Lear made on the way, including those around Suez (15-17 January), of the wadis around Abu Zenima (20 January) and of Wadi Feiran (23 January).

Dated by Lear '22 Jany 1849', the present drawing probably depicts the valley, Wadi Musallam, which – of the features that are near to Wadi Feiran – is closest in spelling to the artist's inscription, 'Wady Mussereen'. He made at least two other drawings on the same day, one ostensibly inscribed 'Wady Buderak' (which was auctioned by Sotheby's in 1988) and another numbered '102' (which is in the collection of the Houghton Library, Harvard University). However, given that the present drawing is numbered '96', it might be assumed that he made at least seven drawings on this day.

Lear and Cross arrived at St Catherine's Monastery on 27 January 1849, and stayed there for three nights. However, during that time, Lear caught a cold, so they decided to turn back to Suez. And on their arrival, Lear was exhibiting signs of fever. They had 'hoped to make Gaza, quarantine, and the Holy Land' but, 'having stayed there for eight days … the weather turned bad and Lear suddenly became miserable and gave up. From Alexandria, he took ship for Malta' (Peter Levi, *Edward Lear: A Life*, London: Tauris Parke Paperbacks, 2013 (revised ed), page 121). He would finally visit Palestine in spring 1858.

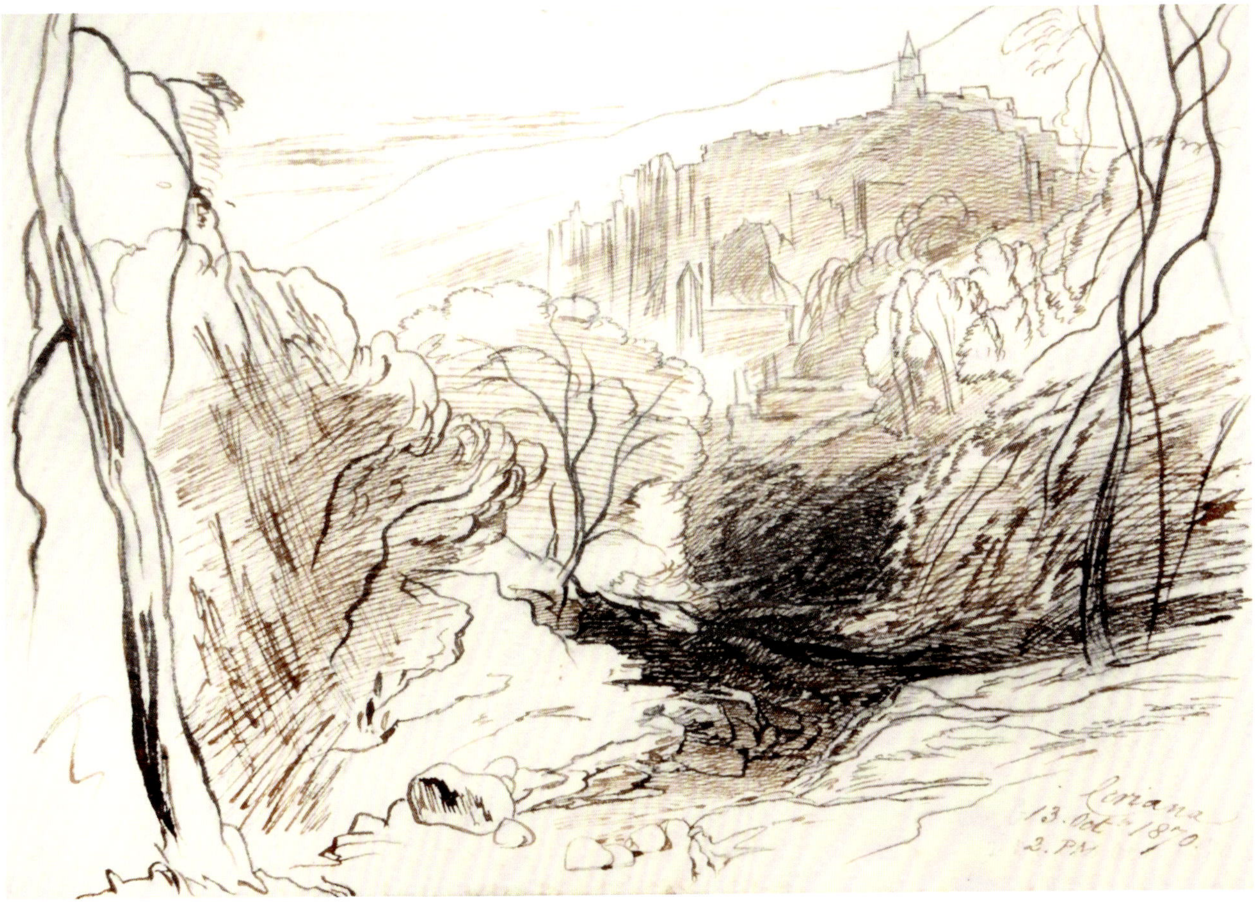

02 **Ceriana**
Inscribed with title and dated '13 Octbr 1870 2pm'
Pen and ink with pencil
7 x 9 ¾ inches

Ceriana

During the autumn of 1870, Edward Lear became impatient with the delay on the completion of his new house in San Remo, on the Ligurian coast of the newly unified Italy. He considered going away, to America or elsewhere, but instead made sketching trips in the surrounding area, and also found diversion in the company of his friends, the Congreves.

One of the trips that Lear made was to Ceriana, a village to the north of San Remo, for at least three days from 13 to 15 October. It is picturesquely sited on the steep lower slopes of Monte Bignone, and can be seen at a distance from the valley below and from the opposite hill.

Lear made at least four drawings during his stay – and probably more, given his industriousness – the first that is recorded being the present one. According to the artist's meticulous annotations, he produced it on Thursday '13 Octbr 1870' at around '2pm', and immediately followed it with one around '3pm' (which is now in the collection of the National Gallery of Art in Washington DC). For both, Lear sat along the bottom of the valley and looked up, through the trees, to the spire of Sant'Andrea, which tops the village and pierces the horizon. The first drawing concentrates on atmosphere and represents the village in silhouette; the second is more detailed and highlights individual features, including the needle-like tower of Santo Spirito.

Early on the Friday morning, Lear returned to the valley bottom, but moved further downstream to sit just below the tower of Santo Spirito. Then from '7 to 9 am', he produced a drawing (auctioned at Christie's in 2007) that greatly emphasises the way the many buildings of Ceriana cling to the hillside.

Lear rose again early on the morning of Saturday 15 October, and seems to have left Ceriana to cross the valley to the lower slopes of Monte Neveia, to the east. Then from '6.30 to 8 am' he made a drawing (now in the Ashmolean Museum, Oxford) that takes in a view through woodland and back towards the village.

By Tuesday 18 October, Lear had returned to the coast, as is evidenced by a drawing that he made of Paggia, early on that day.

GABRIELE CARELLI

Gabriele Mariano Nicolai Carelli (1820/21-1900), sometimes known as Gabriel Carelli

To the anglophone public, Gabriele Carelli is the best-known member of a dynasty of Italian landscape painters. First taken up by the Duke of Devonshire, he soon developed a distinguished clientele for his fresh topographical watercolours of Europe and the Middle East. From 1880, Queen Victoria became a great devotee of his work.

Gabriele Carelli was born in Naples, the second son of the painter, Raffaele Carelli (1795-1864), a member of the 'scuola di Posilippo'. Like his elder brother, Consalvo or Gonsalvo (1818-1900), he first studied under his father. In 1837, he moved, with Consalvo, to Rome to continue his studies, and remained there for three years. Returning to Naples, he launched his career, in 1841, by showing an interior of a chapel at the Mostra Borbonica. By the mid 1840s, he was listed alongside his father as having a studio at Largo del Vasto in the Neapolitan district of Chiaia.

Since the mid 1830s, Raffaele Carelli had been patronised by William Cavendish, 6th Duke of Devonshire, and travelled with him on tours of Sicily (1834) and Asia Minor (1839). Early in 1847, Gabriele Carelli also received his patronage, and travelled with him to England as his personal painter. During the months that he spent in the country, he became acquainted with the Devonshire estates and befriended some of the Duke's employees – notably the gardener, Joseph Paxton.

Gabriele Carelli probably returned to Italy in October 1847. In the following May, he and his younger brother, Achille (1856-1936), joined in the failed nationalist revolt against the Bourbons. It is said that their father had wanted the family to migrate to England to avoid the revolt, but in the end had to hide his sons in his studio so that they would evade capture. Once the trouble had receded, the artists returned to their work, Gabriele developing under the influence of the Belgian painter, Frans Vervloet, who was working in Naples and had joined the 'scuola di Posilippo'. Among other exhibits during this period, Gabriele showed two works at the Esposizione di Belle Arti di Napoli, in 1851.

From 1860, Gabriele Carelli spent increasingly longer times in England and developed a distinguished clientele. However, until 1866, he retained a base in Naples. Among other Neapolitan artists, John Murray's *A Handbook for Travellers in Southern Italy* for 1865 recommended the following:

> Carelli (Gonsalvo), 66, Carelli (Gabriele and Achille), 57, Riviera di Chiaia – a family of artists; Gonsalvo and Gabriele are excellent drawing masters in crayon and water-colours, who paint views in oil and water-colours of the costumes and scenery round Naples (page 82)

By July 1866, Gabriele had moved to England, and he soon settled at 'Woodcote', Kenilworth, Warwickshire. He either rented this property from Henry Hicks, a coal merchant, or shared it with him, and continued to use the address until 1883. His London addresses for the same period include 18 Burton Street, Bloomsbury (1875), 12 Petersham Terrace (now Gloucester Road), South Kensington (1877) and 13 St George's Square, Pimlico (1880-81). He married Martha Kent in 1868, and she gave birth to their son, Conrad (1869-1956), a year later. Eventually, Gabriele would become a British subject.

Though he was unsuccessful in his candidature to the New Society of Painters in Water Colours in 1866, Gabriele Carelli would exhibit interiors and landscapes at a number of London venues, including four works at the Royal Academy (1866-80), and in Liverpool and Manchester. He also continued to exhibit in Italy, and was awarded a prize from the Società Promotrice di Belle Arti in Naples in 1871. His exhibits were based on sketches that he made on regular and extensive travels across Britain and Europe, and to North Africa and the Middle East.

Following a tour of Spain in 1879-80, Gabriel Carelli was brought to the notice of Queen Victoria. (According to an obituary of Carelli in *The Builder* in 1900, this was through Lady Waterpark, a Lady-in-Waiting to her Majesty.) He sold her a number of watercolours and, in the years 1880-83, also fulfilled a commission to record the Royal Mausoleum at Frogmore.

Other projects of the period include illustrations to his wife's article, 'Urbino', written to coincide with the 400th anniversary of the birth of Raphael, and published in the American magazine, *Manhattan*, in December 1883.

Late in the century, Carelli and his family wintered in Menton, on the French Riviera. He would die there in December 1900. Martha died 12 years later.

Their son, Conrad, became an artist, and worked in a looser version of his father's style. For a while he lived and exhibited in Menton.

Consalvo's son, Giuseppe Carelli (1858-1921), was also a painter.

Henry Graves and Co held a memorial show of Carelli's watercolours in 1902.

Gabriele Carelli's work is represented in the Royal Collection.

Further reading

Oreste Ferrari, 'Carelli, Raffaele', *Dizionario Biografico degli Italiani*, Rome: Istituto della Enciclopedia, 1977, vol 20, pages 65-67 (which includes reference to Gabriele Carelli on pages 66-67)

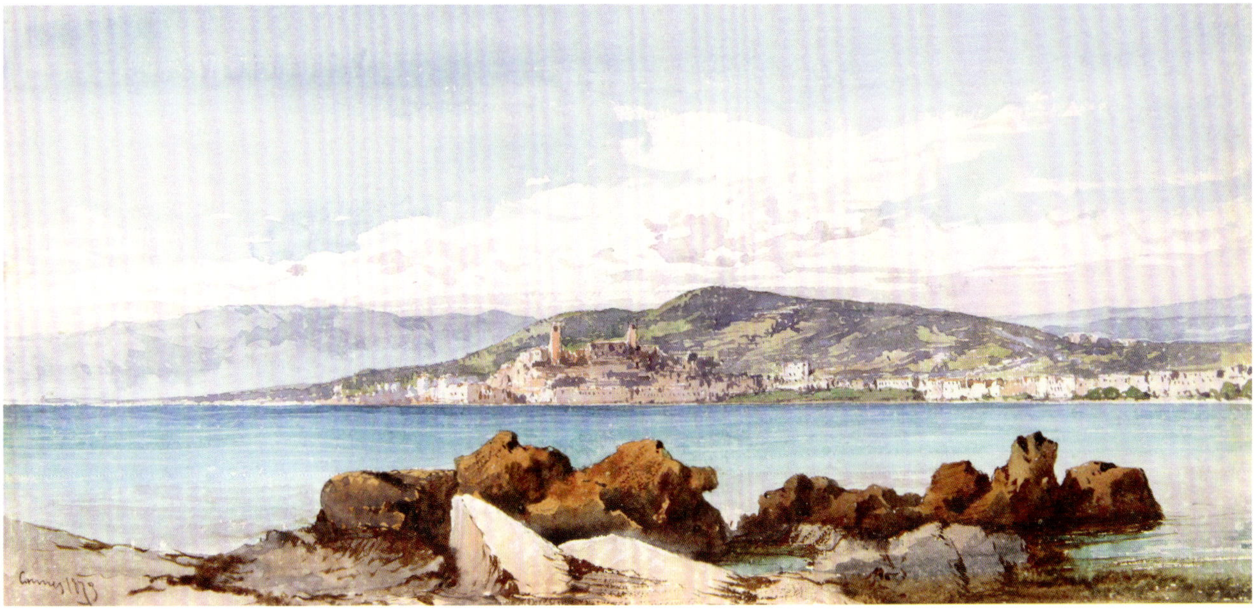

03 Cannes
Inscribed with title and dated 1879
Watercolour
6 ½ x 13 ¾ inches

04 Tangiers
Signed and inscribed with title
Watercolour
9 ¾ x 13 ¾ inches

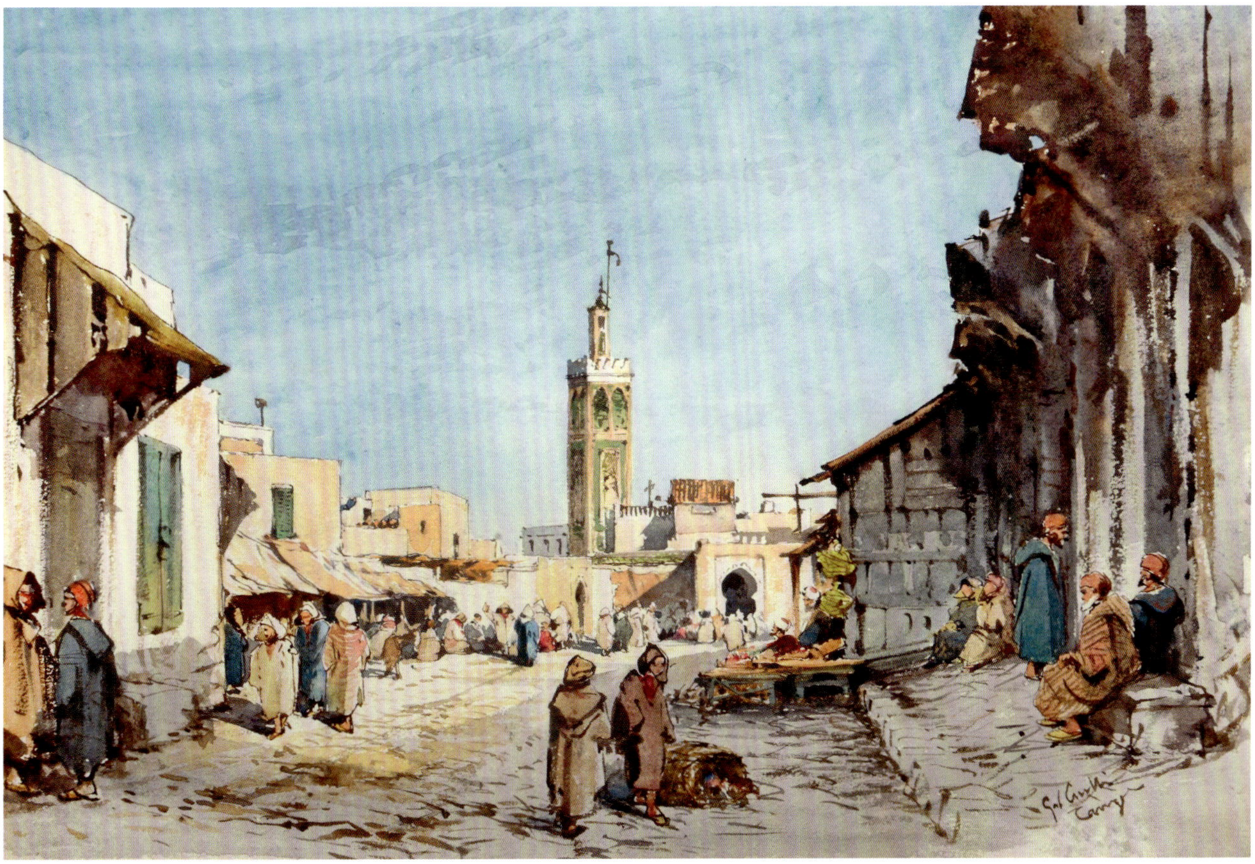

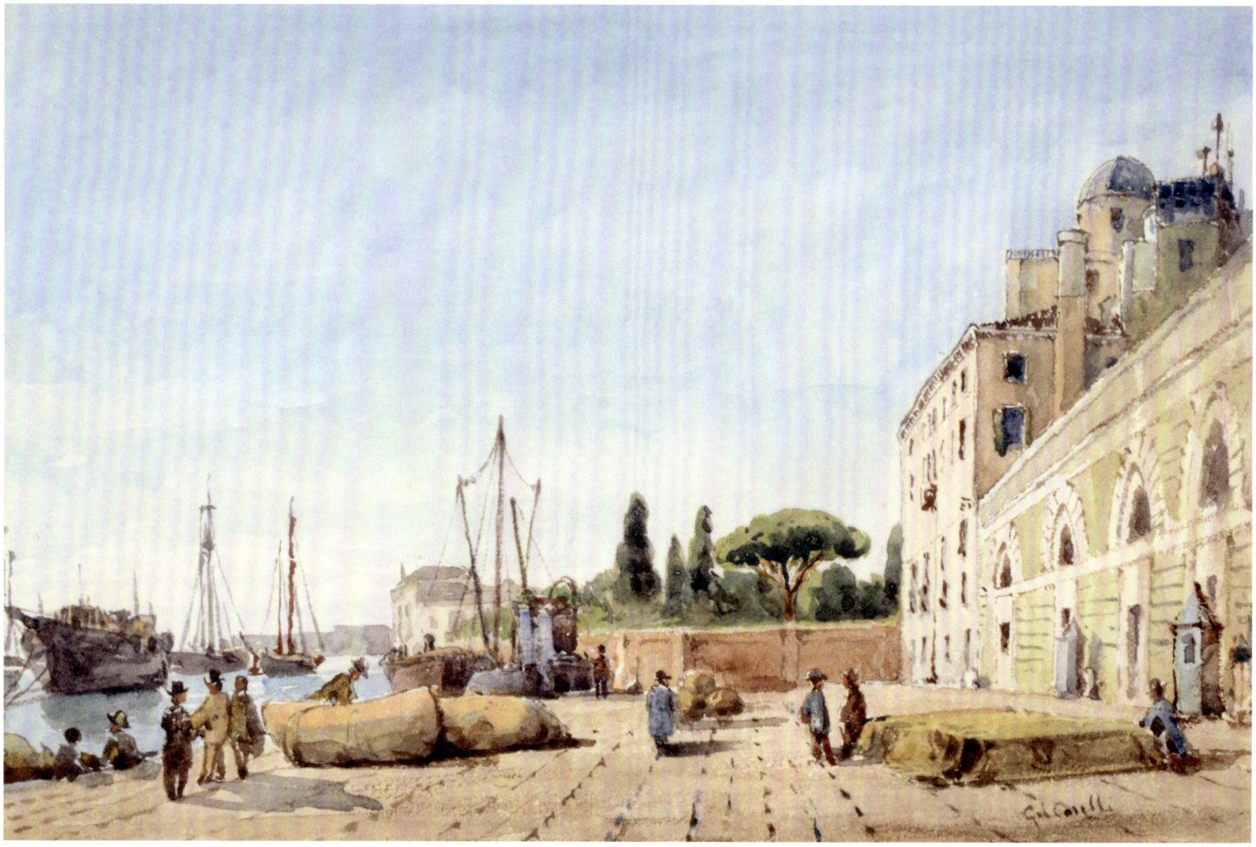

05 **Dogana, Venice**
Signed
Watercolour
6 ¾ x 10 inches

06-08 are all taken from a sketchbook, 1891-92, covering England, the French Riviera, Venice and Egypt

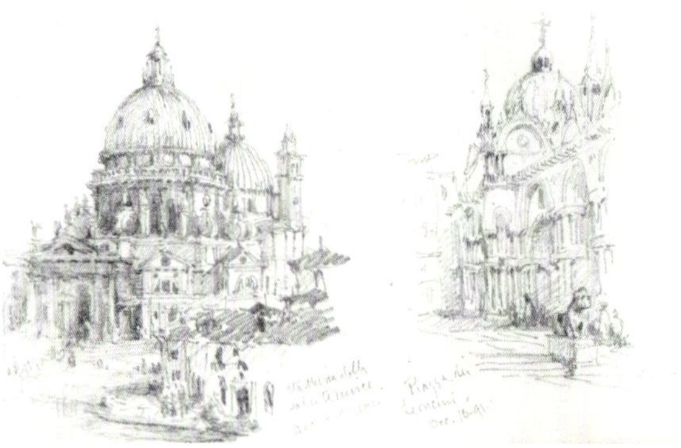

06 **Sta Maria della Salute Venice**
Piazza dei Leoncini
Inscribed with title and dated 'Dec 3rd 1891' and 'Dec 1891'
Pencil
3 ½ x 5 ¾ inches

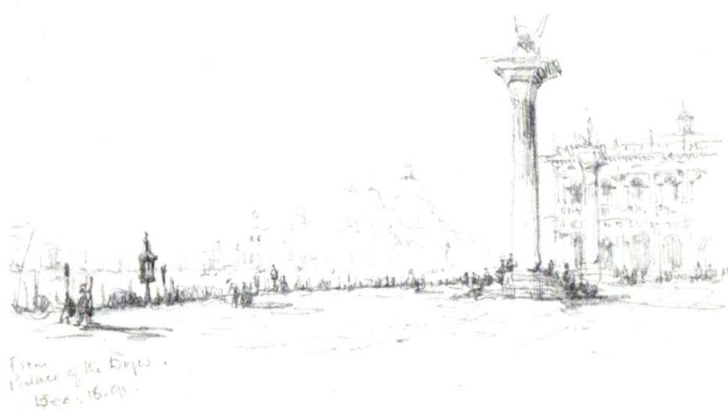

07 **From Palace of The Doges**
Inscribed with title and dated 'Dec 16 91'
Pencil
3 ½ x 5 ¾ inches

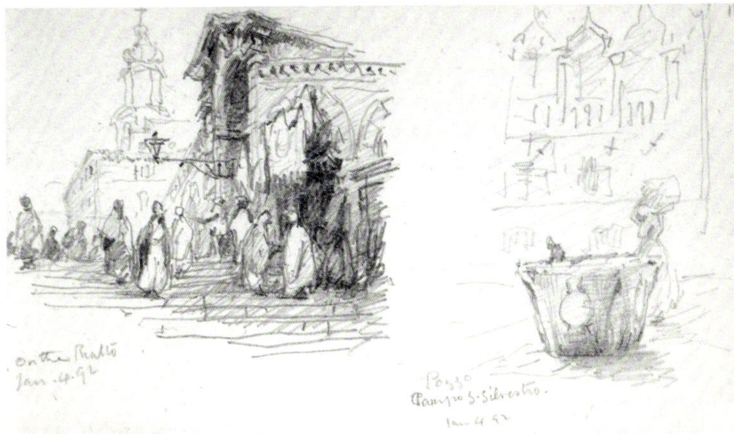

08 On the Rialto
Pozzo, Campo San Silvestro
Inscribed with title and twice dated 'Jan 4 92'
Pencil
3 ½ x 5 ¾ inches

09-13 are all taken from a sketchbook, 1897-98, covering England, France and Italy

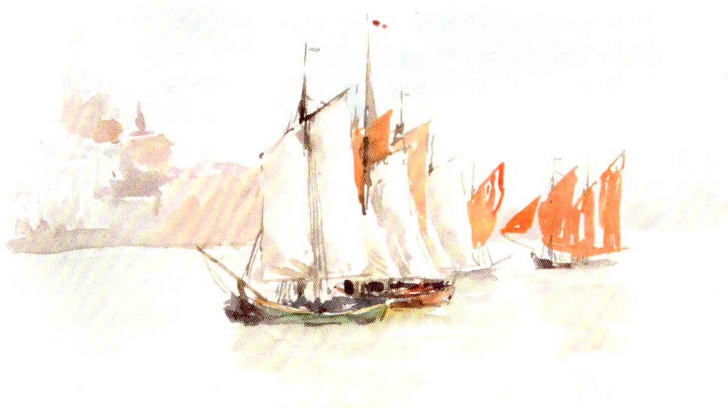

09 From Window
Inscribed with title and dated 'Dec 8 97' on facing page in original sketchbook
Pencil
3 ½ x 5 ¾ inches

Reverse:
Inscribed 'Zattere' and 'Charcoal Boat' and dated 'Dec 14 97' and 'Dec 15'
Pencil
2 ¾ x 4 ¼ inches

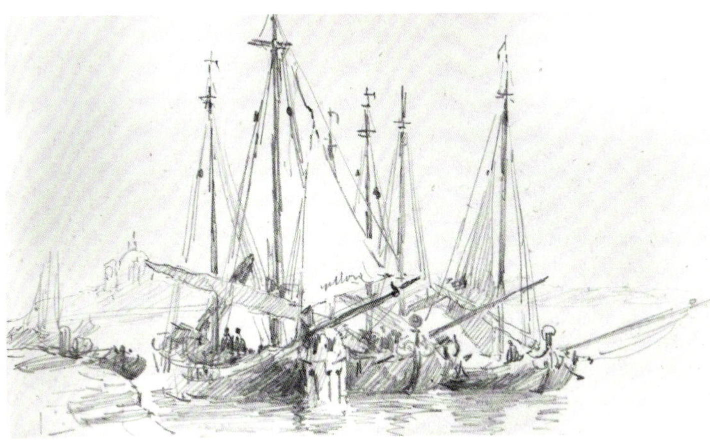

10 Zattere 'Alla Spirito Santo'
Inscribed with title and dated 'Feb 16' on facing page in original sketchbook
Inscribed 'I Gesuati from Calle Trevisan' and dated 'Feb 17' on reverse
Pencil
3 ½ x 5 ¾ inches

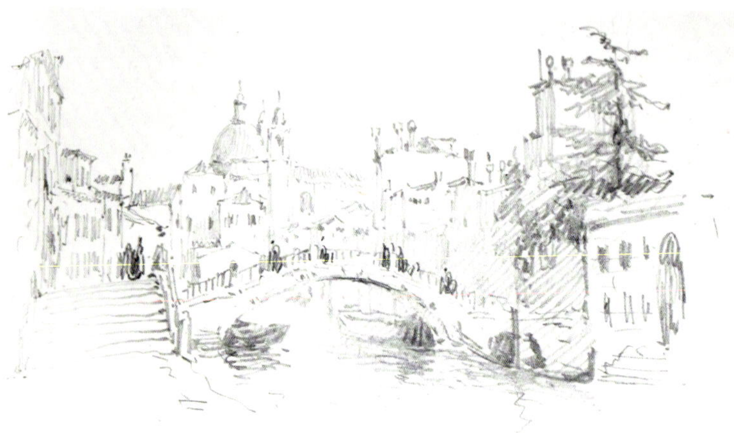

11 I Gesuati from Calle Trevisan
Inscribed with title and dated 'Feb 17' on facing page in original sketchbook
Inscribed 'Agli Incurabili' and dated 'Feb 24' on reverse
Pencil sketch of ship's rigging on reverse
Pencil
3 ½ x 4 ½ inches

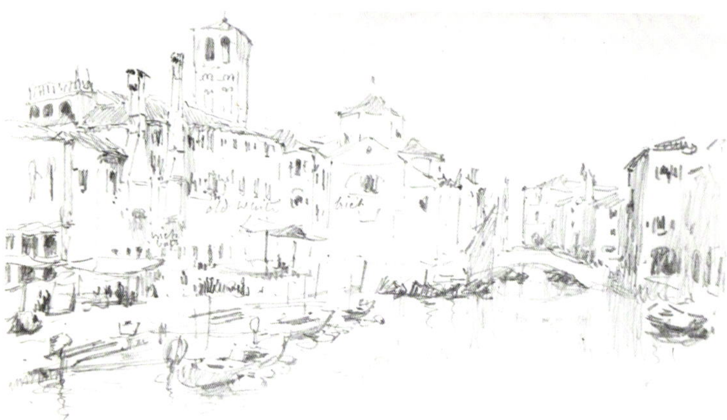

12 In Pescheria
Chioggia
Inscribed with title and dated 'April 5th' on reverse
Pencil
3 ½ x 5 ¾ inches

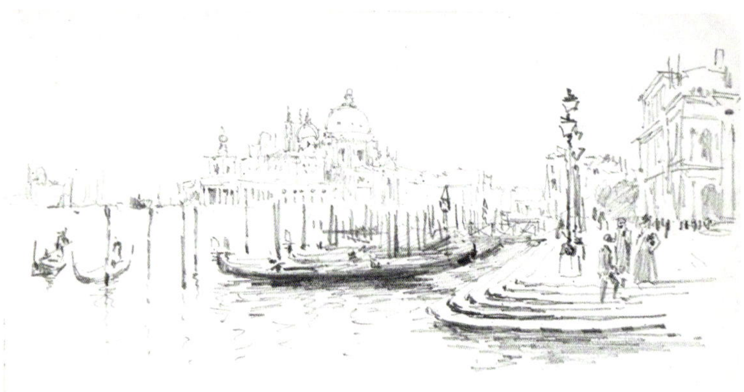

13 From Riva
Inscribed with title and dated 'April 11 – 98' on facing page in original sketchbook
Inscribed 'Zattere' and 'From Giudecca', and dated April 11 98' on reverse
Pencil
3 ½ x 5 ¾ inches

CONSTANCE FREDERICA GORDON-CUMMING

Constance Frederica Gordon-Cumming (1837-1924)

Constance Frederica Gordon-Cumming was one of the most intrepid and enterprising women travellers of the Victorian period, who also had the skill and industry to record her journeys in word and image. Encouraged by her many distinguished connections, during the height of the British Empire, she visited India, Ceylon and many of the countries of the Pacific Rim, between 1868 and 1880. The extent of her achievement is still in the process of evaluation.

Known as 'Eka' to her friends, Constance Frederica Gordon-Cumming was born at Altyre, near Forres, Morayshire, Scotland, on 26 May 1837. She was the 12th child of Sir William Gordon-Cumming, 2nd baronet of Altyre and Gordonstoun, and his first wife, Eliza Maria Campbell. She received her early education at home, probably from resident tutors, and taught herself to paint, with the help of several visiting artists, including Edwin Landseer. Following the death of her mother in 1842, she went to live with her eldest sister, Anne Seymour, who, in 1843, married Oswin Baker-Cresswell of Cresswell and Harehope, Northumberland. However, Jane Eliza Mackintosh, her stepmother from 1846, persuaded her to return to Altyre in 1848, and then sent her to school. So, until 1853, she resided at Hermitage Lodge in Fulham, run by the three Stevens sisters, which she would describe in her memoirs as 'a first-rate school near London'. A year after leaving school, she attended her first London 'season' and her first 'Northern Meeting' at Inverness.

Following the death of her father in 1854, Gordon-Cumming returned to Northumberland to live with her sister, Seymour. On Seymour's death in 1858, she stayed with her sister, Alice Jenkinson, in the Vale of Severn, and then with another sister, Eleanora 'Nelly' Grant, at Castle Grant, on Speyside. In 1867, Nelly's husband, George, 'lost much of his capital in a stock exchange speculation' (Laracy 2013, page 74), so they moved first to Comrie, Perthshire, and then, in 1869, a little further east, to Crieff. During this period, Gordon-Cumming developed as a painter, and began to exhibit in Edinburgh (from 1866) and Glasgow (from 1867).

In spring 1868, Gordon-Cumming undertook a painting tour of the Western Isles, initially in the company of her half-brother, Frederick. Then, in November 1868, she left Southampton to make her first voyage abroad, to India, where she joined her half-sister, Emilia Sergison, and Emilia's husband, Warden, who had been serving in the 4th Hussars. She spent a year exploring the country, and returned to England in February 1870 with portfolios full of paintings and notes for her first article and first substantial book: 'Camp Life in the Himalayas' (*Good Words*, February 1870) and *From the Hebrides to the Himalayas* (1876). So she established a pattern of life in which she travelled widely and published extensively.

During her time in England, Gordon-Cumming probably used the home of her brother, William, at Auchintoul, as a base for visiting other relatives and friends. Then, in the autumn of 1872, she accepted an invitation from 'the widowed Rev Hugh Jermyn, formerly the parson of Altyre and latterly Bishop of Colombo … to visit him and his daughter in Ceylon' (Laracy 2013, page 77). She arrived in Colombo in February 1873, and finally returned to London in July 1874. The opportunity to join the Bishop and his daughter on their official visits across Ceylon formed the substance of her experience on the island, and the basis of her later book, *Two Happy Years in Ceylon* (1892).

During her winter in England, over 1873-74, Gordon-Cumming received an invitation from Arthur Hamilton-Gordon, to join him and his wife, on their journey to Fiji, where he was to become its governor. This instigated her third and most extensive tour abroad. Leaving England in March 1875, they travelled via Singapore and Sydney. While Hamilton-Gordon was keen to move on to Fiji, Gordon-Cumming spent over three months in Australia, and took the opportunity to visit the Blue Mountains and the sheep station of Duntroon. Between September 1875 and March 1878, she explored Fiji, New Zealand and the South Seas – partly in the company of the Bishop of Samoa – before leaving for California. *At Home in Fiji* (1881) and *A Lady's Cruise in a French Man-of-War* (1882) record this period; *Granite Crags* (1884) covers the months that she spent painting in California's Yosemite Valley. She showed the results in what comprised the Yosemite's first ever art exhibition.

From California, Gordon-Cumming set out for Japan, arriving in Nagasaki on 6 September 1878 and departing from Yokohama for China in mid December. Exploring China between December 1878 and June 1879, 'she ranged northwards along the coast from Hong Kong and Canton to Tsientsin, and inland to Peking' (Laracy 2013, page 82). While in Peking, she met William Hill Murray, a Scottish missionary, who had invented the Numeral Type system, through which blind and illiterate Chinese learned to read and write. She was so inspired by this meeting that she helped support his school for the remainder of her life and wrote two books on the subject of the blind in China, as well as the more general record of her stay in the country, *Wanderings in China* (1886).

Gordon-Cumming returned to the United States via Japan, arriving in San Francisco in late September 1879. However, just a week later, on 1 October, she embarked for Hawaii, and spent two months touring the islands, and studying its volcanoes. These she described in *Fire Fountains: The Kingdom of Hawaii* (1883). Crossing the United States from 2 December 1879 to 2 March 1880, she arrived in Liverpool on 13 March.

From that time, Gordon-Cumming lived at Crieff, with her widowed sister, Nelly (until Nelly's death in 1889), and then on her own. For the following 15 years, she wrote most of her books and many articles, and produced paintings and drawings, her creative output bringing her fame. She showed work at various exhibitions, and most notably at the Indian and Colonial Exhibition, which was held in South Kensington in 1886, and included large numbers of her watercolours in various of the national sections. Her final publication was the autobiographical volume, *Memories* (1904), which among other subjects included the main record of her time in Japan.

Though Gordon-Cumming was sometimes criticised as a writer in her lifetime, her achievement was recognised in 1914, when she was made a Life Fellow of the Royal Geographical Society.

She died in Crieff, Perthshire, on 4 September 1924, and is buried nearby.

Her work is represented in the collections of the Museum of Archaeology and Anthropology (Cambridge).

Further reading

Elizabeth Baigent, 'Cumming, Constance Frederica Gordon- (1837-1924)', H C G Matthew and Brian Harrison (eds), *Oxford Dictionary of National Biography*, Oxford University Press, 2004, vol 14, pages 631-632; Hugh Laracy, *Watriama and Co. Further Pacific Island Portraits*, Canberra: ANU E Press, 2013

14

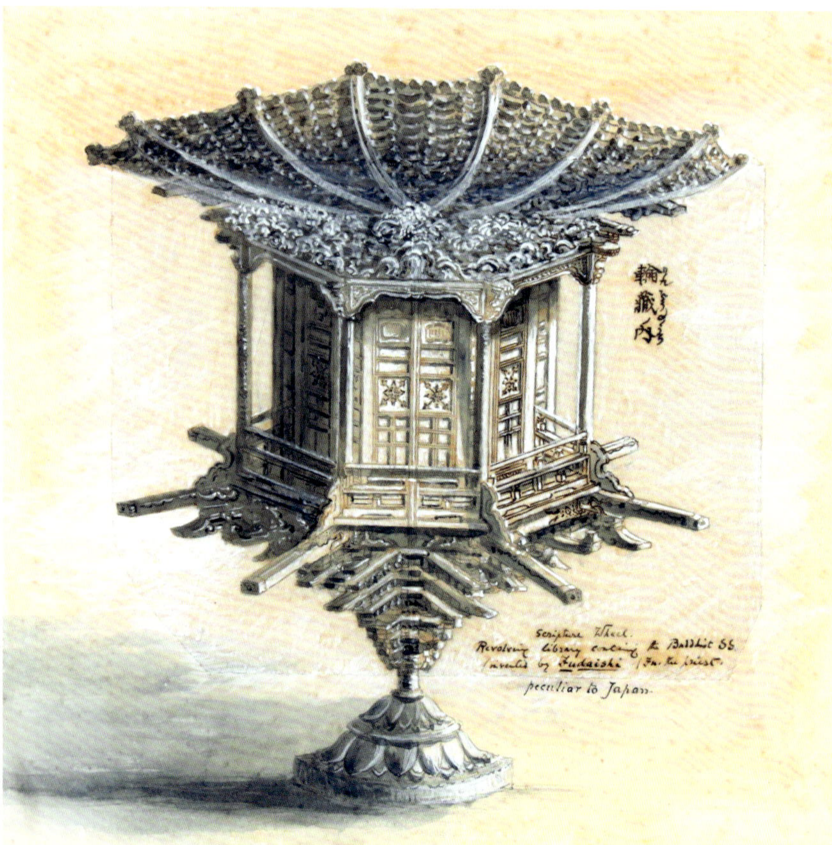

14 Scripture Wheel
Revolving library containing the Buddhist SS (invented by Fudaishi) FN. The Priest. Peculiar to Japan
Inscribed with title and further inscribed in Japanese
Pen ink and watercolour with bodycolour
13 ¼ x 13 ¾ inches

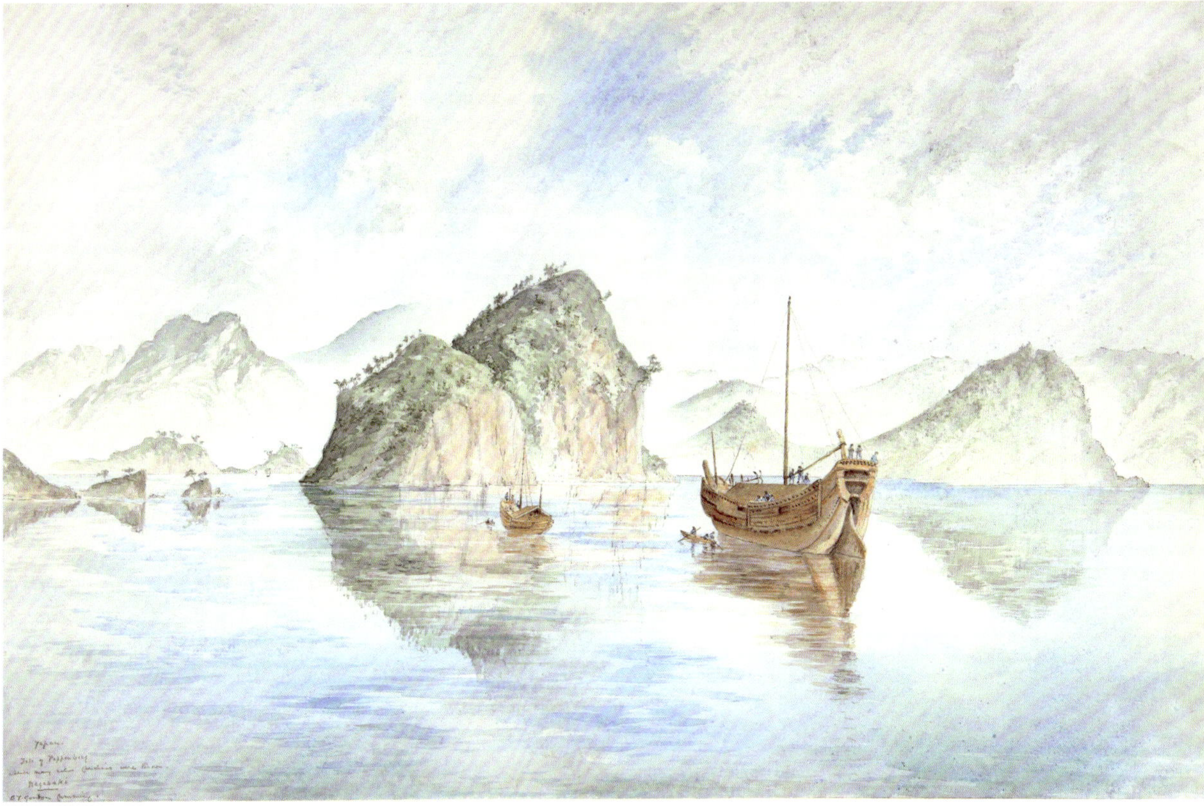

15 Nagasaki, Japan: Isle of Pappenberg
Whence many native Christians were thrown
Signed and inscribed with title
Watercolour
14 ½ x 23 inches

16 Nagasaki, Japan: Isle of Pappenberg
Signed and inscribed with title
Signed on reverse
Watercolour
12 ¼ x 23 inches

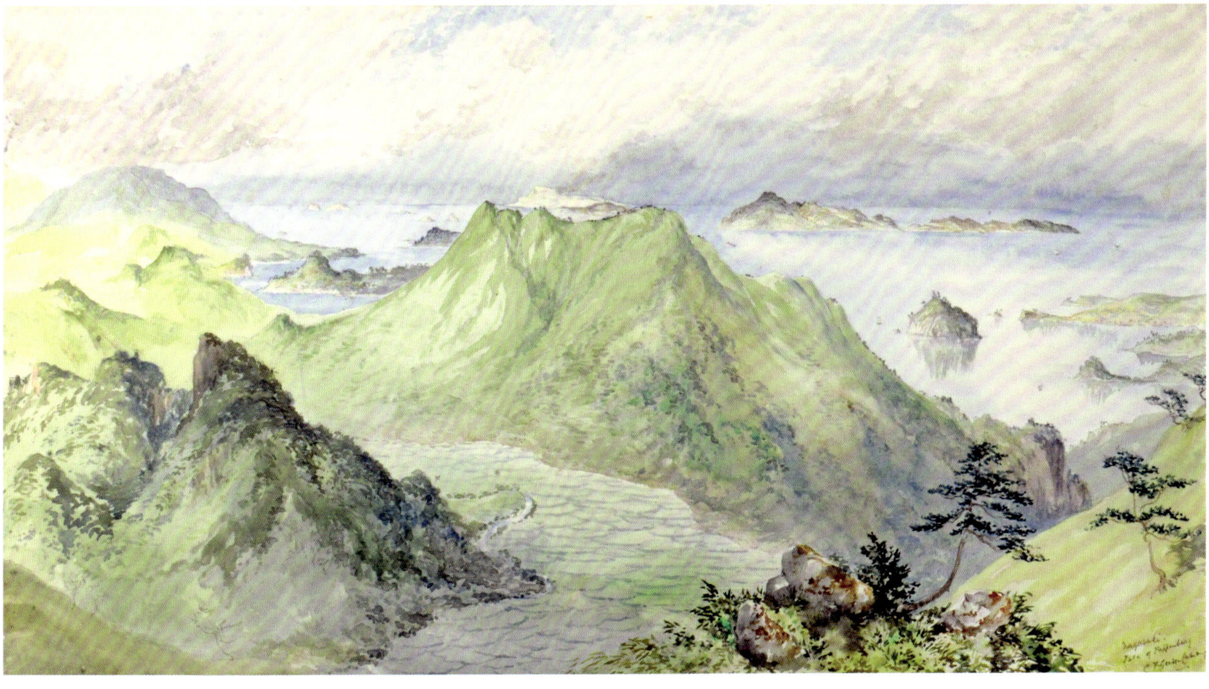

'Having now ample proof that the "rotatory cylinder" has held a well-established position in old Japan, I naturally looked for it at all the principal temples. Before visiting the beautiful shrines of Nikko (where the loveliest Imperial tombs and temples are cradled in the most exquisite scenery), I came on a startling statement concerning how many thousand times the assembled priests had recited the whole Buddhist canon in the course of a great festival. The statement excited no comment, and was apparently accepted as a poetic fiction, but in the light of the helpful wheel, it seemed to me all plain. So on reaching the lovely temple grounds I eagerly looked out for this aid to the task of vain repetitions.

Climbing a succession of long flights of steep stone stairs, and passing by a tall red pagoda with the usual series of dark projecting roof, I reached a large open court, surrounded by many buildings for sacred uses, one of which precisely resembled those in which I had already found the scripture-wheels. Peering in through the gilded fretwork which acted the part of windows, I could faintly discern a massive object, resplendent in scarlet and gold lacquer.

Being now convinced that I had solved the mystery of those many thousand repetitions of the sacred canon, I asked to have the door opened; after some delay the priest was found who had charge of the key; and sure enough there was the wheel! a most gorgeous piece of lacquer work in richest colours, resting on a stone pedestal of lotus-leaves, and containing the holy books in the form of upright scrolls. The priest, as usual, did the honours most courteously, but without affecting a particle of reverence for this labour-saving apparatus. Evidently this phase of superstition had lost its hold on the people, and the priests make no effort to retain a form which they, too, have discovered to be but a hollow sham.

In the same court there is a very handsome large bronze candelabra, enclosed in a great bronze lantern which stands beneath stately cryptomeria trees, and is only protected by a light ornamental roof, supported by carved stone pillars. In general form it resembles a scripture-wheel, and revolves on its own axis, so many of the pilgrims give it a sun-wise turn, though apparently only as a matter of form.

Here, too, I noticed the wheel in its simplest form, as the symbolic decoration on the bronze gateways leading to the magnificent tomb of one of the Shoguns.'

(Constance Frederica Gordon-Cumming, *Memories*, Edinburgh & London: William Blackwood & Sons, 1904, pages 258-259)

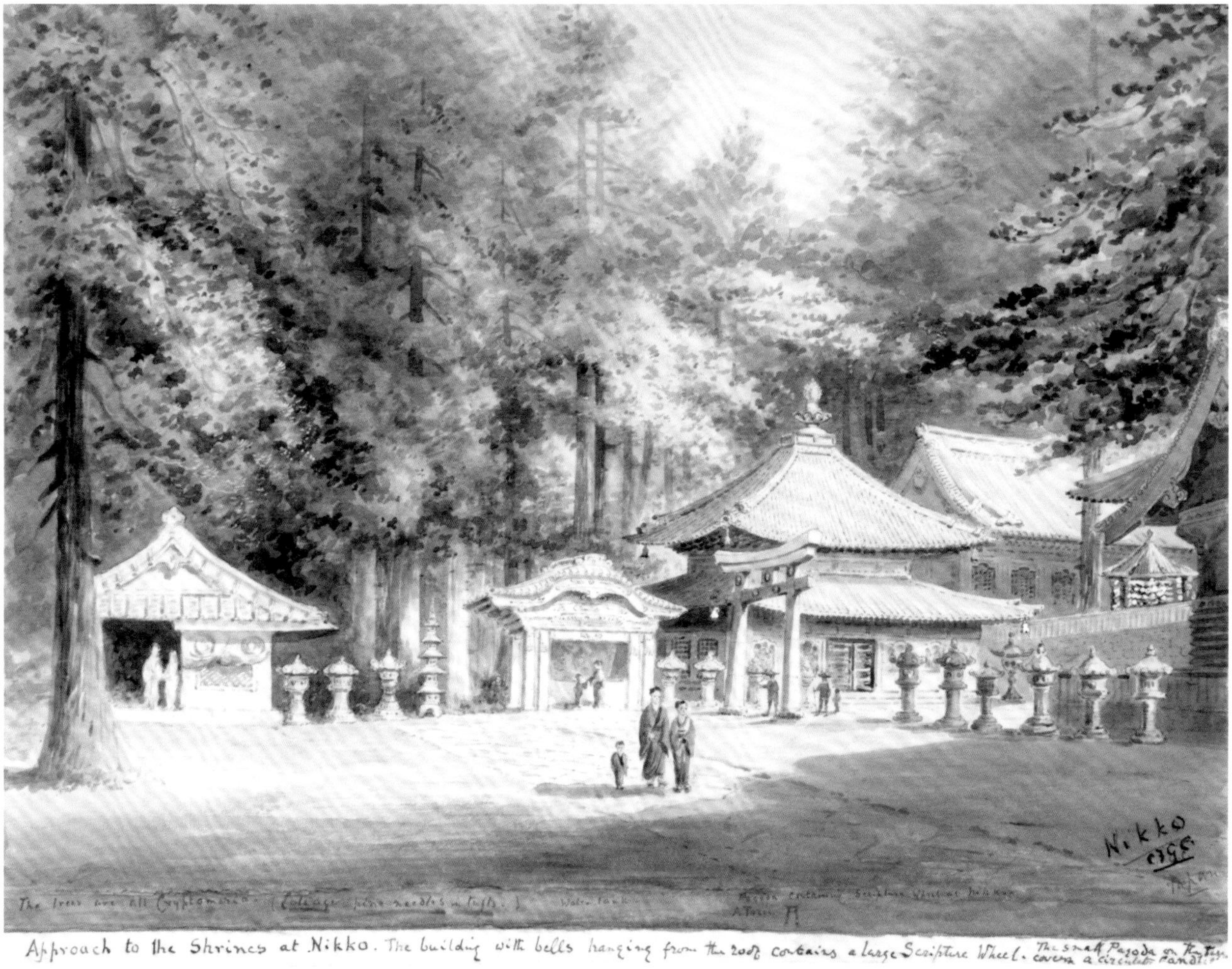

17

17 Approach to the Shrines at Nikko
The building with bells hanging from the roof contains a large scripture wheel. The small pagoda on the left covers a circular candle
Signed with initials and inscribed with title, 'Nikko Japan', 'The trees are all Cryptomeria (foliage: pine needles in tufts)', 'Water Tank' and 'Pagoda containing Scripture Wheel'
Watercolour with bodycolour
10 x 13 ¼ inches

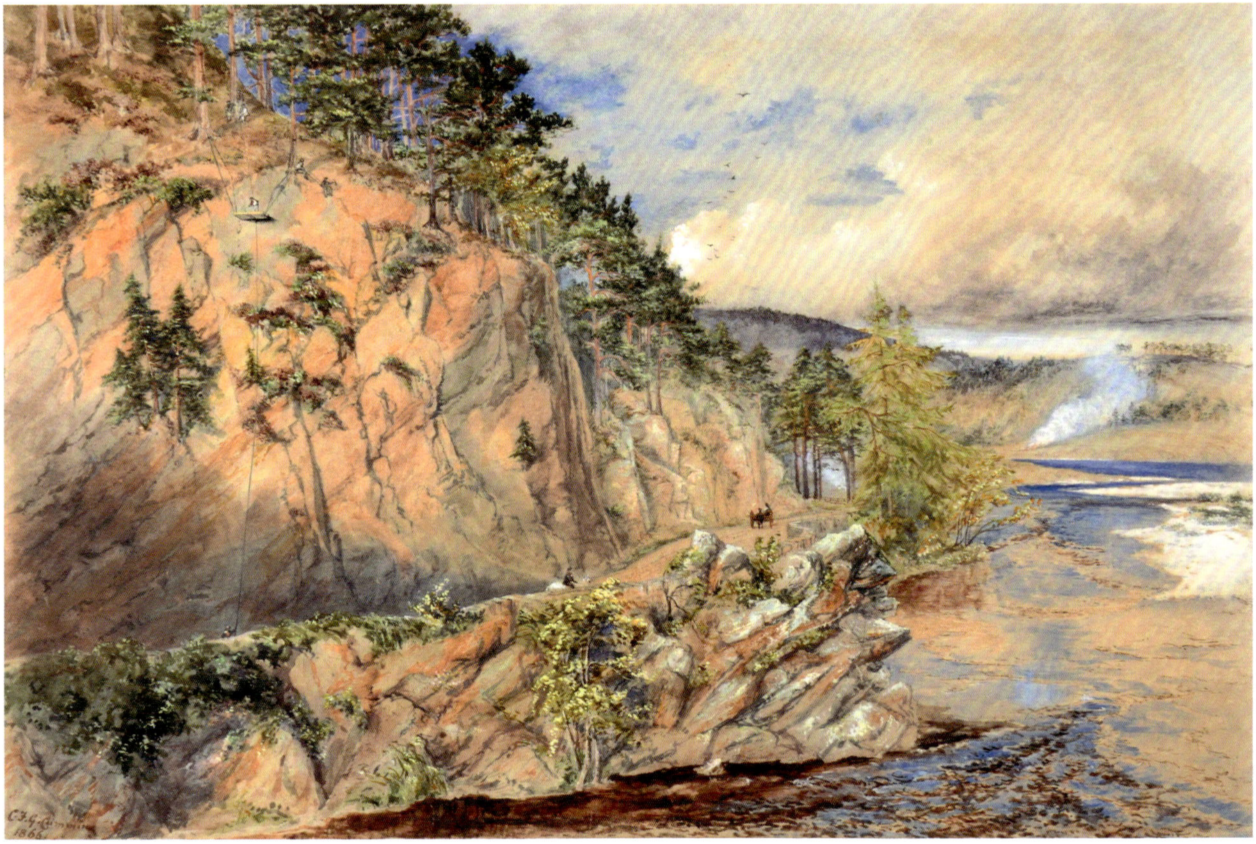

18 Rock of Craig Ellachie on the Spey
Signed and dated 1866
Inscribed with title on reverse
Watercolour and bodycolour
14 ½ x 21 inches

'The George Grants being now comfortably settled at Easter Elchies, on the banks of the Spey, early in January 1859 I joined them there at what proved to be their happy home for the next eight years. It is one of the many minor properties of the Earls of Seafield, and so at that time belonged to George's brother, from whom he rented it. It is a comfortable old house, commanding a beautiful view looking in one direction down the river to Craigellachie, a noble wooded crag, with the river sweeping round its base, and a fine bridge at right angles to the crag. On the further bank lies the village of the same name, and beyond, above beautiful Arndilly, rises the fine heathery mountain Ben Agan.'

(Constance Frederica Gordon-Cumming, *Memories*, Edinburgh & London: William Blackwood & Sons, 1904, page 159)

Publications by Constance Frederica Gordon-Cumming: A Preliminary Check List

1870
'Camp Life in the Himalayas'
Published in *Good Words*, February 1870

1872
(with Walter Easton)
The Great Serpent Mound at Loch Nell, Argyllshire …
Jedburgh: printed by Walter Easton

(with John S Phené)
The Reptile Tumuli of Britain and America
Jedburgh

1876
From the Hebrides to the Himalayas: a sketch of eighteen months' wandering in western isles and eastern highlands
London: Samson Low, Marston, Searle & Rivington (2 vols)

1880
'New Year's Day in Canton'
Published in *The Leisure Hour*, 3 January 1880, pages 8-13

1881
At Home in Fiji … With maps and illustrations
Edinburgh & London: William Blackwood & Sons (2 vols)

'The Greatest Active Volcano'
Published in *Scribner's Monthly*, New York, vol 21, April 1881, pages 926-936

'The Largest Excinct Volcano: an Ascent of Haleakala'
Published in *Scribner's Monthly*, New York, vol 21, June 1881, pages 272-275

Circa 1882
Sketches in Egypt, Arabia, and Palestine
York

1882
'Across the Yellow Sea'
Published in *Blackwood's Edinburgh Magazine*, May 1882

A Lady's Cruise in a French Man-of-War
Edinburgh & London: William Blackwood & Sons (2 vols)

'The Last King of Tahiti'
Published in *The Contemporary Review*, vol 41, May 1882, pages 819-836

'Mysteries of the South Pacific'
Published in *The Leisure Hour*

'Of Furred and Feathered Foes in New Countries' [New Zealand]
Published in *The Gentleman's Magazine*, vol 252, May 1882, pages 554-566

'Oiling the Waves: safeguard in tempest'
Published in *The Nineteenth Century*, vol 11, April 1882

'Wheat, wine, wool'
Published in an unidentified Californian magazine in September 1882

1883
'Alligator-Farming'
Published in *Cassell's Family Magazine*, June 1883

'Early Spring in California' [uncredited]
Published in *The Cornhill Magazine*, vol 47, April 1883, pages 410-423

Fire Fountains: The Kingdom of Hawaii; its volcanoes, and the history of its missions
Edinburgh: William Blackwood & Sons (2 vols)

[Funerary Customs, an article on]
Published in an unidentified magazine in June 1883

'Granite Crags'
Published in *Temple Bar*, October 1883, pages 244-261

In the Hebrides
London: Chatto & Windus

'The Locust War in Cyprus',
Published in *Nineteenth Century*, August 1883

'Notes of a Wanderer in Skye'
Published in *Temple Bar*, September 1883

'On Cuttle-fish as a Dainty Dish'
Pulbished in *Cassell's Family Magazine*, July 1883

'Our Borrowed Plumes. Fine feathers make fine birds in many lands'
Published in *The Leisure Hour*, August 1883

'Pottery of Fiji'
Published in *The Leisure Hour*

'Two British Pilgrimages in the Nineteenth Century' [to Iona and Lindisfarne]
Published in *The Cornhill Magazine*, August 1883

'Unfathomed Mysteries' [on Spiritualism in Boston]
Published in *Blackwood's Edinburgh Magazine*, May 1883

'Wild Tribes of the Sierras'
Published in *The National Review*, vol 2, December 1883, pages 412-421

1884
'Destruction of the American Bison'
Published in *Good Words*, vol 25, June 1884, pages 388-391

Granite Crags … [an account of travels in California] With illustrations
Edinburgh & London: William Blackwood & Sons

'A Lady's Railway Journey in India'
Published in *Macmillan's Magazine*, February 1884

'A Legend of Inverawe and Ticonderoga'
Published in *The Atlantic Monthly*, Boston, September 1884

'A Legend of Vanished Waters' [Loch Spynie]
Published in *The Scottish Review*, vol 4, July 1884, pages 115-137

'Mechanical Modes of Worship',
Published in *The Contemporary Review*, October 1884

'The Newspapers of the World'
Published in *Cassell's Family Magazine*, August 1884

'New Zealand in Blooming December'
Published in *The Century*, New York, 1884, vol 27, pages 919-924

'Prophecies of a Highland Seer. Very remarkable facts in Ross-shire'
Published in *Belgravia*, September 1884

'Sanatorium of the Southern Ocean'
Published in *The Cornhill Magazine*, October 1884

'The World's Oil Supply'
Published in *The Nineteenth Century*, September 1884

1885
'Buddhist Monasteries'
Published in an unidentified magazine, March 1885

'A Chapter of Chinese Travel'
Published in *Blackwood's Edinburgh Magazine*, October 1885

'Locusts and Farmers of America'
Published in *The Nineteenth Century*, vol 17, January 1885, pages 133-153

'The Lowlands of Moray, in the Fourteenth and Nineteenth Centuries'
Published in *The National Review*, vol 4, January 1885, pages 642-657

'Offerings of the Dead'
Published in *The British Quarterly Review*, January 1885

'The Postmen of the World'
Published in *Cassell's Family Magazine*, July & August 1885

'Rambles in Canton'
Published in *Belgravia*, November 1885, pages 54-70

'Reminiscences of Foo-Chow'
Published in *The Cornhill Magazine*, January 1885

'Temple of Heaven, Peking'
Published in *The London Quarterly Review*, April 1885

Via Cornwall to Egypt
London: Chatto & Windus

'The World's Wonderlands in Wyoming and New Zealand'
Published in *The Overland Monthly*, San Francisco, vol 5, no 25, January 1885

1886
'The Eruption of Mount Tarawera in 1886' [Destruction of the Pink and White Terraces, New Zealand]
Published in *The Leisure Hour*, vol 35, October 1886, pages 651-664

'The Great Yellow River Inundation … With Chinese Map'
Published in *The Leisure Hour*, March 1886

'The Hot Lakes of New Zealand'
Published in *Sunday at Home*, October & November 1886

In the Himalayas and on the Indian Plains
London: Chatto and Windus

'A Night of Horror at a Highland Castle'
Published in *Belgravia*, October 1886

'Revered Footprints' [Held Sacred]
Time, vol 15, July 1886

'Sunny Days in Malta'
Published *The National Review*, vol 8, September 1886, pages 77-99

'Sudden Destruction, or Volcanic Frolics'
Published in *The Monthly Packet*, September 1886

Wanderings in China … with illustrations
Edinburgh & London: William Blackwood & Sons (2 vols)

1887
'Divining Rods, Ancient and Modern'
Published in *The Quiver*, July 1887

'Earthquakes in Divers Places'
Published in *The Leisure Hour*, June 1887

'Earth's Fiery Fountains of Molten Rock'
Published in *Atalanta*, vol 1, no 1, October 1887, pages 14-18

'The Ending of the Carnival' [on the Riviera]
Published in *The Leisure Hour*, May 1887

'In the Fiji Isles'
Published in W C Proctor (ed), *Round the Globe Through Great Britain*, London: Isbisters' Home Library

'The Last Commandment'. A Word to Every Christian
London: Church Missionary Society

'On the Social Position of Divers Animals'
Published in *Cassell's Family Magazine*, May 1887

'Our Oldest Colony' [Bombay]
Published in *Macmillan's Magazine*, vol 55, January 1887, pages 218-223

'Strange Medicines'
Published in *The Nineteenth Century*, vol 21, June 1887, pages 901-918

Work for the Blind in China: showing how blind beggars may be transformed into useful Scripture Readers
London: Gilbert & Rivington

1888
'Earth's Boiling Fountains, Part I'
Published in *Atalanta*, vol 1, no 5, February 1888, pages 261-263

'Earth's Boiling Fountains, Part II'
Published in *Atalanta*, vol 1, no 6, March 1888, pages 310-315

'The Home of the Blizzard'
Published in *The Leisure Hour*, April 1888

'Professions for Dogs'
Published in *Blackwood's Edinburgh Magazine*, November 1888, pages 694-707

1889
Notes on Ceylon
London: Church Missionary Society

Notes on China and its Missions
London: Church Missionary House

'In the Old Muniment Room of Wollaton Hall, Part I'
Published in *The New Review*, vol 1, October 1889, pages 490-504

'In the Old Muniment Room of Wollaton Hall, Part II'
Published in *The New Review*, vol 1, December 1889, pages 631-644

'Striking "Ile"' [Petroleum Springs]
Published in *Atalanta*, vol 2, no 10, July 1889, pages 675-679

1890
'The Cruise of the Castle Jermyn'
Published in *Atalanta*, vol 3, no 35, August 1890, pages 663-669

'Real Estate in Volcanic Regions' [Japan]
Published in *The Cornhill Magazine*, vol 61, February 1890

'Some Eventful Voyages',
Published in *Blackwood's Edinburgh Magazine*, March 1890

'Summer in Normandy'
Published in *The Cornhill Magazine*, vol 62, no 15, August 1890, pages 177-190

'Wolves and Were-Wolves'
Published in *Temple Bar*, November 1890

1891
'Footprints of Old' [Fossil and other]
Published *The Sun*, March 1891

'Kandy: The Mountain Capital of Ceylon'
Published in *The Victorian Magazine*, no 1, December 1891, pages 63-67

'Musical Instruments and their Homes'
Published in *Blackwood's Edinburgh Magazine*, vol 149, April 1891

'On Quiet Rivers in Ceylon'
Published in *The Cornhill Magazine*, vol 63, no 16, April 1891, pages 396-419

'Police Work in Ceylon'
Published in *The National Review*, vol 17, July 1891, pages 620-638

1892
'Disaster at the Oil City in Pennsylvania'
Published in *Atalanta*, vol 5, no 58, July 1892

'A Fiery Flood in Pennsylvania' [full report of the disastrous fire and flood at Oil City and area on 5 June 1892]
Published in *Atalanta*, vol 5, no 59, August 1892, pages 675-678

'How Mother Earth Rocked her Cradle in 1891, Part I' [In Japan]
Published *The Newberry House Magazine*, vol 7, no 1, July 1892

'How Mother Earth Rocked her Cradle in 1891, Part II' [In Japan]
Published *The Newberry House Magazine*, vol 7, no 2, August 1892

Two Happy Years in Ceylon
Edinburgh & Ceylon: William Blackwood & Sons (2 vols)

1895
The Blind in China. Letters on Miss C F Gordon-Cumming's advocacy of the Murray numeral method of printing the spoken languages of China (Correspondence from the Glasgow Herald)
Helensburgh: J Lamont

'Perthshire After the Great Gale'
Published *Atalanta*, vol 8, no 89, February 1895, pages 299-301

1898
The Inventor of the numeral type for China by the use of which illiterate Chinese both Blind and Sighted Can Very Quickly be Taught to Read and Write Fluently
London: Downey and Co

'Iridescent Surf at Cromer'
Published in *Nature*, vol 58, no 1495, 23 June 1898, page 174

1900
The Church's Great Commission
London: Church Missionary Society

1904
Memories ... with Illustrations
Edinburgh & London: William Blackwood & Sons

JOHN MACWHIRTER

John MacWhirter, RA RE RI HRMS RSA (1837-1911)

John MacWhirter was a highly popular painter of romantic landscapes, and especially watercolours of the Highlands of Scotland and Continental Europe.

John MacWhirter was born at Slateford, near Edinburgh, on 27 April 1837, a son of George McWhirter, a paper maker, and his second wife, Agnes Laing. One of his elder sisters, Agnes Eliza MacWhirter (1833-1882) was a still life painter. Both he and his sister altered the spelling of their surname from McWhirter to MacWhirter on becoming professional artists.

MacWhirter was educated at Peebles Grammar School until the death of his father, when he entered an apprenticeship with Oliver & Boyd, an Edinburgh firm of booksellers and publishers. However, a few months later, in 1851, he enrolled at the Trustees' Academy School of Art, where he was taught by John Ballantyne and Robert Scott Lauder. While there, he established friendships with a number of fellow students: George Paul Chalmers, Peter Graham, William Quiller Orchardson, John Pettie and William McTaggart.

Spending long periods drawing out of doors, MacWhirter exhibited his first painting – *Old Cottage at Braid* – at the Royal Scottish Academy, in 1854, at the age of 17. Two years later, he made the first of many trips abroad, and would travel – mostly on foot – in Germany, Austria, and through the Alps to Italy. At first he attempted to work in Pre-Raphaelite detail, influenced particularly by Millais, but later adopted a broader style. Nevertheless, he remained constant to his principle of drawing directly from nature.

During the 1860s, MacWhirter also worked as an illustrator, contributing to a number of periodicals, including *Good Words*, *The Golden Thread* and *The Sunday Magazine*, and the books, *The Postman's Bag* (1862), *Wordsworth's Poetry for the Young* (1863) and *Pen and Pencil Pictures from the Poets* (1866). He would return to illustration occasionally during subsequent decades.

First visiting London in 1864, MacWhirter began to exhibit at the Royal Academy in the following year. At the end of the decade, he settled in the English capital, and lived at 1 Titchfield Road (1869-75), though returned regularly to Scotland, and spent much time painting in the hilly countryside of Perthshire. Once in London, he soon attracted the notice of the critic, John Ruskin, with detailed studies of flowers that he had made in Norway in 1862-63; Ruskin bought 25 of these to use as teaching aids and then donated them to the Ashmolean Museum.

In 1872, MacWhirter married Catherine Cowan Menzies, known as 'Katie'. They had two daughters and two sons, their eldest child, Agnes, marrying the painter, Charles Sims, in 1897. The MacWhirters lived in St John's Wood, first at 6 Marlborough Road (1875-80), and then in a house at 1 Abbey Road, designed for them by William Flockhart, and built between 1881 and 1911. Catherine joined MacWhirter on his later travels, including an ambitious trip across the United States in 1877, from New York via Salt Lake City to San Francisco.

Exhibiting widely and regularly in London and provincial centres, MacWhirter was elected an associate of the Royal Scottish Academy in 1867 and a full academician in 1882; an associate of the Royal Academy in 1879, and a full academician in 1893; also a member of the Royal Society of Painter-Etchers and Engravers in 1881, the Royal Institute of Painters in Water Colours in 1882 and an honorary member of the Royal Society of Miniature Painters in 1902. He held three solo shows at the Fine Art Society (1887, 1898, 1901), and two solo shows at the Leicester Galleries (1910, 1911).

He published *Landscape Painting in Water-Colour* in 1900 and *The MacWhirter Sketch Book* in 1906.

He died at home on 28 January 1911, his wife surviving him.

During each of the last five years of his life, he spent time beside Lake Como, and painted watercolours of the surrounding countryside.

His work is represented in numerous public collections, including the Ashmolean Museum (Oxford) and Manchester Art Gallery; and The McManus (Dundee) and The National Trust for Scotland (Edinburgh).

Further reading

Janet Cooksey, 'MacWhirter, John (*b* Slateford, 27 March 1839; *d* London, 28 Jan 1911)', Jane Turner (ed), *The Dictionary of Art*, London: Macmillan, 1996, vol 20, page 34; John McWhirter, 'MacWhirter [McWhirter], John (1837-1911)', H C G Matthew and Brian Harrison (eds), *Oxford Dictionary of National Biography*, Oxford University Press, 2004, vol 36, pages 48-49

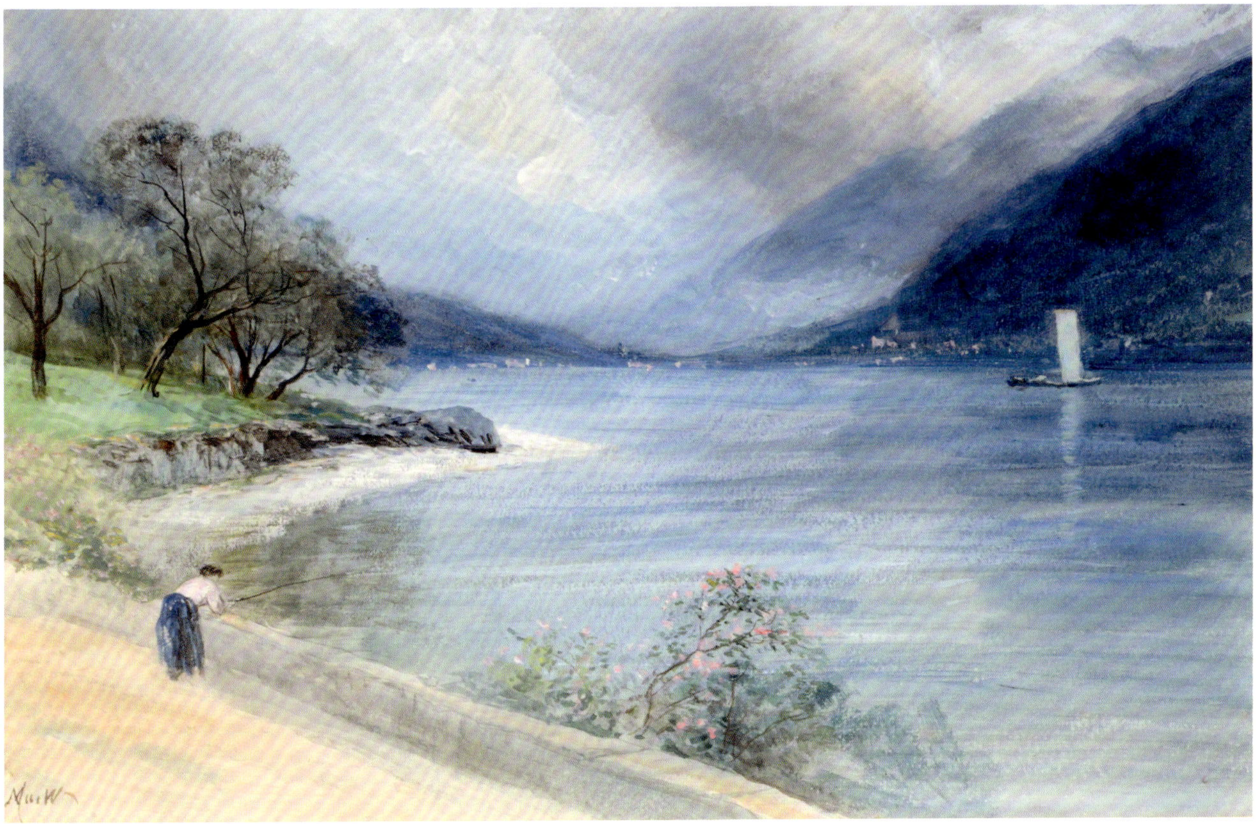

19 Lake Como, Stormy Weather
Signed 'MacW'
Watercolour and bodycolour on paper laid down on board
14 x 20 inches
Provenance: The Fine Art Society, March 1971

JOHN WILLIAM NORTH

John William North, ARA HRSW RWA RWS (1842-1924)

John William North was one of the most successful of late Victorian painters at capturing the experience of the rural atmosphere, in both oil and watercolour. Though he was best known for his English landscapes – and especially those of Somerset – his intense, almost tactile, approach to representing dense foliage equally suited the lush vegetation of the Bay of Algiers, which he visited regularly during the late 1870s.

John William North was born in the London suburb of Walham Green, Fulham, on 1 January 1842. At the age of 11, he was placed in the care of his uncles, when his draper father, mother and younger brother migrated to Canada. One great-uncle owned a farm in Hertfordshire, and early visits there set the pattern for the rural sojourns in which he nurtured his art. Leaving school at the age of 13, he studied at the Central School of Art at Marlborough House and, by 1858, was apprentice to the wood engraver Josiah Wood Whymper. He began his career in 1862 with the Dalziel Brothers, the leading firm of wood engravers, for whom he provided contributions to leading periodicals and volumes, including *Wayside Posies* (1867). From 1865, he also exhibited paintings, mainly watercolours, at such leading venues as the Royal Academy (elected an associate in 1893) and the Royal Society of Painters in Water-Colours (elected an associate in 1871 and a member in 1883). Later he would be elected an honorary member of the Royal Scottish Society of Painters in Water-Colours and a member of the Royal West of England Academy.

Back in 1860, North had encountered the Quantock Hills, Somerset, for the first time, on a walking tour with Edward Whymper, son of the engraver. He so loved the area that he lodged regularly at Halsway Manor Farm, often working there in the 1860s with fellow apprentices George Pinwell and Frederick Walker. These artists were bound together, in illustration and painting, by a response to their environment, for they evolved a form of landscape with figures that was grounded in topographical particulars yet imbued with the spirit of pastoral poetry. (Retrospectively, in 1895, on the occasion of an exhibition in Birmingham, the circle of artists centring on Walker and North would be given the name of 'Idyllists'.)

North confirmed his close association with the Quantocks in 1869, when he moved to Woolston Moor Farm, about three miles north of Halsway. He stayed there regularly until 1884, when he married Selina Weetch, the daughter of a Somerset farmer. They then settled at Beggearn Huish House, at Nettlecombe.

However, his friendship with Walker also led North, in the early 1870s, to take fishing trips to the Scottish Highlands, and to travel to Algiers. North arrived in Algiers on Christmas Day 1873, joining Walker, who had gone there for the sake of his health. When Walker became homesick and returned to England in the following February, North remained, buying a piece of land on which he built himself a house. He resided there for several months of each of the following six years, and maintained contact with the town until late in the century.

The premature deaths of Pinwell and Walker, in 1875, made North assess his career and strike out independently. He turned increasingly to pure landscape, excluding the figures that had emphasised his involvement in illustration. He also worked increasingly in pure watercolour, eschewing bodycolour, and evolving a loose, abstracted handling. He employed a similar approach in his occasional use of oil, a medium he took up at the suggestion of George Frederick Watts.

Four years after the death of his wife in 1894, North moved to Bilbrook, near Washford. He established the OW Paper and Arts Company, in order to manufacture and market a type of watercolour paper, made substantially of linen, which was ideal for his own practice but generally found hard to use.
He remained preoccupied with such experiments to the neglect of his painting until the company folded at the outbreak of the First World War. The few works that he completed after the turn of the century are considered to have a visionary quality. He spent the decade from 1904 at Withycombe and then his last years at Stamborough Farm, on the edge of Exmoor, dying there on 20 December 1924.

Further reading

Herbert Alexander, 'John William North', *Old Water-Colour Society's Club*, vol 5, 1927-28, pages 35-52; Christopher Newall, 'North, John William (1842-1924)', H C G Matthew and Brian Harrison (eds), *Oxford Dictionary of National Biography*, Oxford University Press, 2004, vol 41, pages 107-109

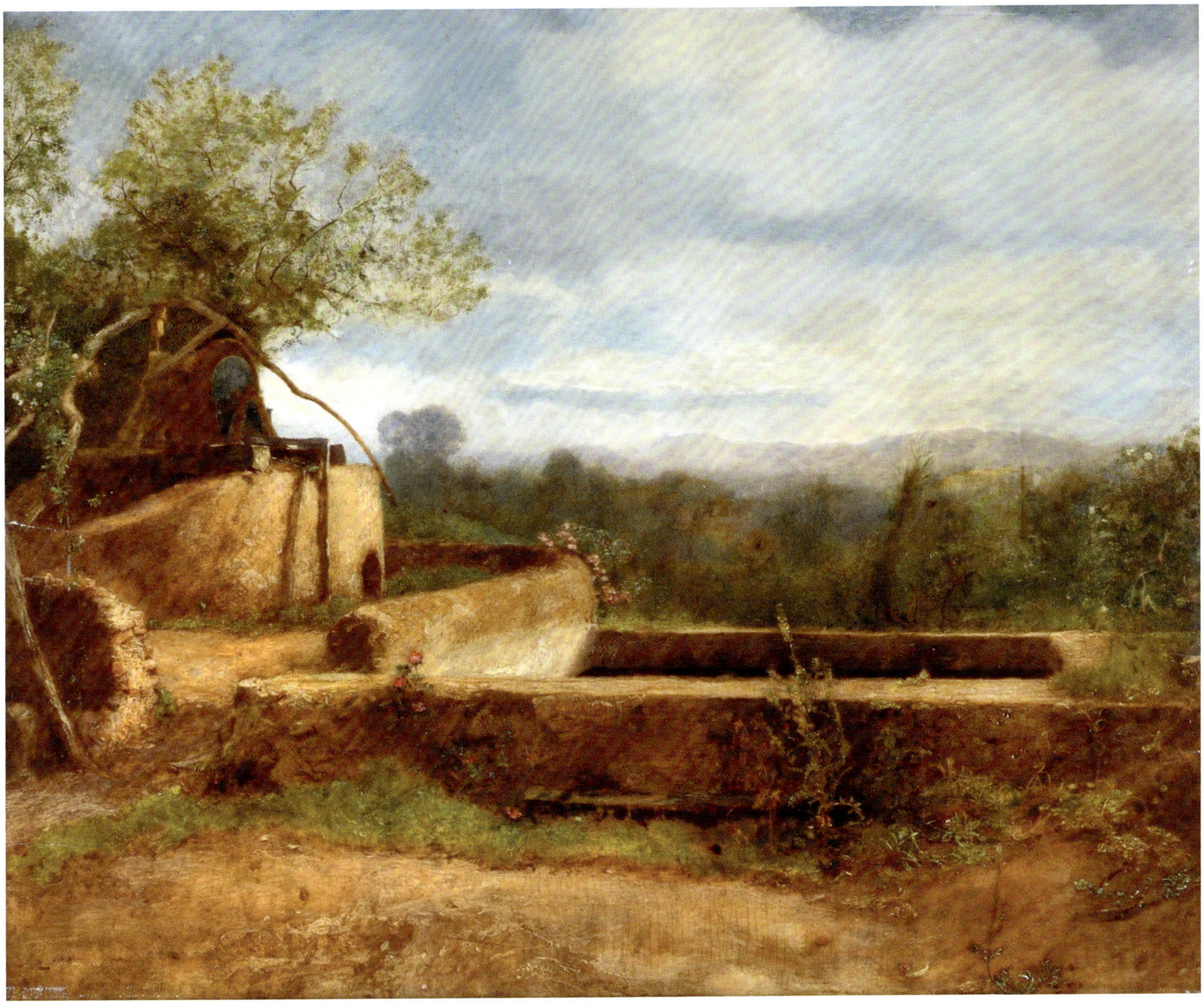

20 **Algerian Afternoon**
Signed, inscribed 'Algiers' and dated 1880
Oil on panel
24 ¾ x 30 inches

Algerian Afternoon

In the winter of 1873, J W North joined his friend and fellow artist, Fred Walker, on a trip to Algiers. Walker hoped that the warm North African climate would counter the effects of his chronic tuberculosis, and that the landscape might provide him with inspiration for his painting in progress, *The Unknown Land*. On their arrival on Christmas Day, the friends shared 'in ecstasies over the flowers and fruitful greenness of the land' (Alexander 1927-28). However, by late February 1874, Walker felt no better and had become homesick. So he left North and returned home in the company of the amateur artists, Barbara Bodichon and Gertrude Jekyll, who had also been wintering in Algiers. He would die on 4 June 1875, with *The Unknown Land* unfinished.

When Walker left, North stayed on in Mustapha Superieur, a beautiful suburb of Algiers frequented by English and French visitors. Buying a piece of land from his neighbour, Ali Cherif, he built himself a house called 'Dar el Ouard' or 'House of the Roses', and lived there for several months each year over the next six years, producing a number of oils and watercolours on Algerian themes. He sold it on his marriage in 1890, though retained a piece of land in Algiers for another five years in the vain hope of building another property. Dar el Ouard now seems to be the residence of the Spanish Ambassador to Algiers.

ALBERT GOODWIN

Albert Frederick Goodwin, RWS (1845-1932)

In synthesising the influences of J M W Turner and the Pre-Raphaelites, Albert Goodwin may be considered one of the most Ruskinian of Victorian landscape painters. Indeed, he was taken up by John Ruskin and, in 1872, given the opportunity to travel with him on an intensive tour of Italy and Switzerland. This set the pattern for many further and extensive travels. Like Ruskin, Goodwin responded to landscape with a religious fervour and understanding; but he interpreted it with even greater eclecticism than did his mentor, even experimenting with the style of James McNeill Whistler, Ruskin's adversary in the field of aesthetics.

Albert Goodwin was born in Boxley Road, Maidstone, Kent, on 17 January 1845, the son of the builder, Samuel Goodwin, and his wife, Rosetta. He was educated locally, in Bedford Place, at a school run by William Henry Wicksteed. On leaving school, he was apprenticed to a local draper, but after six months he left to take up painting. He was influenced by the Pre-Raphaelites, becoming the pupil of Arthur Hughes, who lived for a time in Maidstone, and later Ford Madox Brown. His early landscapes – mainly of Kent, but also of Jersey, Holland and Newcastle – are of an intense, jewel-like precision. Brown told his patron, James Leathart, that he believed that Goodwin would 'become before long one of the greatest landscape painters of the age' (in a letter dated 12 July 1864).

Following the death of his first wife, Mary Ann, in 1869, Goodwin moved to London to work in the studio of Arthur Hughes. It was probably through Hughes that Goodwin met the critic, John Ruskin, and then gave him a lesson in watercolour painting. At about the time that he was elected an associate of the Society of Painters in Water Colours, in 1871, Ruskin commissioned him to producesome landscapes of Oxfordshire. Then, in the following year, Ruskin took him and Arthur Severn on a three-month tour through Switzerland to Italy. Goodwin never forgot this introduction to alpine scenery, which remained for him a standard of beauty, or to the cities of Italy, which he revisited on numerous occasions. As if demonstrating the programme that Ruskin had laid out in *Modern Painters*, Goodwin looked increasingly to the example of Turner; at times, however, he tried to synthesise it with the aesthetic of Whistler. This conflict of influences is dramatised to fascinating effect in Goodwin's privately printed diaries.

Goodwin was a hardworking and prolific artist, driven by religious belief and moral responsilibity to express his talent and provide for his family. He travelled extensively in search of varied, and often exotic, landscapes, and visited Egypt (1876), India (1895), the West Indies and North America (1902, 1912) and New Zealand (1917). Sometimes these sites became settings for literary or biblical subjects, some developed on a large scale and painted in oil. Goodwin exhibited regularly at the Royal Academy (1860-1920) and the Royal Society of Painters in Water-Colours. He became an associate of the RWS in 1871 and a full member a decade later. In addition, he held eight solo shows at the Fine Art Society (1886-1907), three at Leggatt's (1912-22), two at the Rembrandt Gallery (1902, 1904), and others. Later in his career, he reworked and embellished many of his favourite watercolours, adding ink lines, surrounding them with borders, and assembling them in albums. Through his career, he lived in London, Devon and Sussex. He died on 10 April 1932, outliving his second wife, Alice, by 16 years. He was survived by their five daughters and two sons.

His work is represented in numerous public collections, including the British Museum, Tate and the V&A; and The Fitzwilliam Museum (Cambridge), Maidstone Museum & Bentlif Art Gallery, Manchester Art Gallery and The Whitworth Art Gallery (Manchester).

For further information on the life and work of Goodwin, please refer to *Albert Goodwin RWS 1845-1932*, 1986; *Albert Goodwin RWS 1845-1932*, 1996; and *Albert Goodwin RWS 1845-1932*, 2007; all published by Chris Beetles Ltd. Chris Beetles has also published a sumptuous limited edition volume of over 400 pages and more than 200 colour plates, accompanied by extracts from Goodwin's diaries.

22 **A Mountain Stream**
Signed and dated /84
Watercolour
13 ¾ x 20 ½ inches
Exhibited: Royal Society of Painters In Water-Colours, Winter 1884, no 254
Literature: Christopher Wood, *Victorian Painting*, London: Weidenfeld and Nicholson, 1996

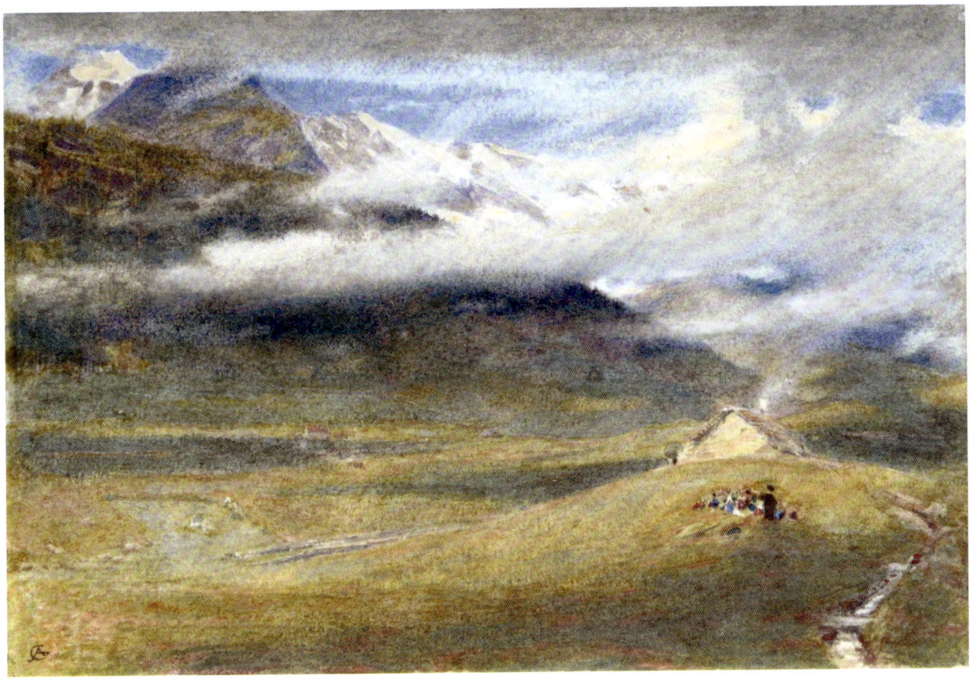

21 **Swiss Valley**
Signed with monogram
Watercolour and bodycolour
4 ¾ x 6 ¾ inches

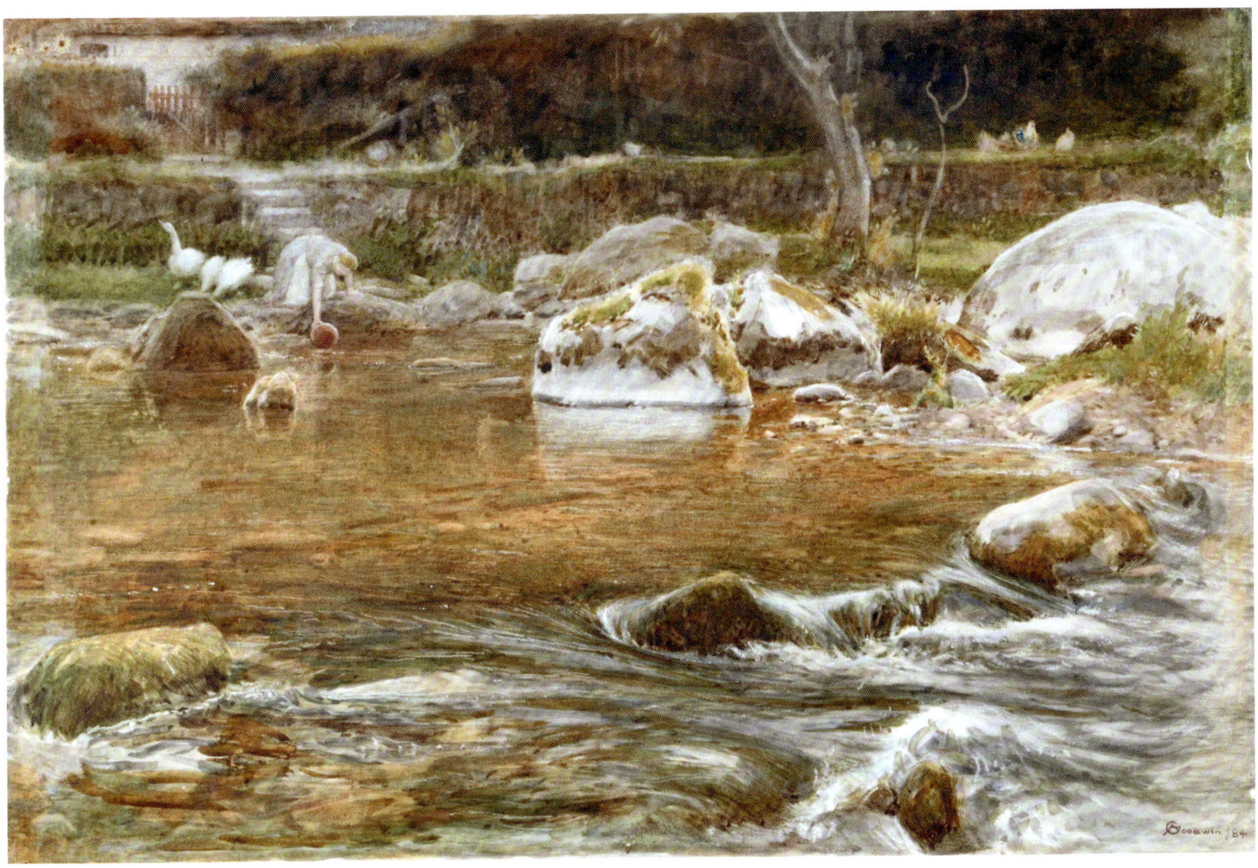

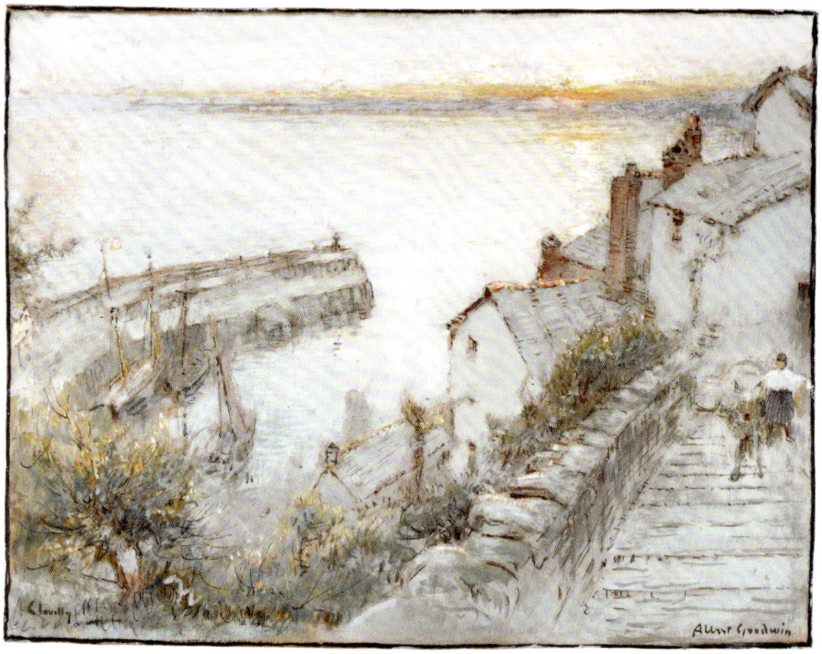

23 **Clovelly**
Signed and inscribed with title
Watercolour, bodycolour and ink
on tinted paper
9 x 11 ¾ inches

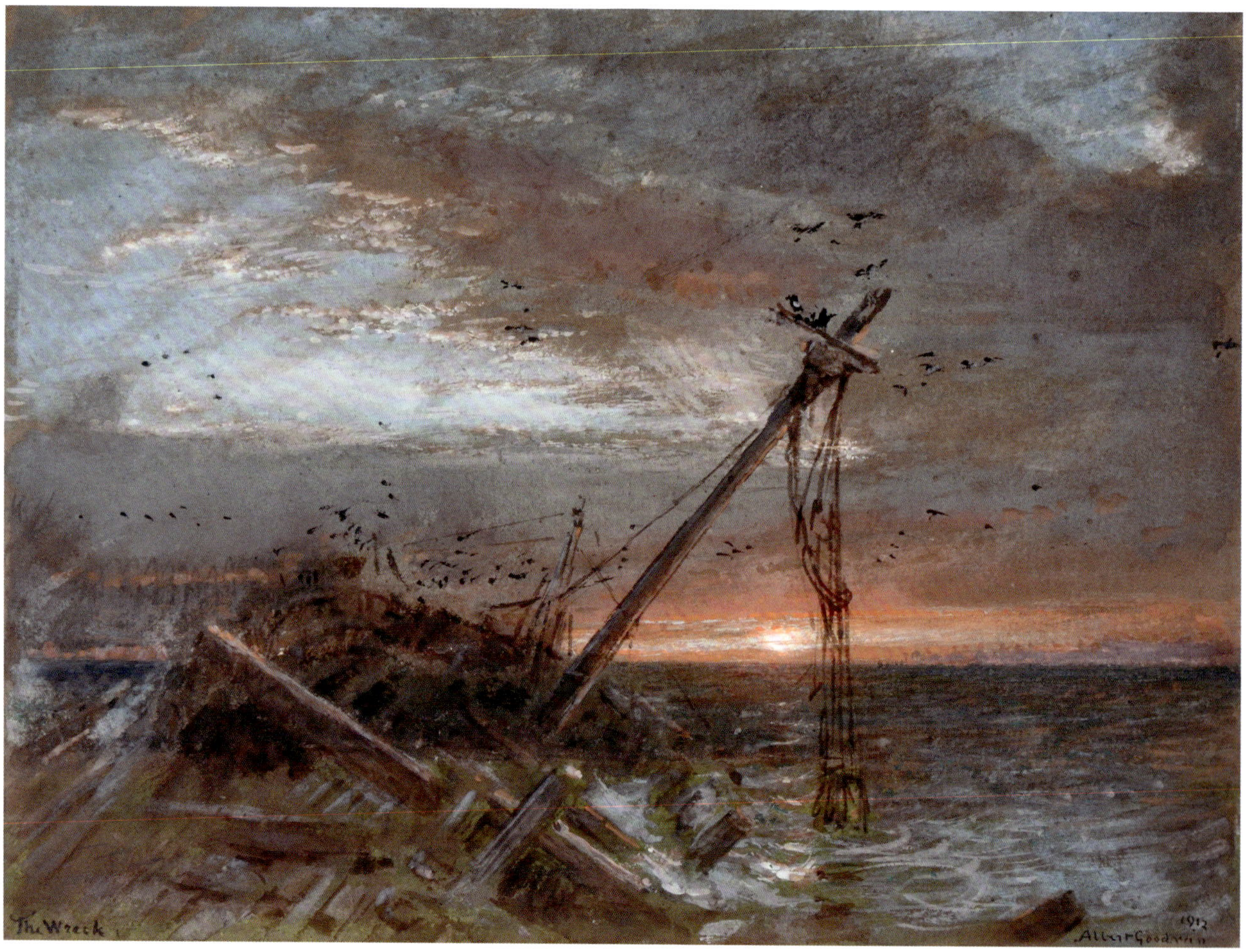

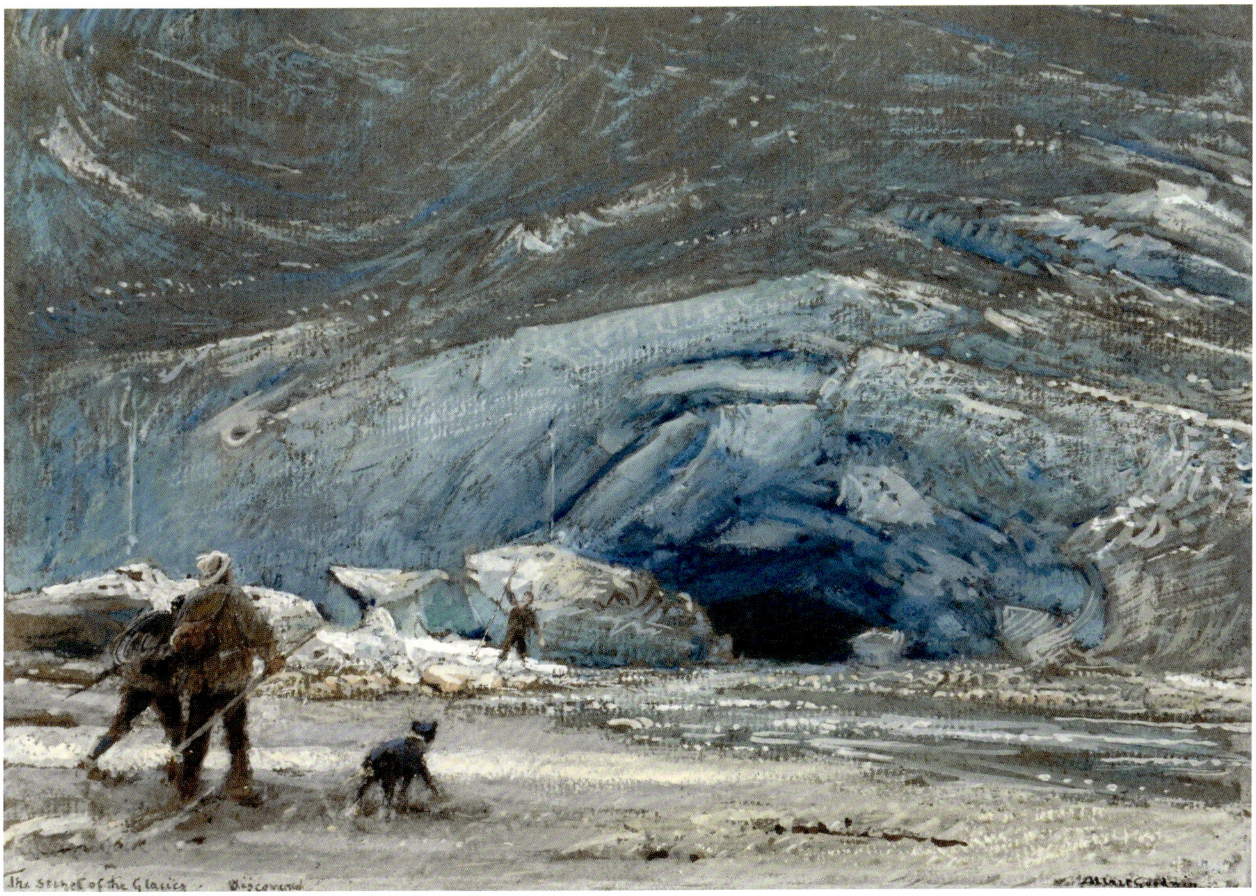

25 The Secret of the Glacier. Discovered
Signed and inscribed with title
Watercolour and bodycolour on tinted paper
10 x 15 inches
Provenance: Matthew Biggar Walker
Exhibited: 'A Collection of Oil Paintings, Water Colour Drawings etc, by Albert Goodwin RWS RWA, lent by M B Walker Esq', City of Birmingham Museum and Art Gallery, 1926, no 22

24 The Wreck
Signed, inscribed with title and dated 1912
Watercolour and bodycolour on tinted paper
10 ¾ x 14 ¼ inches

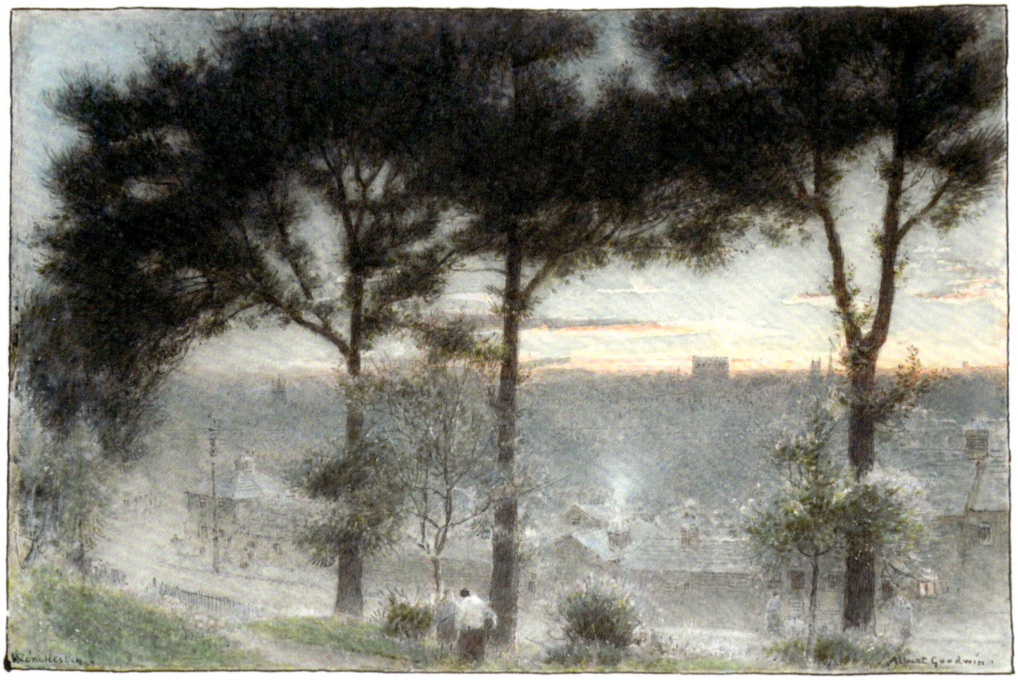

26 Winchester
Signed and inscribed with title
Watercolour with pen ink and bodycolour
9 ¾ x 14 ½ inches

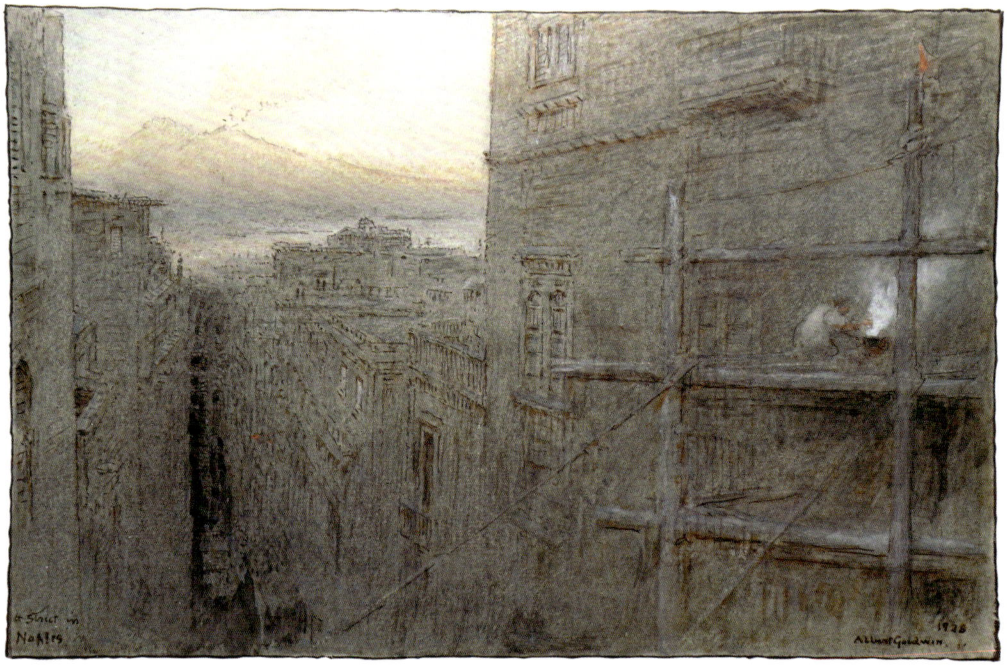

27 A Street in Naples
Signed, inscribed with title and dated 1926
Watercolour with pen ink and bodycolour
enclosed by decorative border
10 x 15 inches

THOMAS HOSMER SHEPHERD

Thomas Hosmer Shepherd (1793-1864)

Thomas Hosmer Shepherd was probably the most talented member of a family of London topographers, his once famous images outstanding in their vivacious detail.

Thomas Hosmer Shepherd was born in France on 16 January 1793, the son of a watchcase maker. On returning to England, the Shepherd family settled in a neighbourhood close to the City Road in London, and Thomas was baptised at St Luke Old Street, on 24 February.

Throughout his career, from 1809 to 1859, Shepherd was patronised by the celebrated interior designer, Frederick Crace, who became equally famous as a collector of views and maps of London. Crace commissioned him to produce watercolours of specific London buildings and locations, and also bought others from him. The fame of the Crace Collection then acted as a springboard for Shepherd's career, as he began to receive commissions from others, including Rudolph Ackermann. From around the time of its foundation in 1809, until its demise in 1828, Shepherd produced a series of street views for Ackermann's magazine, *The Repository of Arts*, sometimes in collaboration with his elder brother, George Sidney Shepherd.

Though he became virtually synonymous with the modern city, Shepherd was equally skilful in representing the countryside. To this end, he made a number of sketching tours, the first in 1810.

Eight years later, Shepherd visited France, probably on his honeymoon, an event apparently commemorated in the naming of the first of his seven children, Frederick Napoleon Shepherd, who was born in June 1819. By 1820, the family had settled at 26 Chapman Street (now Batchelor Street), Islington, one of the new streets on the west side of the Liverpool Road, on the edge of the built up area of the city. He used his home address when advertising as a drawing master.

From this time, Shepherd established himself as a book illustrator, with contributions to the part work, *Londina Illustrata* (1819-25), again in collaboration with his brother, George, among others. Security and success soon arrived, with his first commission from the publisher, Jones & Co, based at the Temple of the Muses, Finsbury Square. The first part of *Metropolitan Improvements* appeared in 1827, and comprised numerous steel engravings after drawings by Shepherd, with a commentary by the architect, James Elmes. Its popularity not only ensured further commissions for Shepherd from Jones but 'induced many publishers to embark on similar works' (an unsigned review in the *Gentleman's Magazine* for March 1829, cited by J F C Phillips, *Shepherd's London*, London: Cassell 1976, page 11).

The sequel to *Metropolitan Improvements*, entitled *London and its Environs*, would begin to appear in 1828.

During 1827, Shepherd made sketching tours of the West Country and Scotland in order to prepare his drawings for *Modern Athens!* (1829) and *Bath and Bristol* (1829-31), published by Jones with commentaries by the well-known antiquarian, John Britton. Yet, while Jones and Shepherd planned other volumes about parts of Great Britain (and Shepherd responded by travelling to Ireland in 1828), no further such publication materialised.

Shepherd began to work with other publishers, often reworking the images of London that he had drawn for Jones, while also broadening his horizons. So he exhibited four watercolours of Scotland at the Society of British Artists, in 1831 and 1832, and produced illustrations of Westmorland and the Rhine, by 1832 (though not necessarily on location).

A decade later, Shepherd moved to 2 Bird's Buildings (now part of Colebrooke Row), north of Camden Passage, Islington – probably to better accommodate his growing family. From that time, he provided some images for the *Illustrated London News*, but became very poor, and was sustained only by the continuing patronage of Crace, who died in 1859.

Shepherd himself died in Islington on 4 July 1864. His wife, Jane Maria, and at least three of his children survived him. They included Frederick Napoleon Shepherd, who carried on the family tradition of topography, and Valentine Claude Shepherd, a wood engraver.

The Crace Collection in the British Museum contains nearly 500 images by Shepherd, including 38 views of Edinburgh for *Modern Athens!* His work is also represented in numerous other public collections, including Kensington & Chelsea Library and the V&A.

Further reading

Brian Reginald Curle and Patricia Meara, *Thomas Hosmer Shepherd, 1793-1864: a descriptive catalogue of watercolours and drawings in the local collections of Kensington and Chelsea libraries*, London: Kensington and Chelsea Public Libraries, 1973; Lucy Peltz, 'Shepherd, George Sidney (1784-1862)', H C G Matthew and Brian Harrison (eds), *Oxford Dictionary of National Biography*, Oxford University Press, 2004, vol 50, page 245 (which includes reference to Thomas Hosmer Shepherd); J F C Phillips, *Shepherd's London*, London: Cassell 1976

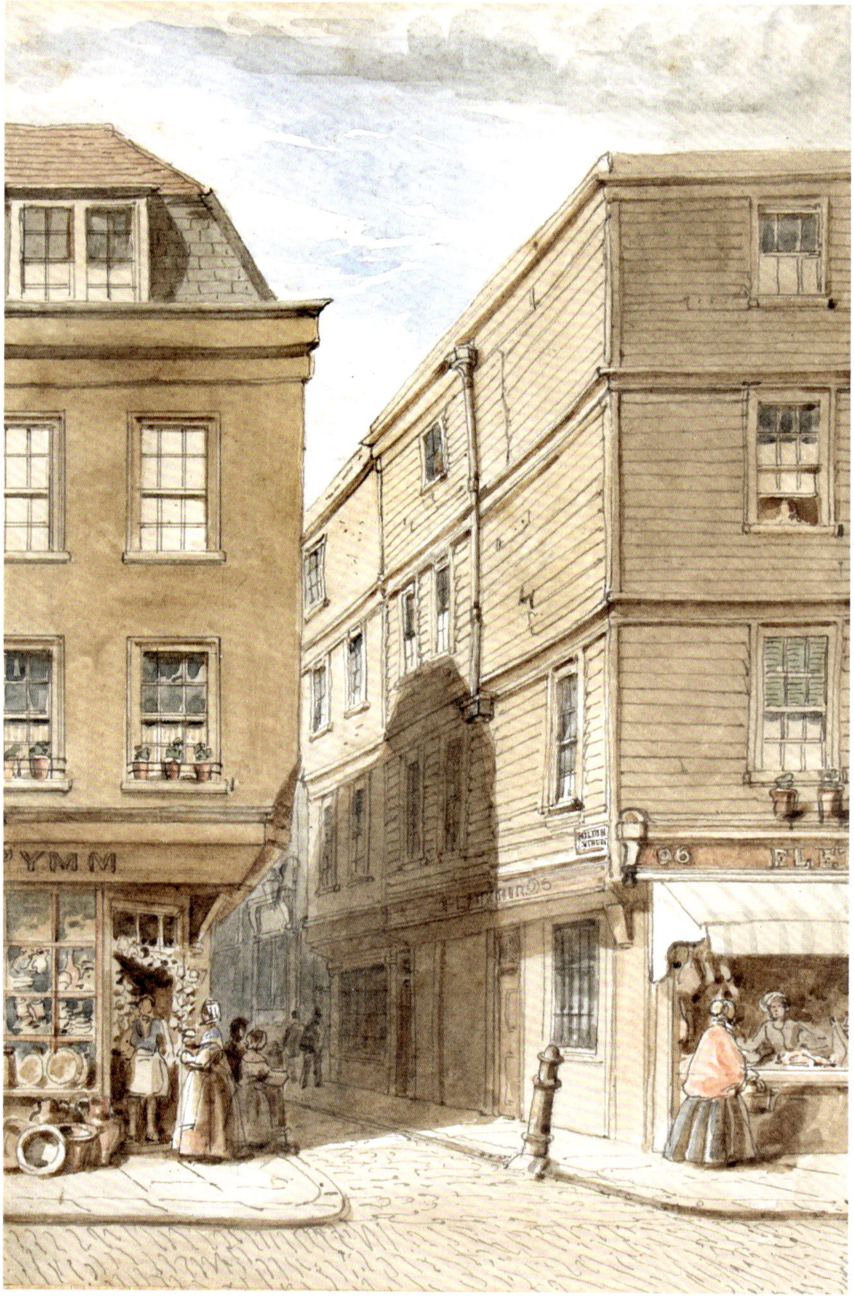

28 Entrance to Milton Street from Fore Street, Cripplegate
Inscribed 'Entrance to Milton Street F Fore St, Cripplegate on reverse
Watercolour and pencil
8 ½ x 5 ¾ inches

Entrance to Milton Street from Fore Street, Cripplegate
East of the Church of St Giles-Without-Cripplegate, and running between Fore Street and Chiswell Street, Milton Street was better known as Grub Street, its name before 1830. As such it became synonymous with the margins of London's literary and journalistic scene from the seventeenth century onwards. By the early eighteenth century, it had become a focus for poor and aspiring writers and for publishers and sellers of cheap books, pamphlets and newspapers, including the *Grub Street Journal* (1730-37).

Thomas Hosmer Shepherd produced his image in the mid nineteenth century. It represents the junction of Milton Street and Fore Street in such detail that the shop on the left can be identified as that belonging to Philip Pymm, a dealer in china, glass and earthenware. The business certainly operated from 97 Fore Street between 1811 and 1871, and Pymm himself may be the figure standing in the doorway. For much of that period, the shop at 96 Fore Street, on the right, was a cheesemonger. By the 1850s, it was run by William Fletcher, whose surname can be seen emblazoned above the ground floor, on both the front and the side of the building.

Andrewes House, one of the apartment blocks on the Barbican Estate, has stood on the site of Fore Street since 1969. It is named after Lancelot Andrewes, who was Vicar of St Giles, Cripplegate, from 1588, and rose to become Dean of Westminster.

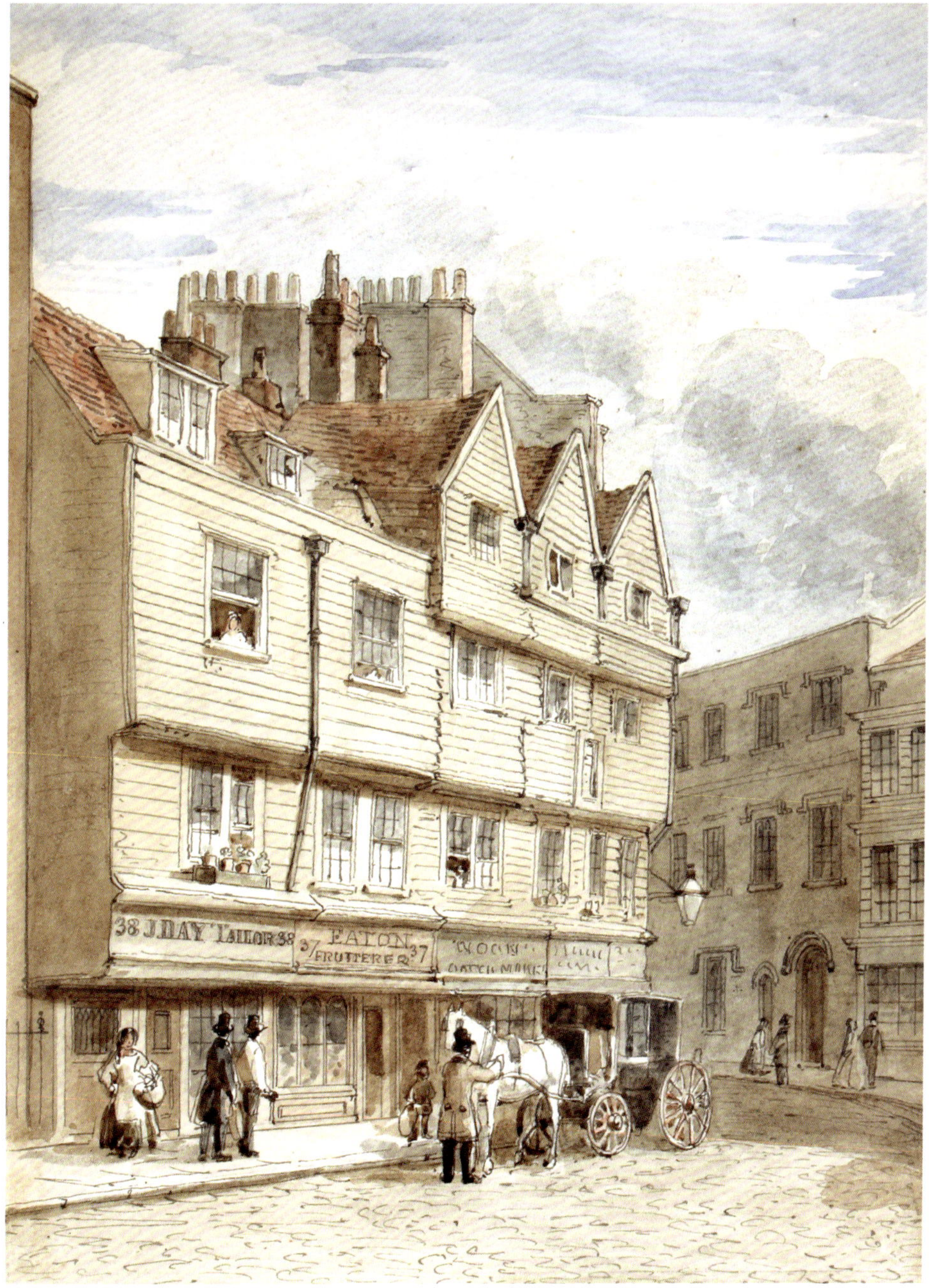

29 Old Building, Red Cross Street and Fore Street, Cripplegate
Inscribed with title on reverse
Watercolour
8 ½ x 6 ¼ inches

Old Building, Red Cross Street and Fore Street, Cripplegate
Red Cross Street ran between Beech Street in the north and Fore Street in the south, on land that is now covered by the Barbican Centre. It seems to have been named after a cross that stood at the north end of the street. However, William Denton, writing in *Records of St Giles' Cripplegate* in 1883, suggests that it derived its name 'from the signs or armorial bearings of the abbey of Ramsey', Huntingdonshire, which had owned property in the street (page 166).

Though this watercolour seems to be a pair with *Entrance to Milton Street*, it has not been possible to date the two with any certainty to the same decade of production. However, it is most likely that Thomas Hosmer Shepherd here represents the configuration of shops late in the 1850s. He produced another, more frontal view of this block of shops in 1850 for the collection of the interior designer, Frederick Crace (which is now in the British Museum). This shows the buildings occupied by different shopkeepers: No 38 by Tune, a ticket and sign writer, No 37 by Lord, a tailor, and No 36 by a greengrocer. A year later, the artist, John Wykeham Archer (1808-1864), painted another, wider view of the block, in which an unnamed tobacconist has replaced Tune at No 38, though Lord, the tailor, remains at No 37. Archer includes what Shepherd's narrower perspective has to omit: the tower of St Giles Cripplegate looming over the buildings to the right.

HERBERT MENZIES MARSHALL

Herbert Menzies Marshall, VPRWS RE ARIBA ROI (1841-1913)

Herbert Menzies Marshall was one of the most atmospheric of the Edwardian painters of urban topography.

Herbert Menzies Marshall was born on 1 August 1841, the youngest son of Thomas Horncastle Marshall, barrister-by-law, and later Judge of the Leeds County Court. The family lived at 33 Park Square, Leeds, and Outwood Hall, near Wakefield.

Marshall was educated at Westminster School and Trinity College, Cambridge, playing first-class cricket for the university, and graduating in 1864 with a second-class degree in the natural science tripos. In the same year, he went to Paris for the purpose of studying architecture, and entered the atelier of Charles-Auguste Questel. On his return from Paris in 1867, he became a student of the Royal Academy Schools, and in the following year received the Travelling Studentship for Architecture. Apparently, 'the result of travelling in Italy and of constant sketching under a bright sun was to weaken his eyesight so much that he was obliged to give up all work for two years, and especially any architectural drawing' (Plarr 1895, page 570). On his return to England, he lived close to the Royal Academy at 22 Old Burlington Street, with the architect, Robert Kerr, and was elected an associate of the Royal Institute of British Architects, though never practised as an architect, and retired in 1871.

Marshall's 'accident induced him to turn his attention to water-colour painting, as being less trying to the eyes, and in 1871 he exhibited his first drawing at the Dudley Gallery' (Plarr 1895, loc cit). He then worked mainly in London, producing series of topographical watercolours for exhibition and publication. He was elected an associate of the Royal Society of Painters in Water-Colours in 1879, a full member in 1882 and acted as Vice-President between 1898 and 1900. He was also elected to the Royal Society of Painter-Etchers and Engravers (1881), and the Royal Institute of Painters in Oils (1901). In addition, he showed regularly at such London dealers as the Fine Art Society, the Abbey Gallery and the Leicester Galleries, and in Paris, winning a silver medal at the Exposition Universelle of 1889.

Lodging at 35 Great Marlborough Street by April 1881, Marshall married Amy Lee, the daughter of a solicitor, at the end of that month. Together, they would have one son and two daughters. By 1883, they were living at 1 Victoria Mansions, Westminster, with the Great Marlborough Street address probably being retained as a studio. In 1896, they probably moved to 39 Grosvenor Road, Pimlico, and were certainly living there by 1900.

In 1904, Marshall was appointed Professor of Landscape Painting at Queen's College, Harley Street, London. By that date, he and his family were living at 83 Philbeach Gardens, Earl's Court. He illustrated a number of books, including Miss Mitton's *The Scenery of London* (1905), E V Lucas's *Wanderer in Holland* (1905) and – with his daughter, Hester – *Cathedral Cities of France* (1907). He died at home on 2 March 1913.

Further reading

Victor G Plarr, *Men and Women of the Time. A Dictionary of Contemporaries*, London: George Routledge, 1895, page 570

'His special aim [is] to show how beautiful and mysterious is the common life of the streets and on the river when seen under the atmospheric effects which are found only in London.'

(Plarr 1895, page 570)

30 **Houses of Parliament**
Signed and dated 1906
Watercolour
10 ½ x 7 ¼ inches

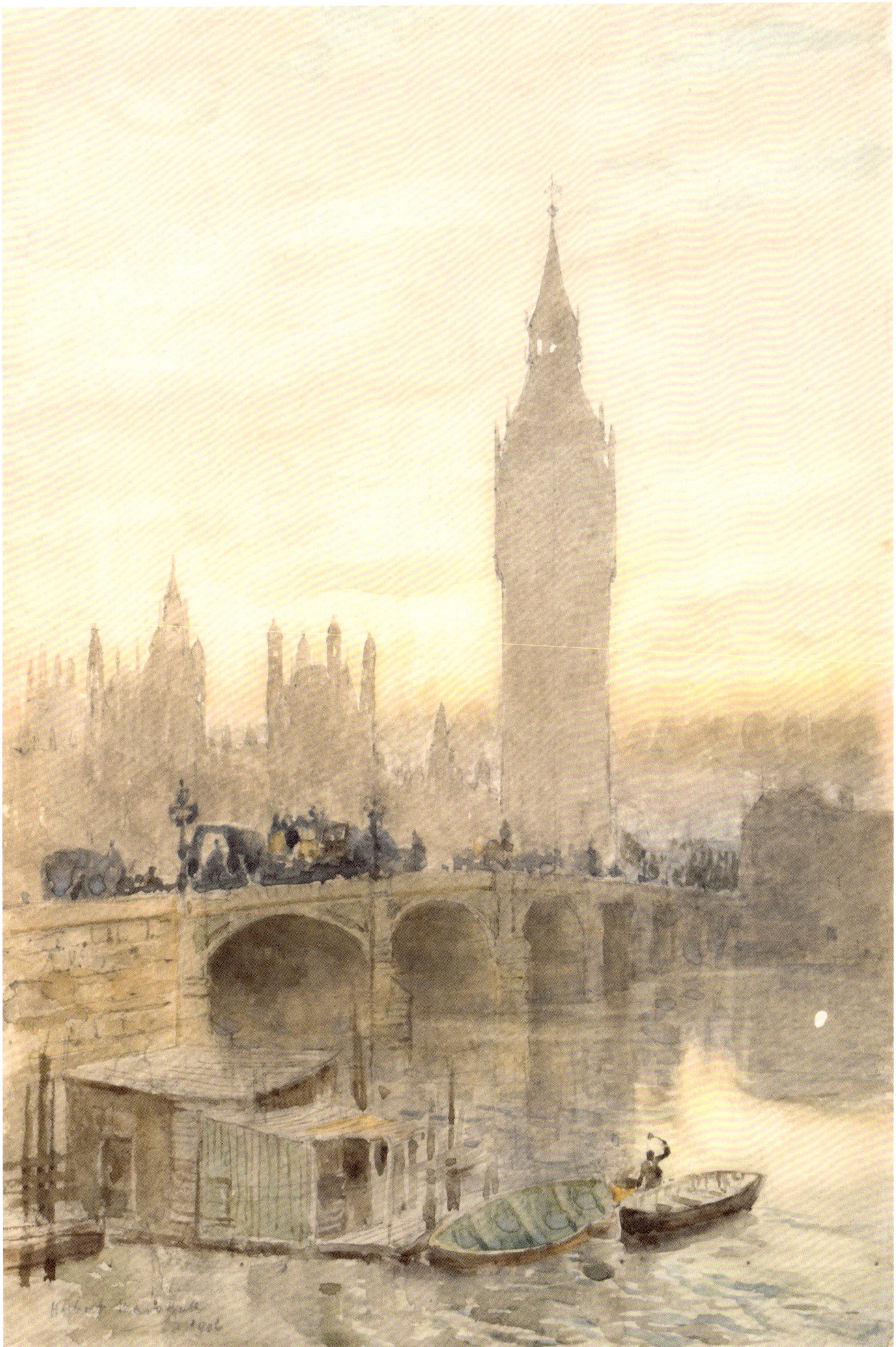

WILLIAM LIONEL WYLLIE

William Lionel Wyllie, RA RBA RE RI NEAC (1851-1931)

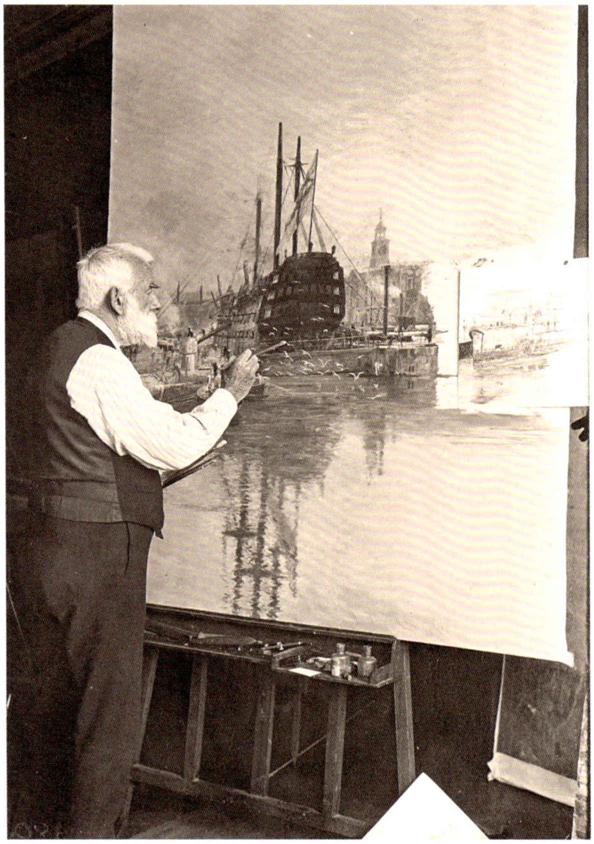

W L Wyllie at work on *Swaying up the Mainyard*, which he exhibited at the Royal Academy Summer Exhibition in 1928

The leading British marine artist of the late nineteenth century, William Lionel Wyllie captured the sea and shipping in a wide range of images from fresh watercolours of Northern France through etchings of the Thames to large-scale canvases of historically significant events.

William Lionel Wyllie was born in London on 5 July 1851, son of the painter William Morrison Wyllie. As a child, he lived at 67 Albany Street, close to Regent's Park, and spent summers at Wimereux, on the French coast, where he began to sketch, encouraged by his father and his half-brother, Lionel Percy Smythe. He studied art at the Heatherley School of Fine Art (1865) and at the Royal Academy Schools (1866-69), where he won the Turner Medal in his final year. He also made a study of the history of shipbuilding to help him with his paintings. His notable influences include Henry Moore, Whistler and Turner, of whom he later wrote a study (1905).

Wyllie worked initially as a marine illustrator for *The Graphic* (1870-90), and from 1883 produced etchings for Robert Dunthorne of the Rembrandt Gallery. In 1884, he published *Tidal Thames*, the first of a number of books that he both wrote and illustrated. Exhibiting at such leading London venues as the Royal Academy, he had five solo shows at the Fine Art Society (from 1883). He was elected to the Society of British Artists (1875); the New English Art Club (1887); the Royal Institute of Painters in Water Colours (1882, resigning in 1884, but being re-elected in 1917); a Royal Academician (ARA 1889, RA 1907); to the Royal Society of Painter-Etchers and Engravers (ARE 1903, RE 1904).

In 1884, Wyllie moved to Gillingham House, near Chatham, settling shortly after at Hoo St Werburgh. He then formed a close association with the Royal Navy, which he sealed, in 1907, on moving to Portsmouth, where he lived in the Tower House. He was Marine Painter to the Royal Yacht Squadron and the Royal Victoria Yacht Club, and did much work, including posters, for the Orient Company, White Star Line and Union Castle Line. Often sailing in the barge Ladybird and in yachts, he made painting trips to Holland and Northern France. In 1917 he painted an aerial view of the Battle of Bourlon Wood, for which Air Marshal Trenchard sent maps and aerial photographs. Between 1924 and 1930 he worked on a Panorama of Trafalgar for the Victory Museum, Portsmouth. He died in London on 6 April 1931.

His work is represented in the Defence Academy of the United Kingdom and the Ministry of Defence Art Collection, and numerous public collections including the Guildhall Art Gallery, the Imperial War Museum, the National Maritime Museum; and the National Museum of the Royal Navy (Portsmouth), Portsmouth Museums and Records Service and the Russell-Cotes Art Gallery and Museum.

Further reading

Stephen Deuchar, 'Wyllie, W(illiam) L(ionel) (*b* London, 6 July 1851; *d* London, 6 April 1931)', Jane Turner (ed), *The Dictionary of Art*, London: Macmillan, 1996, vol 33, page 452;
H B Grimsditch, *rev* Roger Quarm, 'Wyllie, William Lionel (1851-1931)', H C G Matthew and Brian Harrison (eds), *Oxford Dictionary of National Biography*, Oxford University Press, 2004, vol 60, pages 654-655

Chris Beetles is the publisher of the definitive biography of W L Wyllie entitled *W L Wyllie: Marine Artist, 1851-1931*, by Roger Quarm, former curator of pictures at the National Maritime Museum, and John Wyllie, the artist's grandson.

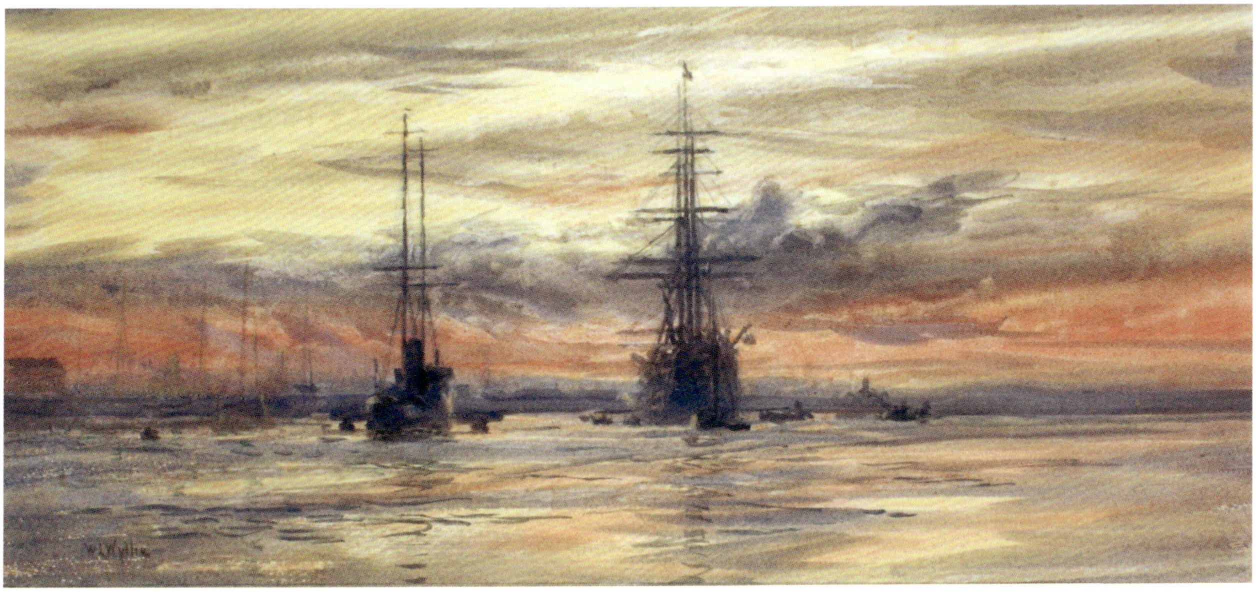

31 **Shipping at Sunset**
Signed
Watercolour
5 x 11 inches

32 **Moonlight**
Oil on paper
10 ½ x 14 inches
Provenance: Aileen Wyllie, the daughter of the artist, and by descent

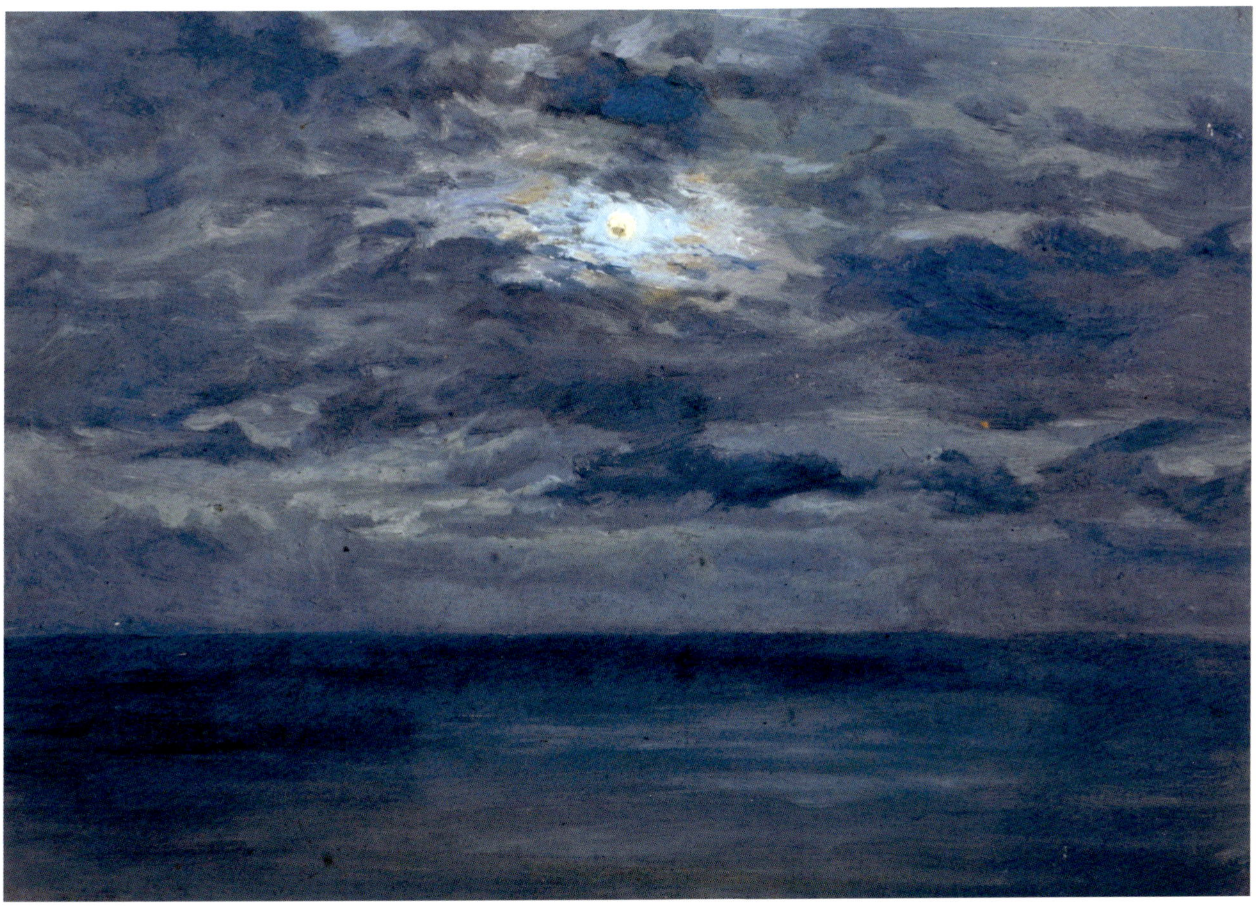

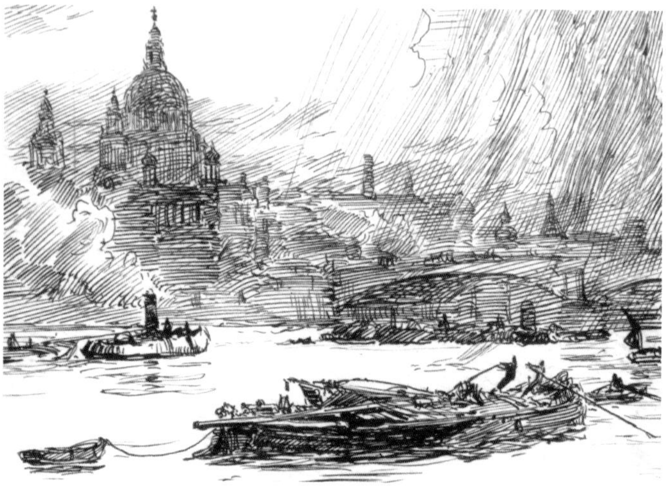

33 St Paul's Cathedral, seen from the River
Pen and ink
4 ½ x 6 ¼ inches
Provenance: Aileen Wyllie, the daughter of the artist, and by descent
Illustrated: W L and M A Wyllie, *London to the Nore*, London: A & C Black, 1905, page 22 (in a wider format, the artwork having been subsequently cropped, probably by the artist)

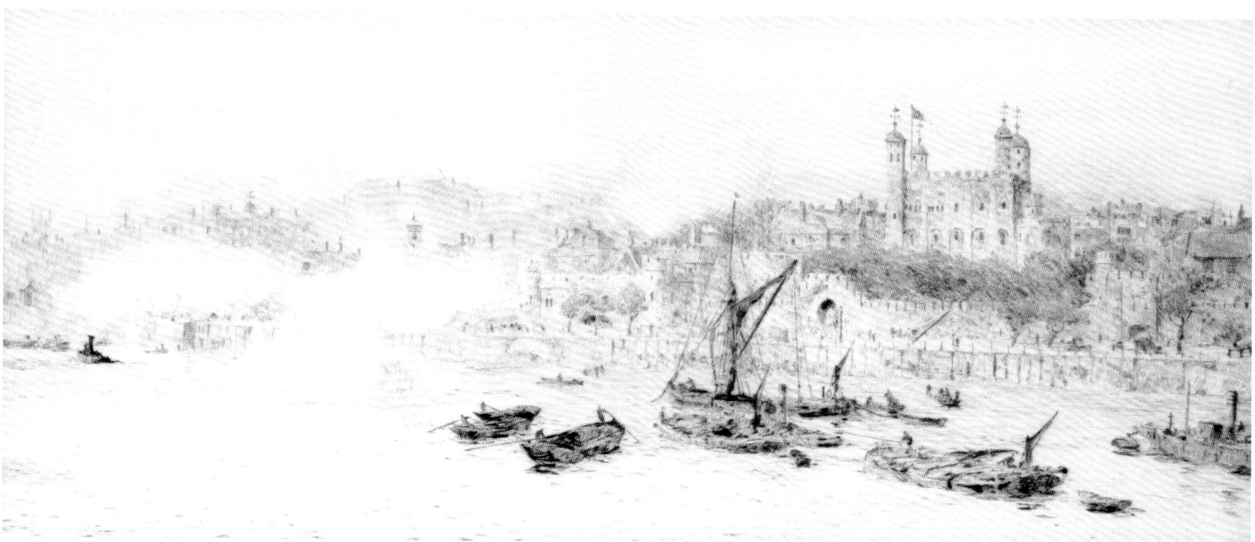

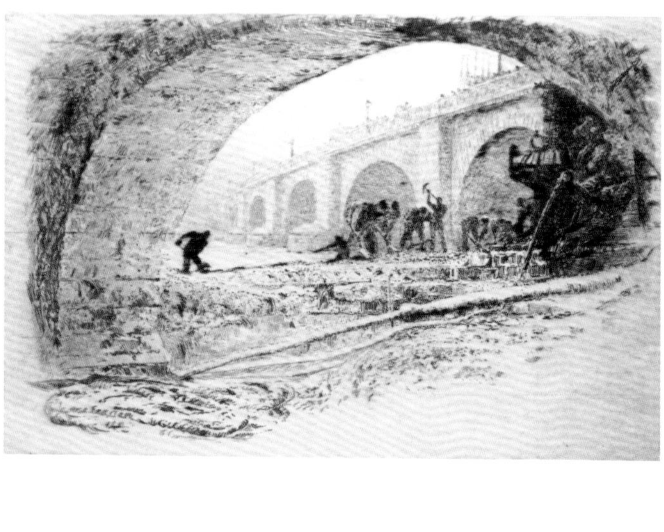

34 Royal Salute, the Tower of London
Inscribed 'Trial proof'
Etching and aquatint
7 x 15 ¾ inches
Provenance: Aileen Wyllie, the daughter of the artist, and by descent

35 The Northern Arch of Old London Bridge
Inscribed 'Trial proof'
Etching
7 x 9 inches
Provenance: Aileen Wyllie, the daughter of the artist, and by descent

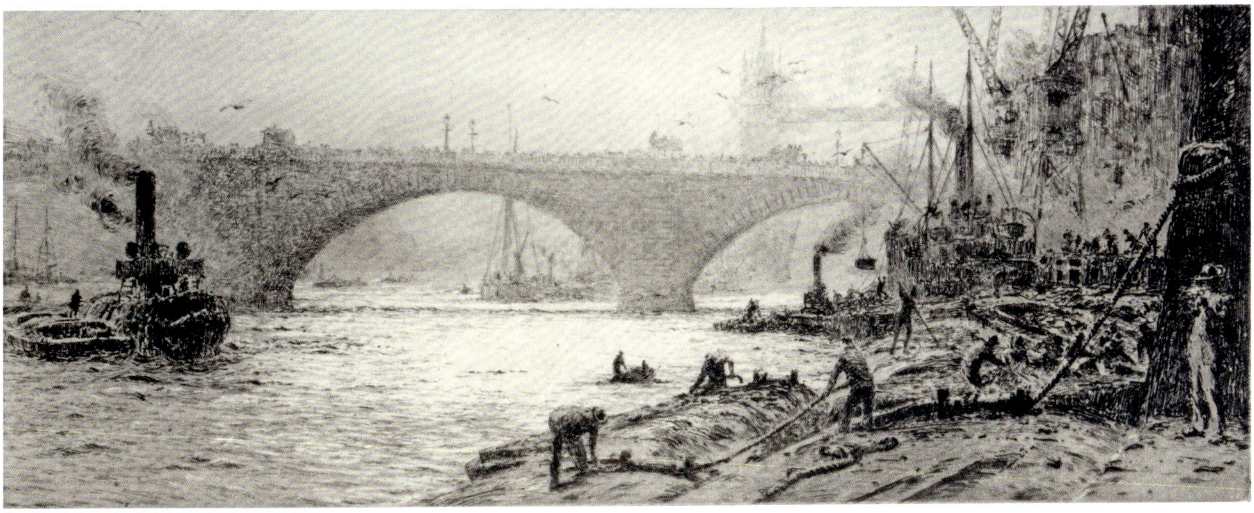

36 London Bridge
Signed
Etching with aquatint
5 x 12 ¾ inches
Provenance: Mawson, Swan and Morgan, Picture Dealers, Newcastle

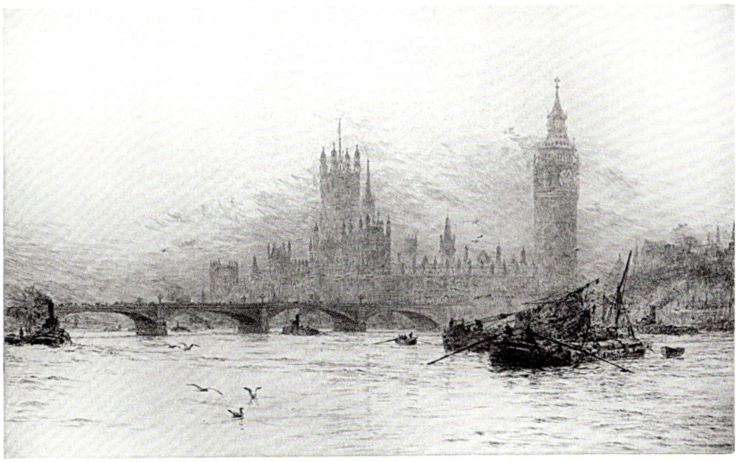

37 Westminster
Signed and inscribed with title
Etching with drypoint
9 ½ x 14 inches

38 Blackfriars to Westminster from the Top of St Paul's Cathedral
Inscribed 'Trial proof'
Etching
7 x 15 ½ inches
Provenance: Aileen Wyllie, the daughter of the artist, and by descent

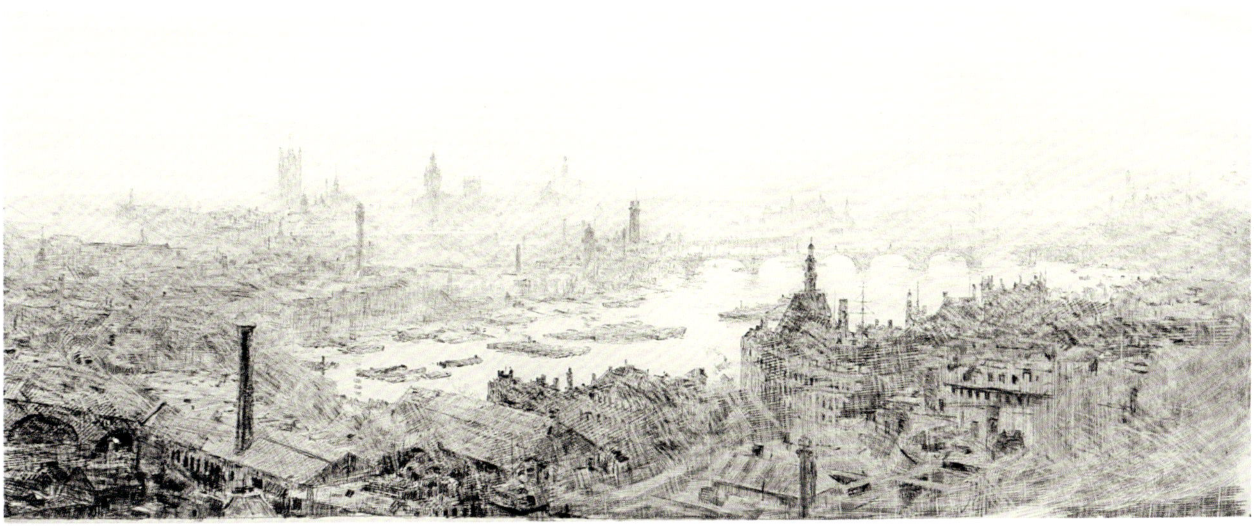

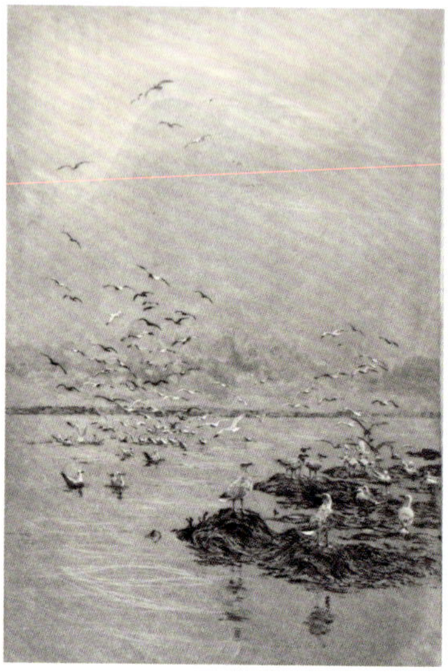

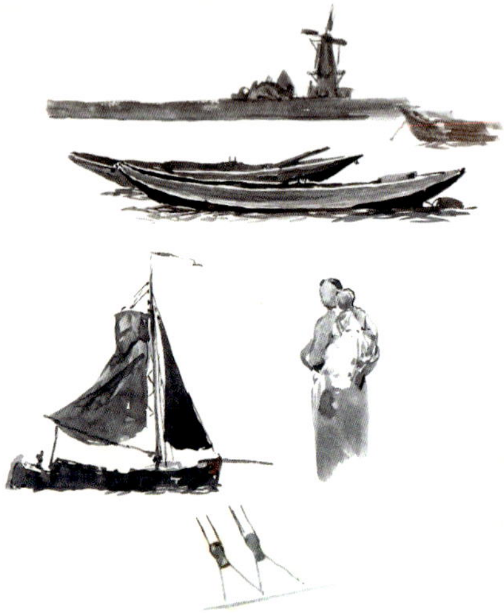

39 Seagulls
Inscribed 'Working proof'
Etching, drypoint and aquatint
12 ¾ x 9 inches
Provenance: Aileen Wyllie, the daughter of the artist, and by descent

40 Sailing Barges on a Still Day
Pen ink and watercolour
9 ½ x 7 ¼ inches

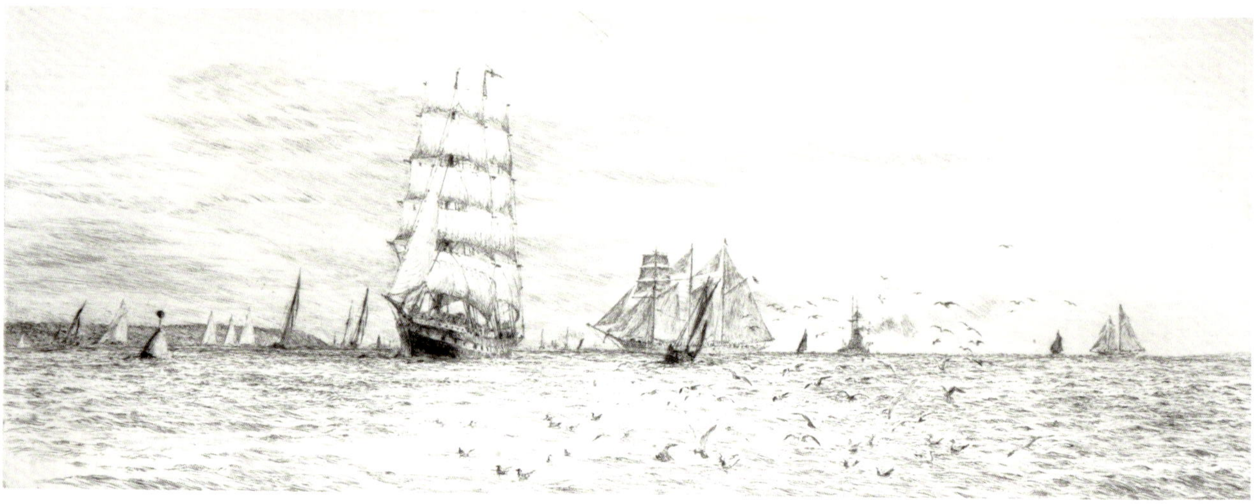

41 Fantôme and Sunbeam
Signed
Etching, 5 x 13 inches

Fantôme and Sunbeam

The Fantôme, was originally launched as Belem in 1896 in Nantes, France. She was built as a cargo ship to transport sugar from the West Indies and cocoa and coffee from South America. In 1914 she was sold to Hugh Grosvenor, 2nd Duke of Westminster (1879-1953), who converted her into his private yacht. In 1922 she was sold to Hon. A E Guinness (1876-1949) who renamed her Fantôme II and sailed her round the world with his three daughters the following year. Guinness was so attached to the Fantôme, that he extended the deckhouse to accomodate his office so that wherever he travelled he could conduct his business without leaving the ship. She remained in the Guinness family until 1951. Eventually, after changing hands several times, she returned in 1979 to her home port of Nantes, again as Belem, flying the French flag after 65 years. Fully restored to her original condition, she began a new career as a sail training ship and is still sailing today.

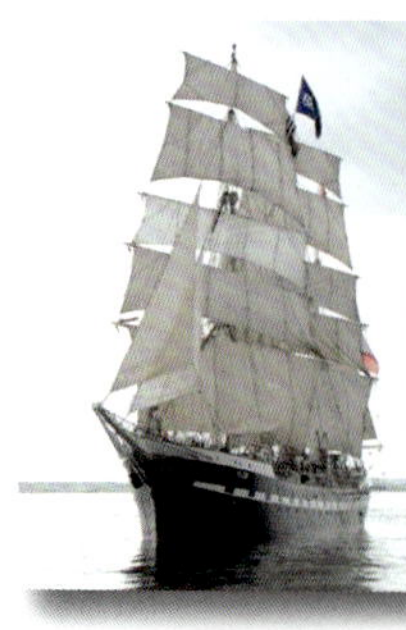

The Sunbeam was commissioned in 1874 by Thomas Brassey (1836-1918), Liberal MP for Hastings and Civil Lord of the Admiralty under Gladstone. In 1876-77 he and his first wife used the Sunbeam to circumnavigate the globe. In 1895, As Governor of Victoria, he sailed the Sunbeam to Australia and, five years later, returned on it to England. During the First World War, at the age of 79, he sailed her to the Greek island of Lemnos so that she could support Indian troops as a hospital ship during the Gallipoli Campaign. In 1922 she was sold to Sir Walter Runciman and Co Ltd and continued to be used as a private yacht until she was broken up in 1930. This etching appears to show Fantôme and Sunbeam off the Cowes headland in the Solent.

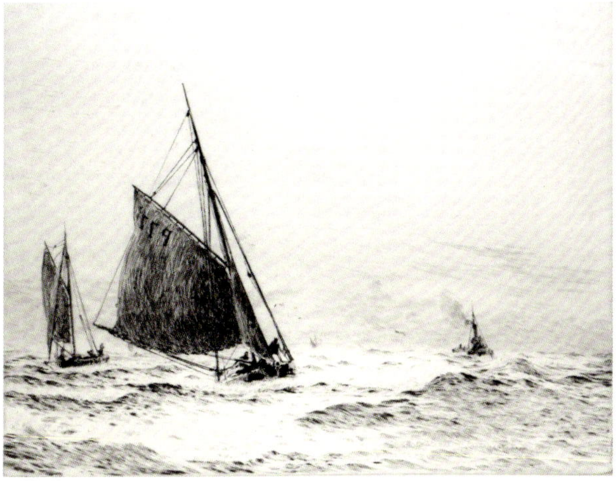

42 **Running Home in Time**
Signed
Etching
7 ½ x 9 ¾ inches

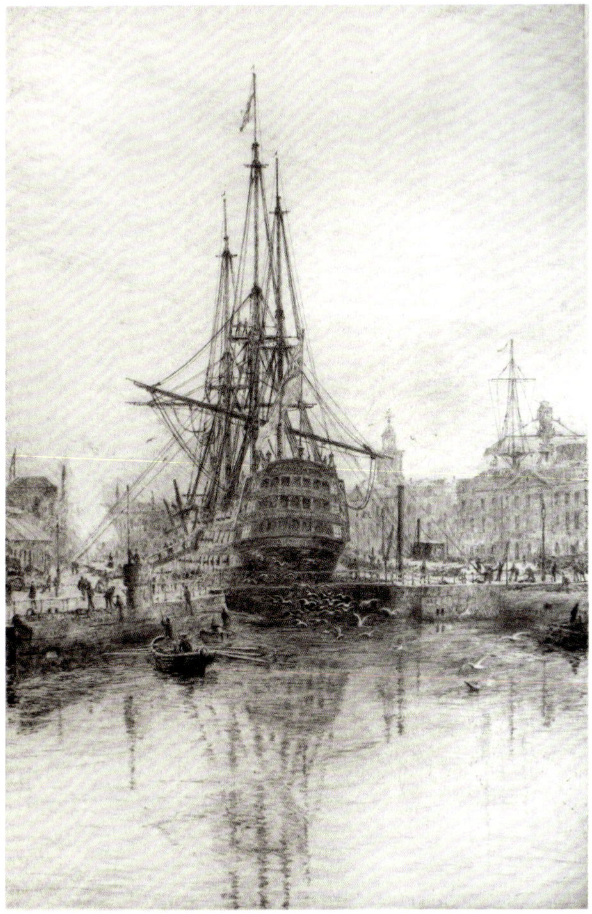

43 **HMS Victory in Portsmouth Harbour**
Signed
Signed and inscribed with title and 'original drypoint' on adhesive label on reverse of frame
Etching with drypoint
14 ½ x 10 ½ inches
Provenance: Robert Dunthorne & Son

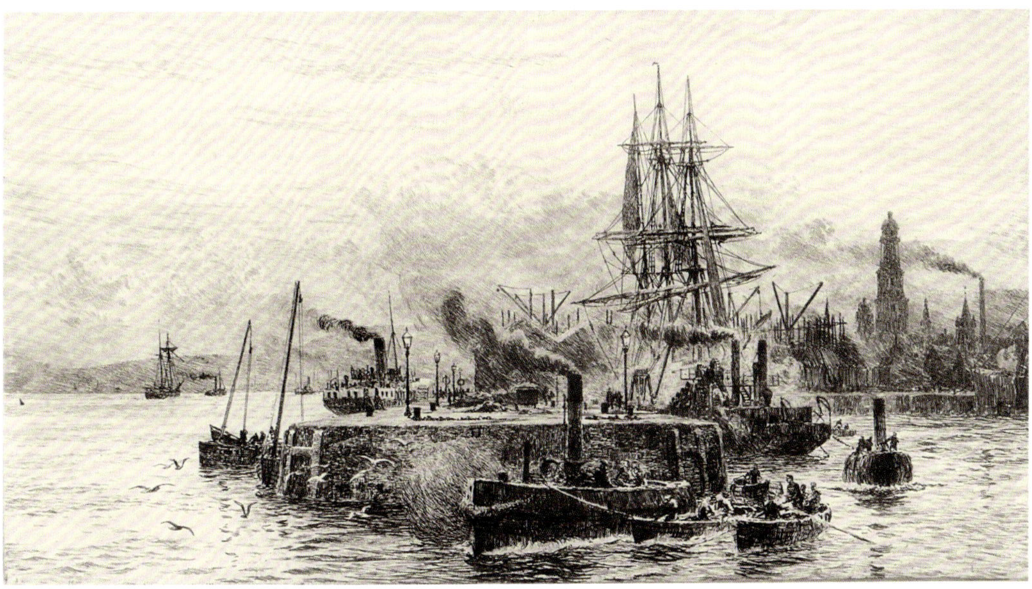

44 **Greenock**
Signed
Etching
7 x 12 inches

WILLIAM WALCOT

William F Walcot, RBA RE (1874-1943)

Working as both painter and printmaker, William Walcot became the most celebrated architectural artist in England during the 1920s and 30s.

William Walcot was born at Lustdorf, near Odessa, on 10 March 1874, the elder son of travelling merchant, Enoch Shannon, known as Frank Walcot, and his Russo-German wife, Catherine. During his childhood, he travelled through Europe with his parents, attending schools in Amiens and Paris in the 1880s. On returning to Russia at the age of 17, he studied architecture under Louis Benois at the Imperial Academy of Fine Arts, St Petersburg (1895-97), and also in Paris at Atelier Redon, in the Ecole des Beaux-Arts. He practised architecture in Moscow for five years, designing the city's Hotel Metropol (1898-1902) and several villas, and subsequently visiting Rome and London. While still in Moscow, he met and married an Irish governess, Margaret Ann O'Neill. However, she suffered from ill health and would die of tuberculosis on the Isle of Wight in 1904.

Settling in London in 1907, Walcot was first employed as a draughtsman to the architect Eustace Frere. He soon became a freelance draughtsman, producing presentation drawings for a number of leading architects to show their clients and to exhibit at the Royal Academy. His treatment of these drawings as works of art rather than technical exercises led to commissions from the Fine Art Society to visit Rome and Venice, and he held a total of eight solo shows with that dealer (1908-28). He also showed watercolours and etchings with leading exhibiting societies, and was elected to the membership of the Royal Society of Painter-Etchers and Engravers (ARE 1918, RE 1920) and the Royal Society of British Artists (1913). He was additionally a Fellow of the Royal Institute of British Architects (1922) and an associate of the British School in Rome. Steeped in the culture and architecture of antiquity, he designed and illustrated luxury editions of *Salammbô* (1926) and *Hérodias* (1928) by Gustave Flaubert for Les Editions d'Art Devambez.

In 1911, Walcot entered a second marriage, with Alice Maria Wheelan, and she would bear him two daughters. However, from 1926, he lived with Ada Grace Chamberlain, known as Margot; together they would have a daughter and son.

The most celebrated architectural draughtsman in England through the 1920s and 30s, Walcot worked from studios in London, Oxford and Rome at the height of his career. However, his practice collapsed on the outbreak of the Second World War, and he went into a decline. Moving with his family to the Ditchling estate of Frank Brangwyn early in the war, he entered St George's Nursing Home, Hurstpierpoint, Sussex, in 1943. While at the nursing home, on 21 May 1943, he fell from a window to his death.

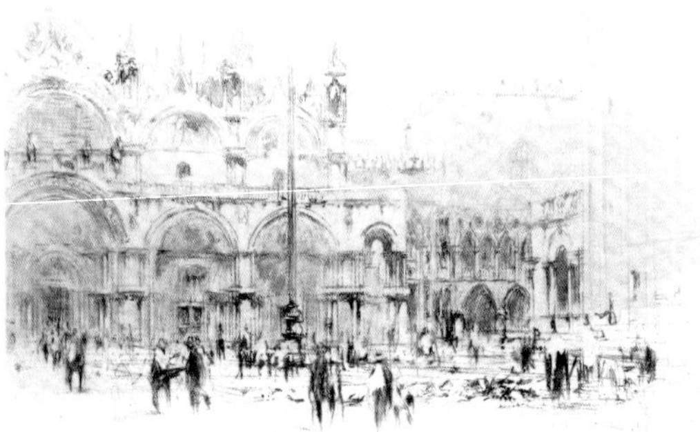

45 **San Marco**
Signed
Etching and drypoint, 4 ¼ x 6 inches
One of the series of four etchings, 'The Venice "Set"', 1920, from an edition of 415. Dickins 66
Exhibited: Fine Art Society, 1922; 'Etchings & Watercolours by William Walcot', Fine Art Society, June 1924

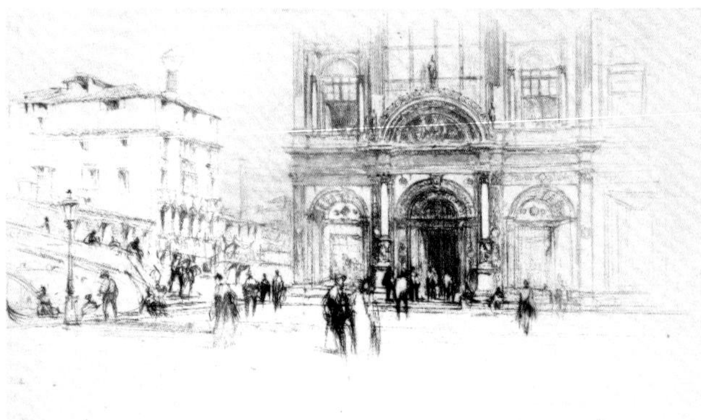

46 **The Hospital of St Mark**
Signed
Etching and drypoint, 4 ¾ x 7 inches
One of the series of four etchings, 'The Venice "Set"', 1920, from an edition of 415. Dickins 68

His work is represented in the collections of The Cleveland Museum of Art (Ohio).

Further reading

Catherine Cooke and Polly Walcot Stewart, 'Walcot, William (1874-1943)', H C G Matthew and Brian Harrison (eds), *Oxford Dictionary of National Biography*, Oxford University Press, 2004, vol 506, pages 760-761; J M Richards, 'Walcot, William [Valkot, V F] (*b* Lustdorf, near Odessa, Russia, 10 March 1874; *d* Hurstpierpoint, W Sussex, 21 May 1943), Jane Turner (ed), *The Dictionary of Art*, London: Macmillan, 1996, vol 32, page 773

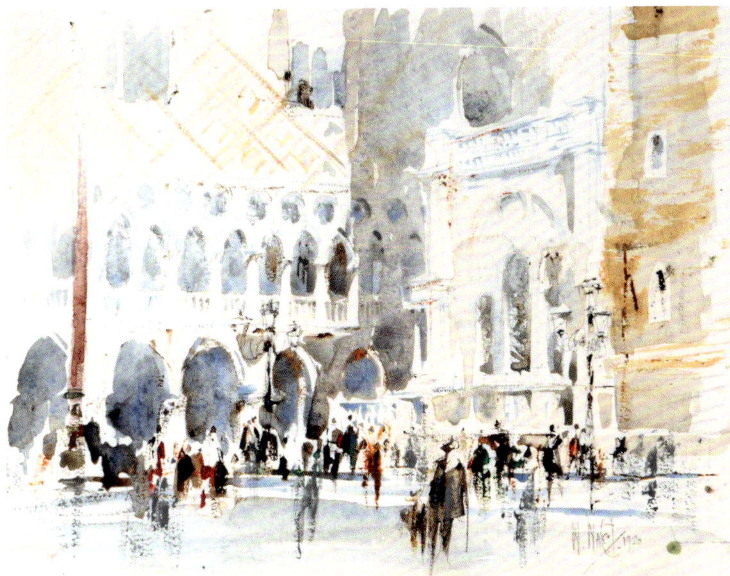

47 St Mark's Square, Venice
Signed and dated 1920
Watercolour with pencil and bodycolour
6 ¼ x 8 inches

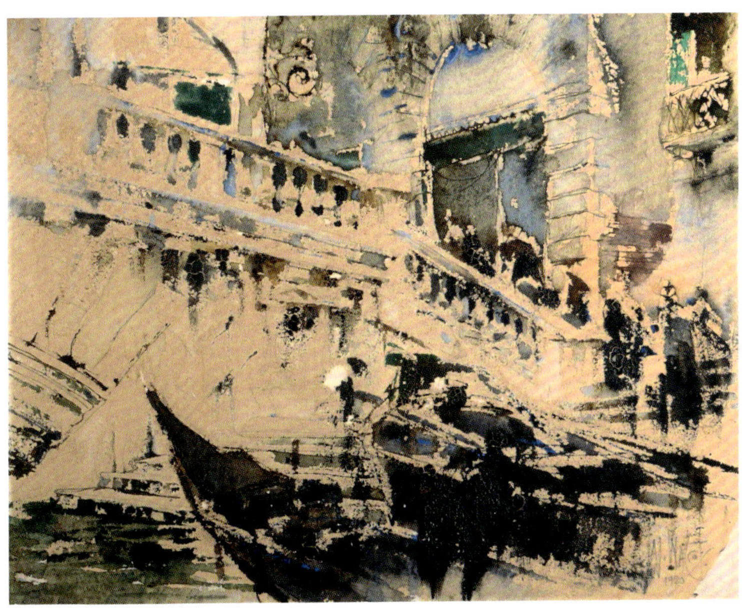

48 Rialto Bridge, Venice
Signed and dated 1920
Watercolour with bodycolour, pencil and gum arabic on tinted paper
11 ¼ x 14 inches

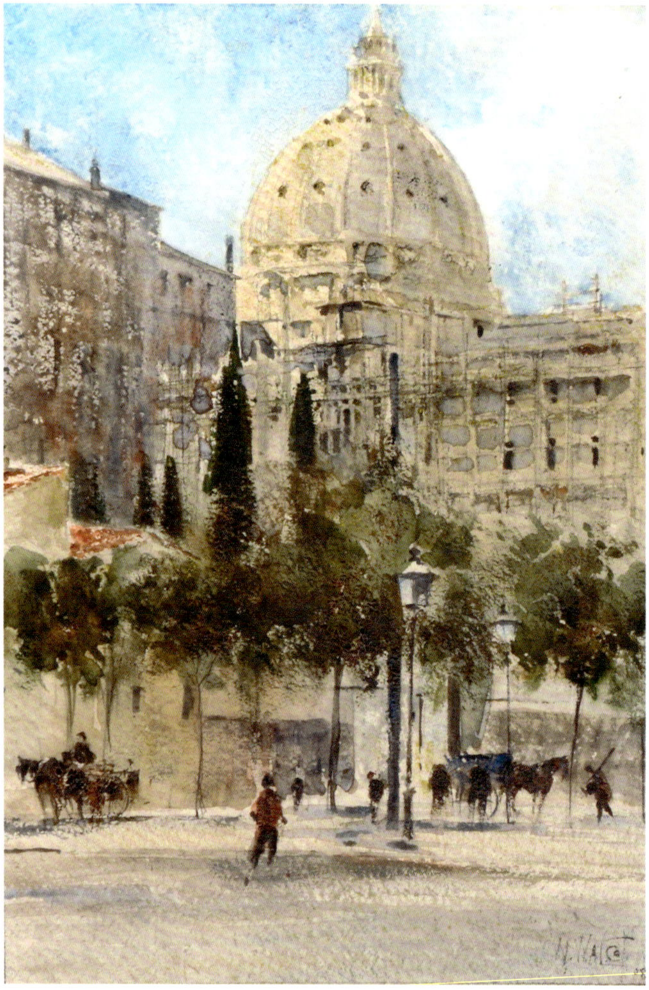

49 Piazza Angelica, Rome
Signed and dated 08
Watercolour with bodycolour, pencil and gum arabic on tinted paper
11 ¾ x 8 ¼ inches
Exhibited: 'Watercolours of London & Rome by William Walcot',
Fine Art Society, London, February 1909, no 1

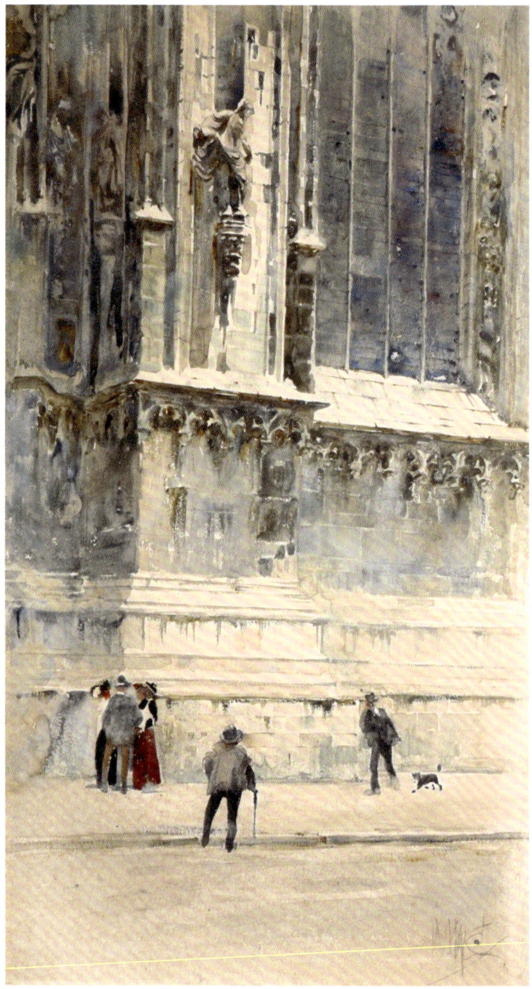

50 Figures before a Cathedral
Signed
Watercolour with bodycolour, pencil
and gum arabic on tinted paper
21 ¼ x 12 ¼ inches

51 Pincio
Signed and dated 08
Watercolour with bodycolour, pencil and gum arabic on tinted paper
10 x 11 ¾ inches

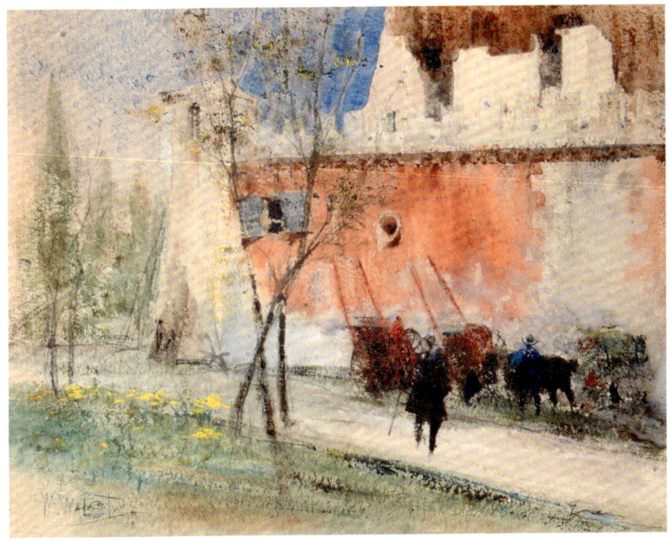

52 The Steps of St Peter's, Sunday Morning
Signed
Watercolour with bodycolour, pencil and gum arabic on tinted paper
9 ¾ x 13 inches
Exhibited: Fine Art Society, London, March 1909, no 19

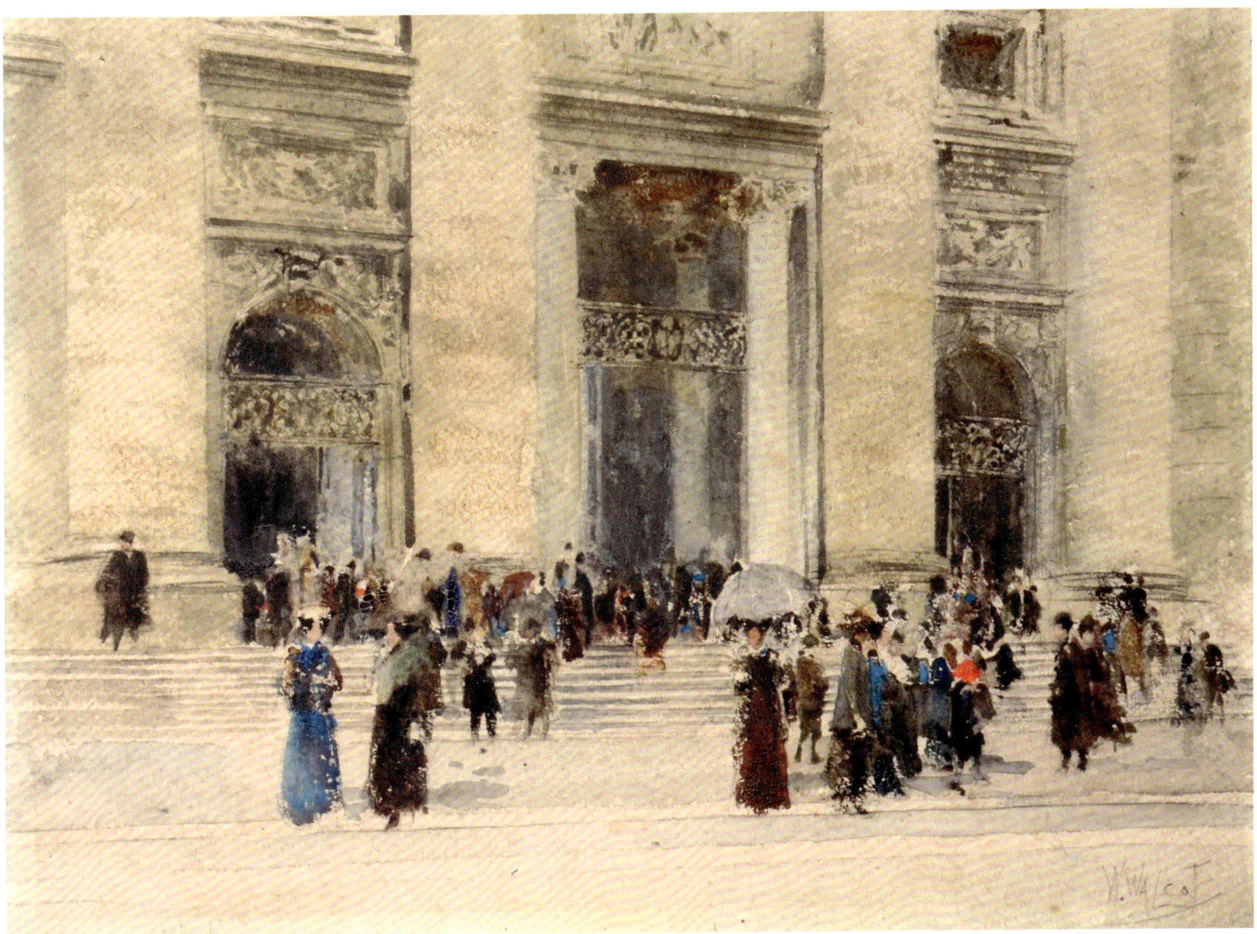

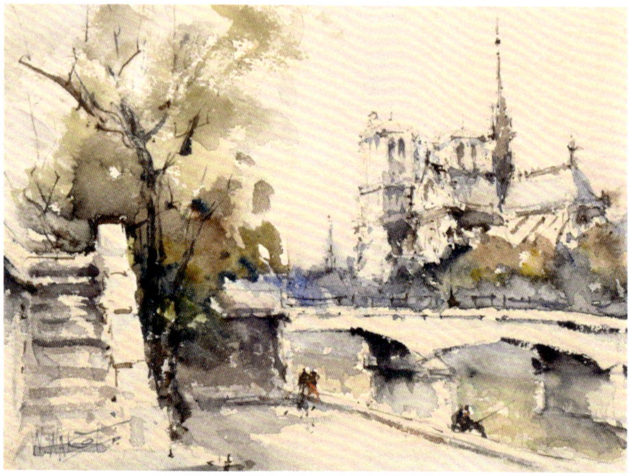

53 **Notre Dame**
Signed
Watercolour and bodycolour on tinted paper
5 ½ x 7 ½ inches

54 **Le Palais de Justice, Brussels**
Signed and dated 1911 twice
Watercolour with bodycolour and pencil on tinted paper
22 x 21 inches
Provenance: Horner Galleries, Sheffield
Literature: *Architectural Water-Colours & Etchings of W Walcot*, London: H C Dickins and Technical Journals, 1919, page 125

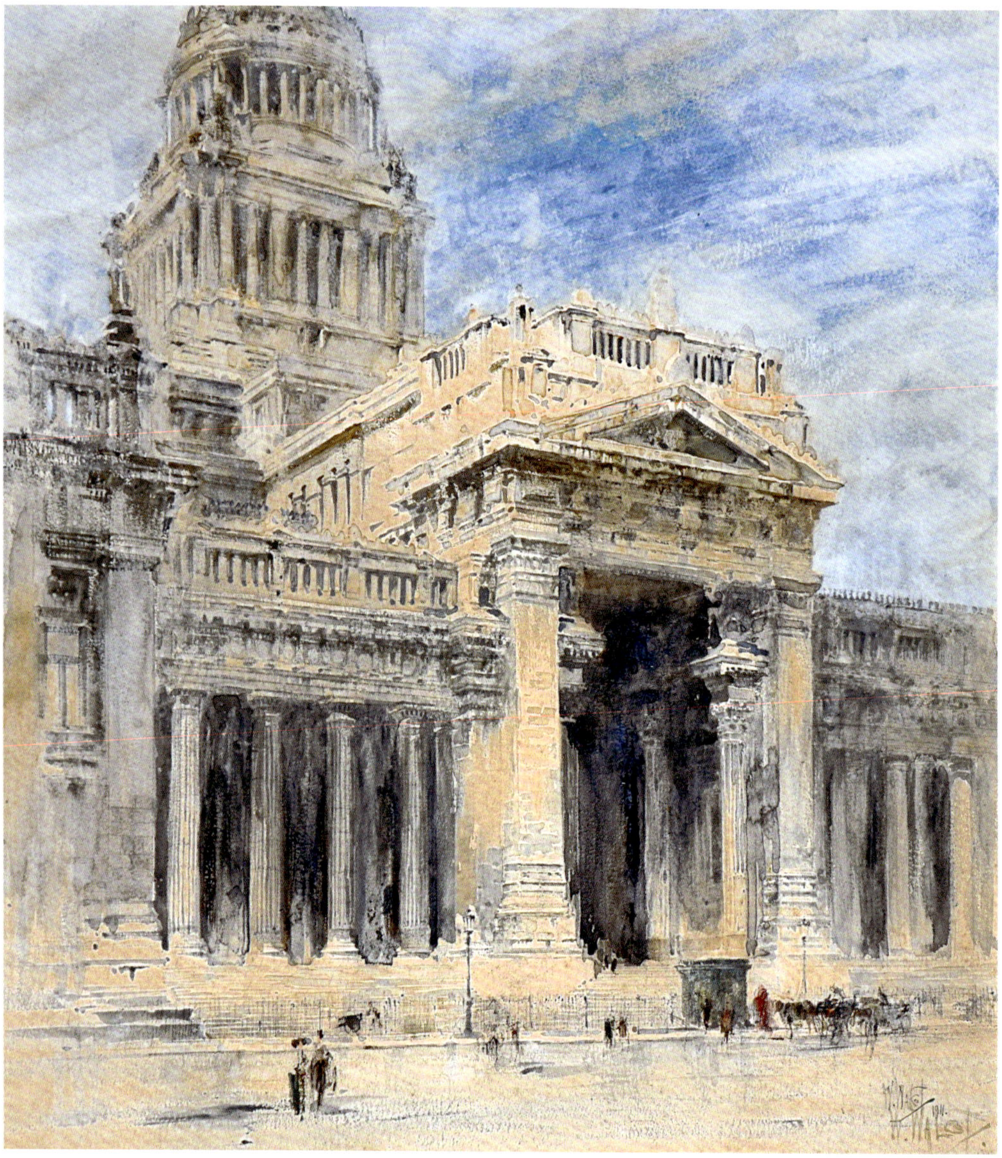

55 La Madeleine, Paris
Signed
Watercolour with pencil and bodycolour
7 ¾ x 9 ¾ inches

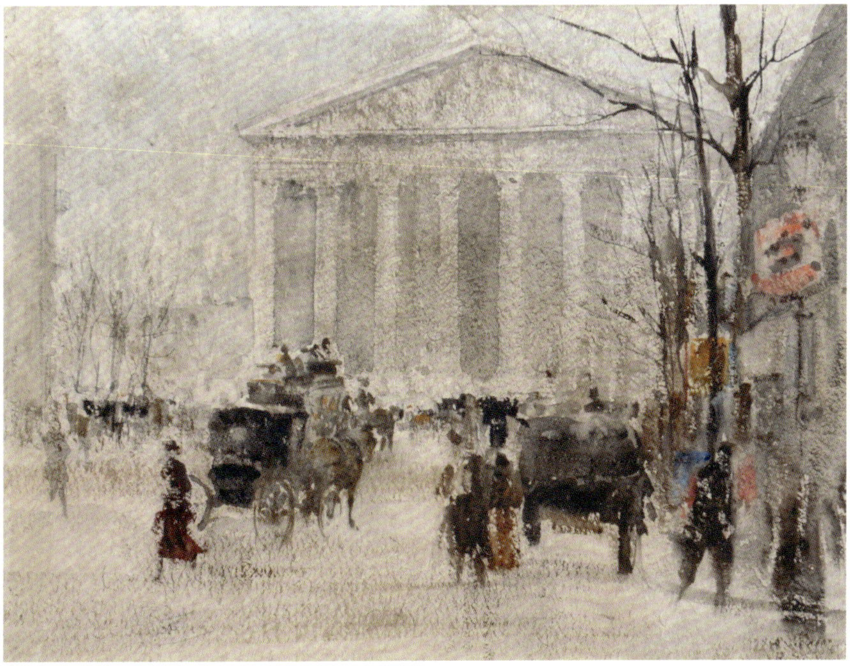

56 La Bourse, Paris
Signed and dated 09
Watercolour with bodycolour, pencil
and gum arabic on tinted paper
15 x 19 ½ inches

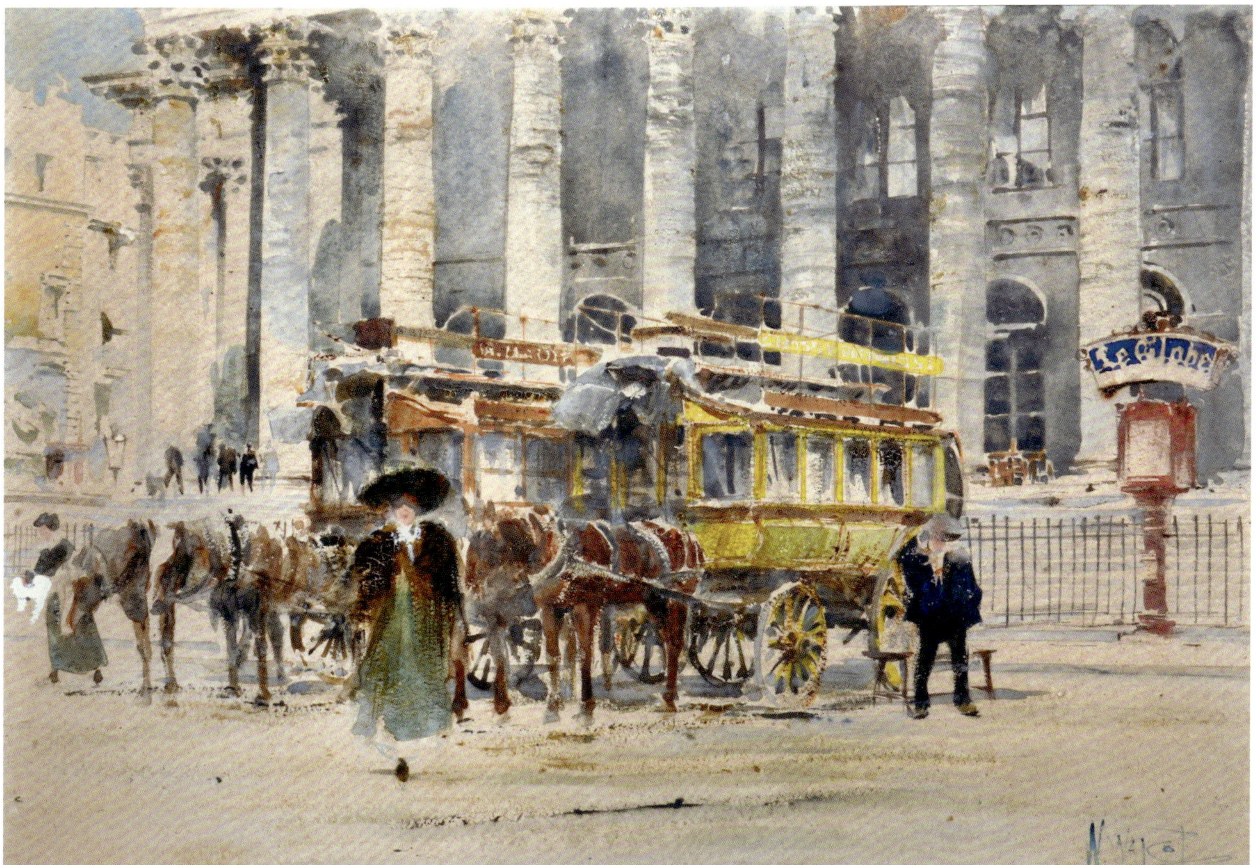

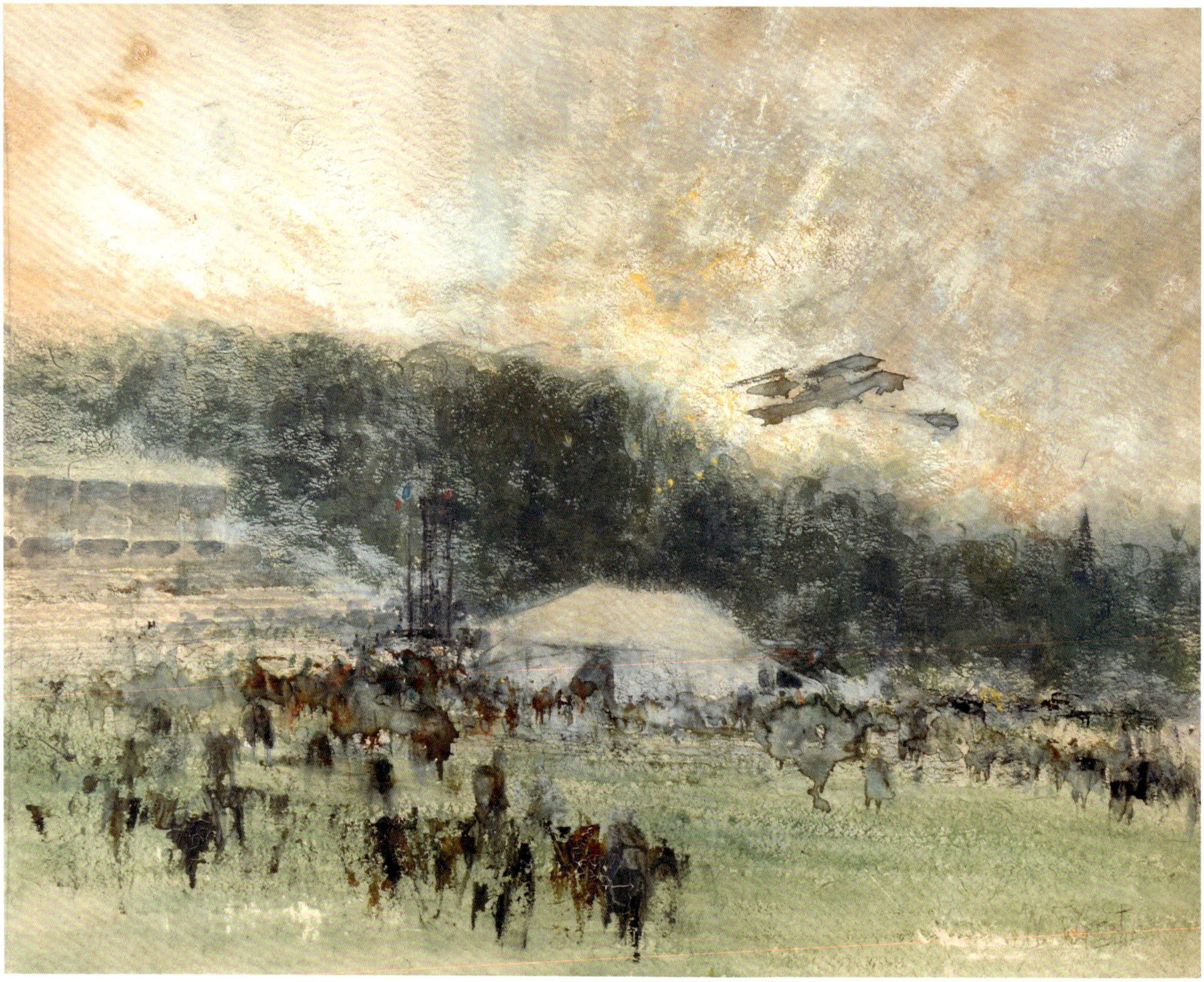

57 The Air Show
Signed
Watercolour with pencil, bodycolour and gum arabic on tinted paper
15 ¼ x 18 ½ inches

The Air Show

It has been suggested that this image shows one of the early Paris air shows. However, the earliest of those, which took place from 1909 until the First World War, mainly comprised fairs at the Grand Palais.

It has also been suggested that the air-borne biplane is a Maurice Farman MF11 Shorthorn, which undertook its first air test in 1913, and was adopted by both the Armée de l'air and the Royal Air Force, for use during the First World War.

'The limitations of the space made it necessary for the approach to the building through this entrance to be along a handsome corridor 14 feet wide leading to an elliptical hall. Doors lead from this hall to lifts and a staircase and to a wrought iron gateway which forms the entrance to the ante-room.'

(Cuthbert Maughan, 'The New Home of Lloyd's', *The Bankers' Magazine*, October 1928, page 530)

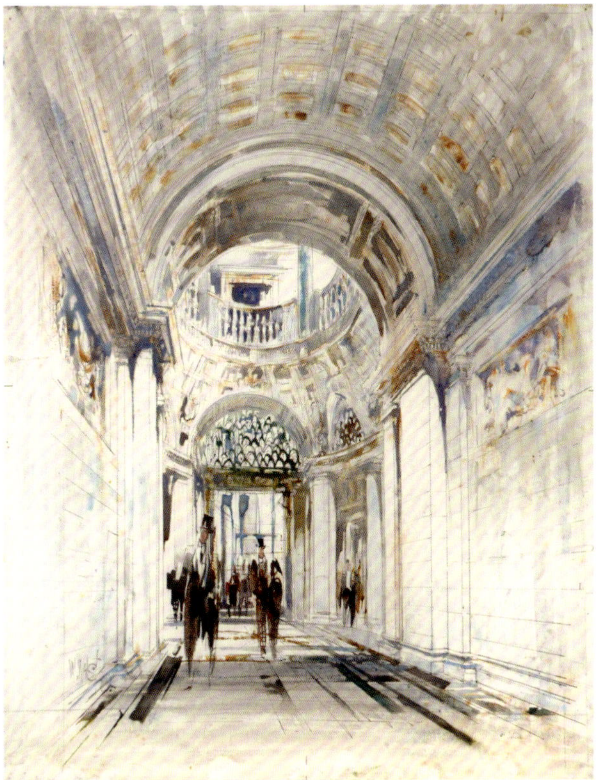

58 **Lloyd's: Entrance Corridor**
Signed
Watercolour with ink and pencil
21 x 18 inches
Exhibited: Summer Exhibition, Royal Academy of Arts, 1931, no 1372

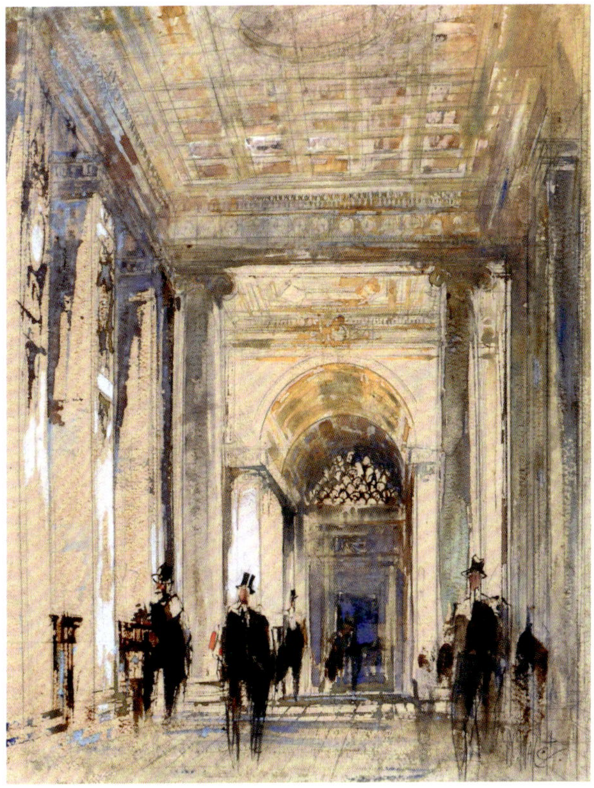

59 **Lloyd's: Ante to The Room**
Signed
Watercolour, bodycolour and pencil on tinted paper
21 x 18 inches
Exhibited: Summer Exhibition, Royal Academy of Arts, 1931, no 1367

Lloyd's

In 1928, work was completed on the new headquarters of the insurance underwriters, Lloyd's of London, at Leadenhall Street, which had been designed by Sir Edwin Cooper (1874-1942). William Walcot not only produced the presentation drawings for the project, but also painted *Mercury* and *Neptune*, two of four ceiling panels for the Underwriting Room. Frederick Taylor painted the others, *Peace* and *Industry*.

Cooper's building was demolished in 1980 to make way for the present headquarters, which were designed by Sir Richard Rogers.

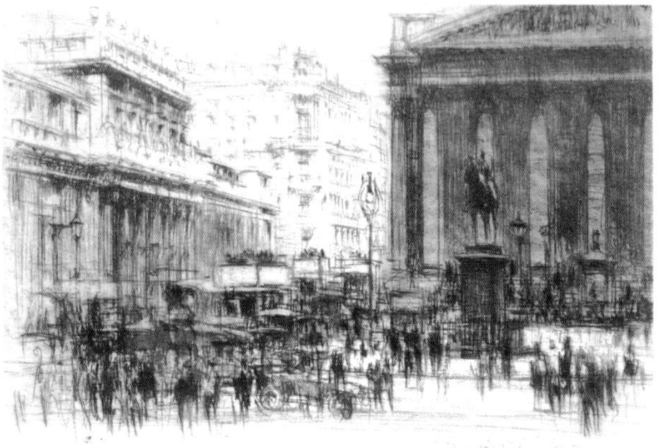

60 Bank of England and The Royal Exchange
Signed in pencil
Etching and drypoint
4 x 5 ¾ inches

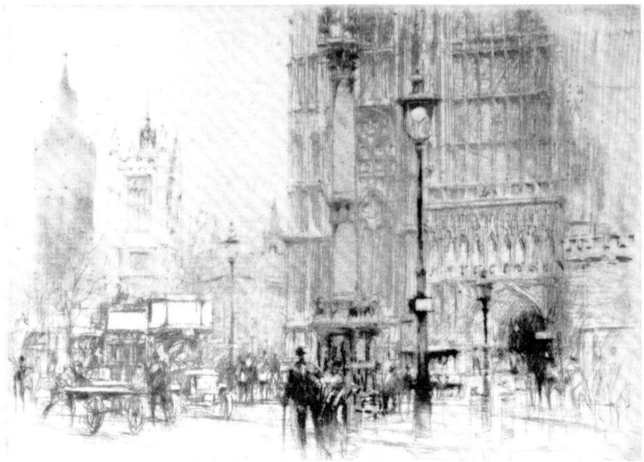

61 Westminster Abbey
Signed
Etching, drypoint and aquatint
3 ½ x 4 ¾ inches
1919, UK edition of 175 + US edition of 75. Dickins 55

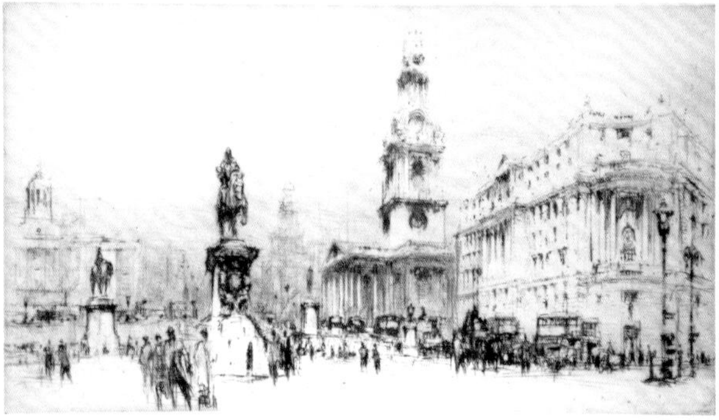

62 Trafalgar Square (with King Charles's Statue)
Signed
Etching and drypoint
6 ½ x 11 ¾ inches

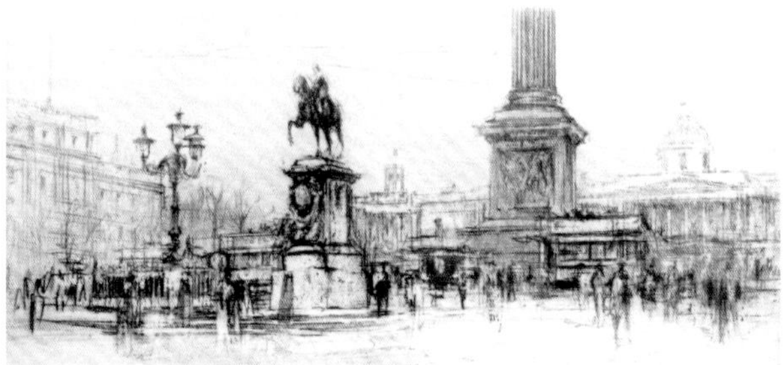

63 Trafalgar Square
Signed
Etching with drypoint and aquatint
3 ¼ x 7 inches
One of the series of six etchings, 'The London "Set"', 1924. Dickins 90

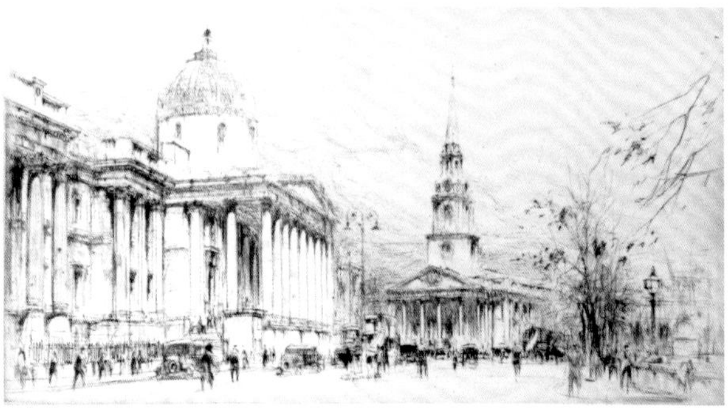

64 National Gallery & St Martin-in-the-Fields
Signed
Etching and drypoint
6 ½ x 11 ¾ inches

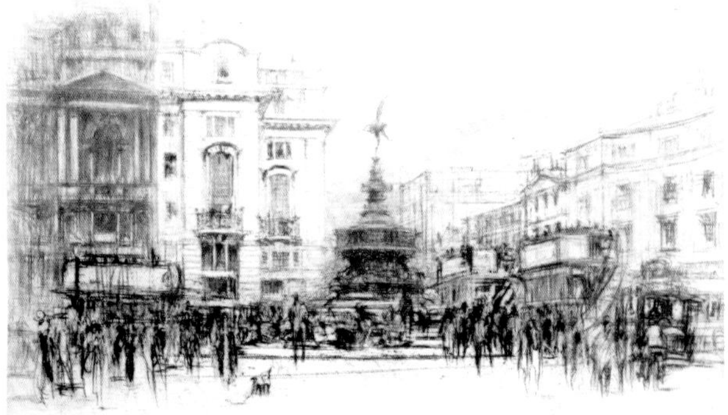

65 Piccadilly Circus (with Criterion Theatre)
Signed
Etching and drypoint
4 ½ x 6 ¾ inches
One of the series of six etchings, 'The London "Set"', 1924. Dickins 92

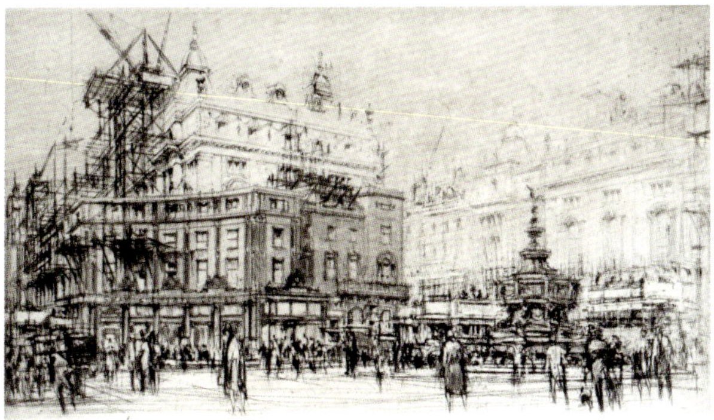

66 **Piccadilly Circus – Rebuilding Swan & Edgar's**
Signed
Etching, drypoint and aquatint
5 ½ x 8 ¼ inches

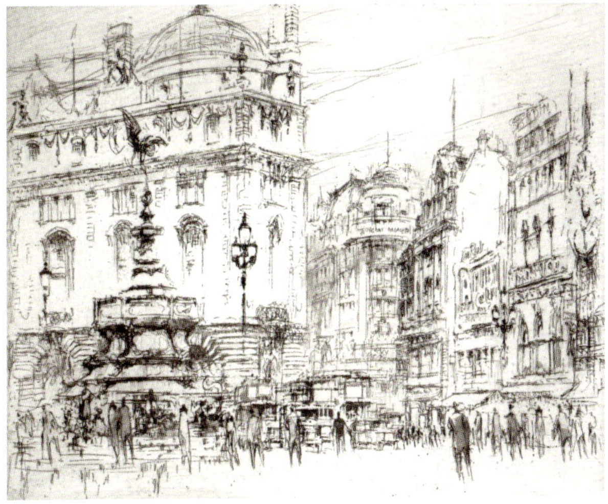

67 **Piccadilly Circus and Glasshouse Street**
Signed
Etching and aquatint
9 ¾ x 12 ¼ inches

68 **Hyde Park Corner**
Signed
Watercolour with pencil and bodycolour
8 x 10 inches
Provenance: Aitken Dott, Edinburgh

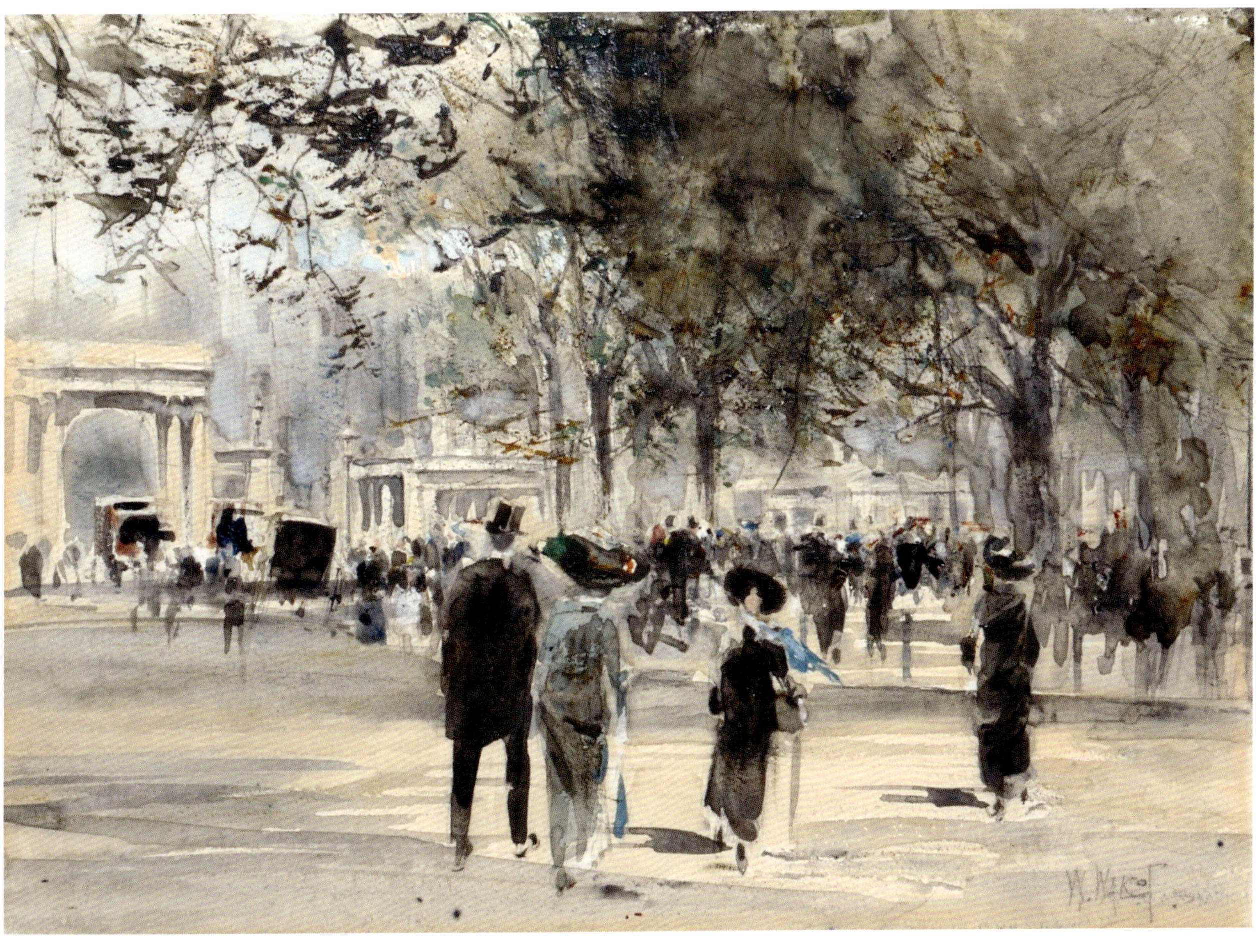

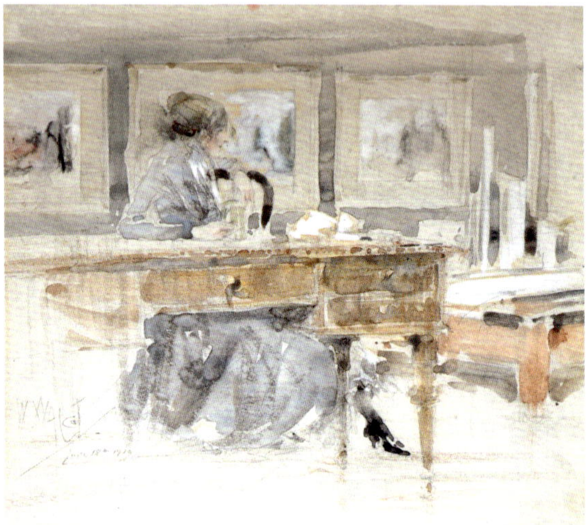

Woman Seated at a Desk
An inscription on the reverse of this watercolour – in a hand other than that of the artist – suggests that the sitter is Millie Millar. Millie Millar may have been related to William Walcot's friend, the American architect, Albert D Millar, who was house architect to Selfridges department store, during the 1920s and 30s. In 1935, Millar and Walcot collaborated on decorating the store in celebration of the Silver Jubilee of the accession of George V.

69 **Woman Seated at a Desk**
Signed and dated 'June 18th 1919'
Watercolour with bodycolour
6 ¾ x 7 ½ inches

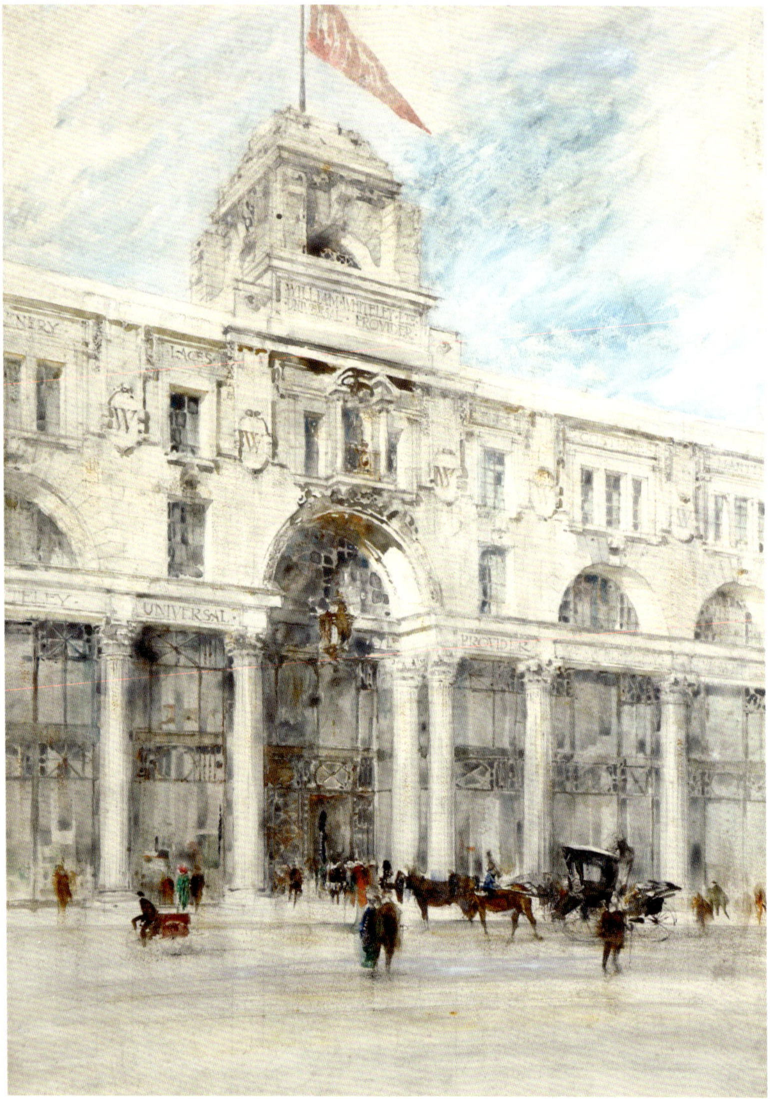

William Whiteley Ltd Universal Provider
The entrepreneur, William Whiteley (1831-1907), founded his first department store in Westbourne Grove, London, in 1867, and soon dubbed himself the 'Universal Provider'. His business empire developed with such success that, in 1899, it was listed on the London Stock Exchange. Tragically, Whiteley himself was murdered on 24 January 1907, by a man claiming to be his illegitimate son. However, his two sons continued to expand the business and, in 1912, opened a magnificent new store, designed by John Belcher (1841-1913) and John James Joass (1868-1952). It is probably in conjunction with this project that Walcot prepared the present architectural perspective. The store was rebuilt again in 1925.

70 **William Whiteley Ltd**
Universal Provider
Watercolour with pencil and bodycolour
17 ½ x 25 inches

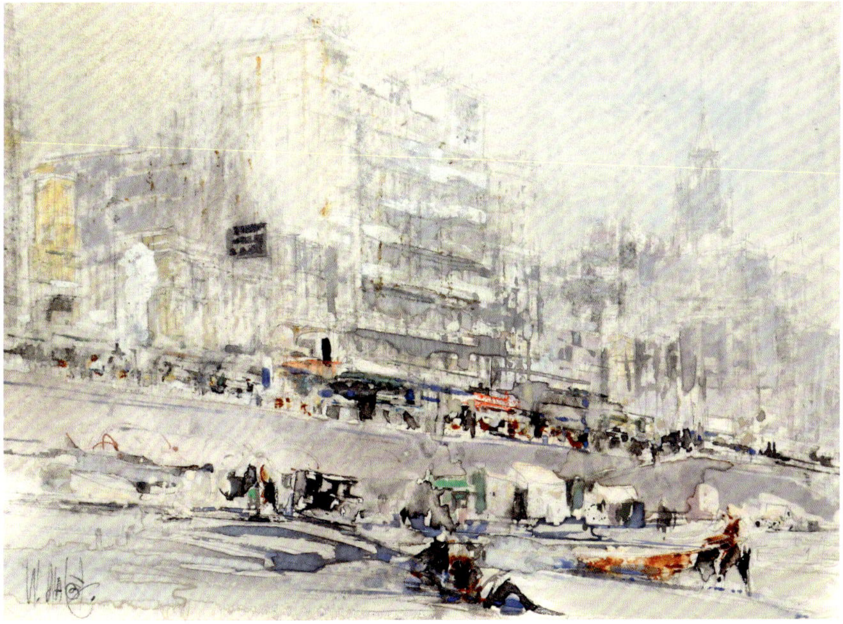

71 **The Grand Hotel, Brighton**
Signed
Inscribed 'Brighton' on reverse
Watercolour with bodycolour and pencil
6 ½ x 8 ½ inches

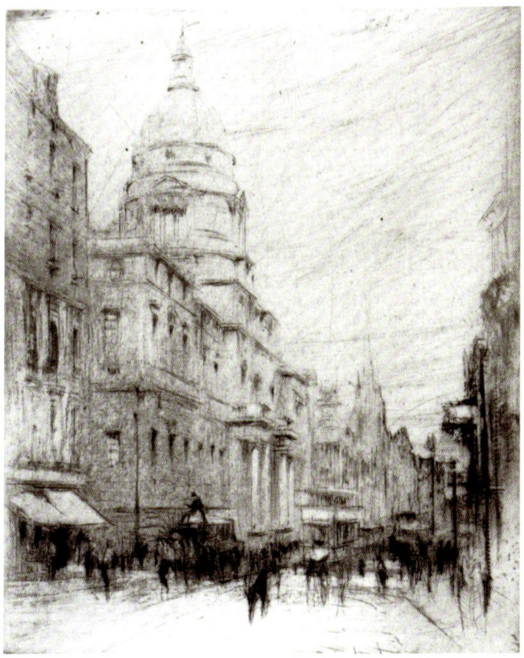

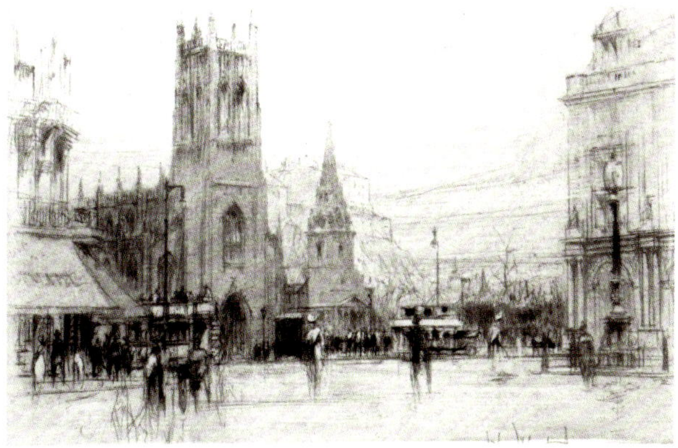

73 **The West End (Edinburgh)**
Signed
Etching, 3 x 4 ¾ inches
One of the series of five etchings, 'The Edinburgh "Set"', 1918, from an edition of 75. Dickins 43

72 **The University (Edinburgh)**
Signed
Etching, 4 ¼ x 3 ½ inches
One of the series of five etchings, 'The Edinburgh "Set"', 1918, from an edition of 75. Dickins 42

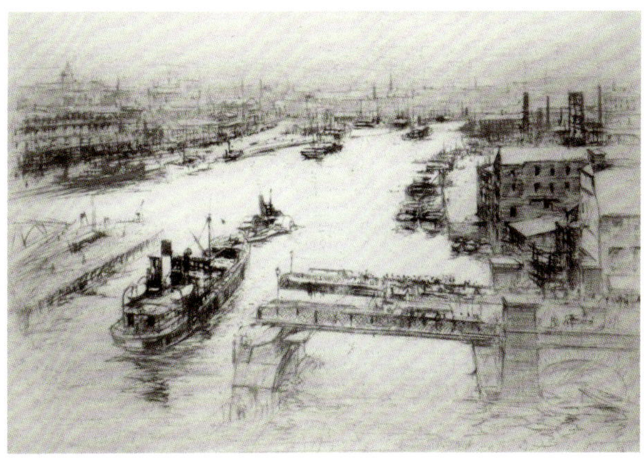

74 **The Tyne**
Signed
Etching and drypoint, 6 ½ x 7 ¾ inches
One of the series of five etchings, 'The Arteries of Great Britain', published by Dickins in 1922, in an edition of 425. Dickins 73

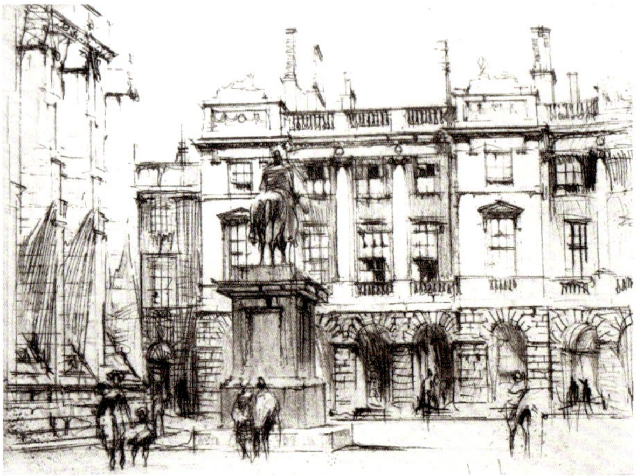

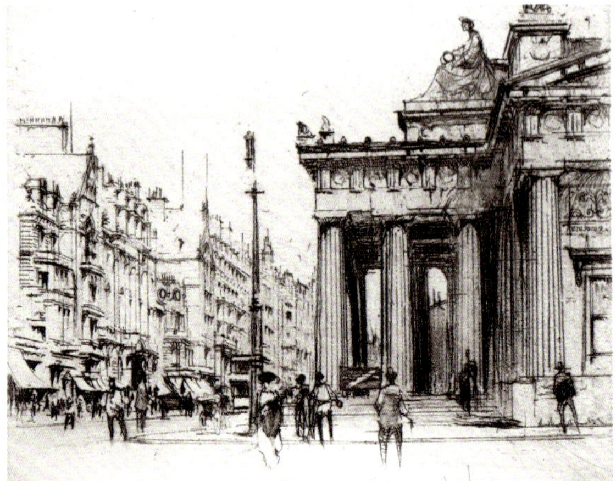

75 **Parliament Square (Edinburgh)**
Signed
Etching, 3 ¼ x 4 ¼ inches
One of the series of five etchings, 'The Edinburgh "Set"', 1918, from an edition of 75. Dickins 44
Literature: *Architectural Water-Colours and Etchings of W Walcot*, London: H C Dickins & Technical Journals, 1919, page 25

76 **Royal Scottish Academy**
Signed
Etching
3 x 3 ¾ inches
One of the series of five etchings, 'The Edinburgh "Set"', 1918, from an edition of 75. Dickins 45

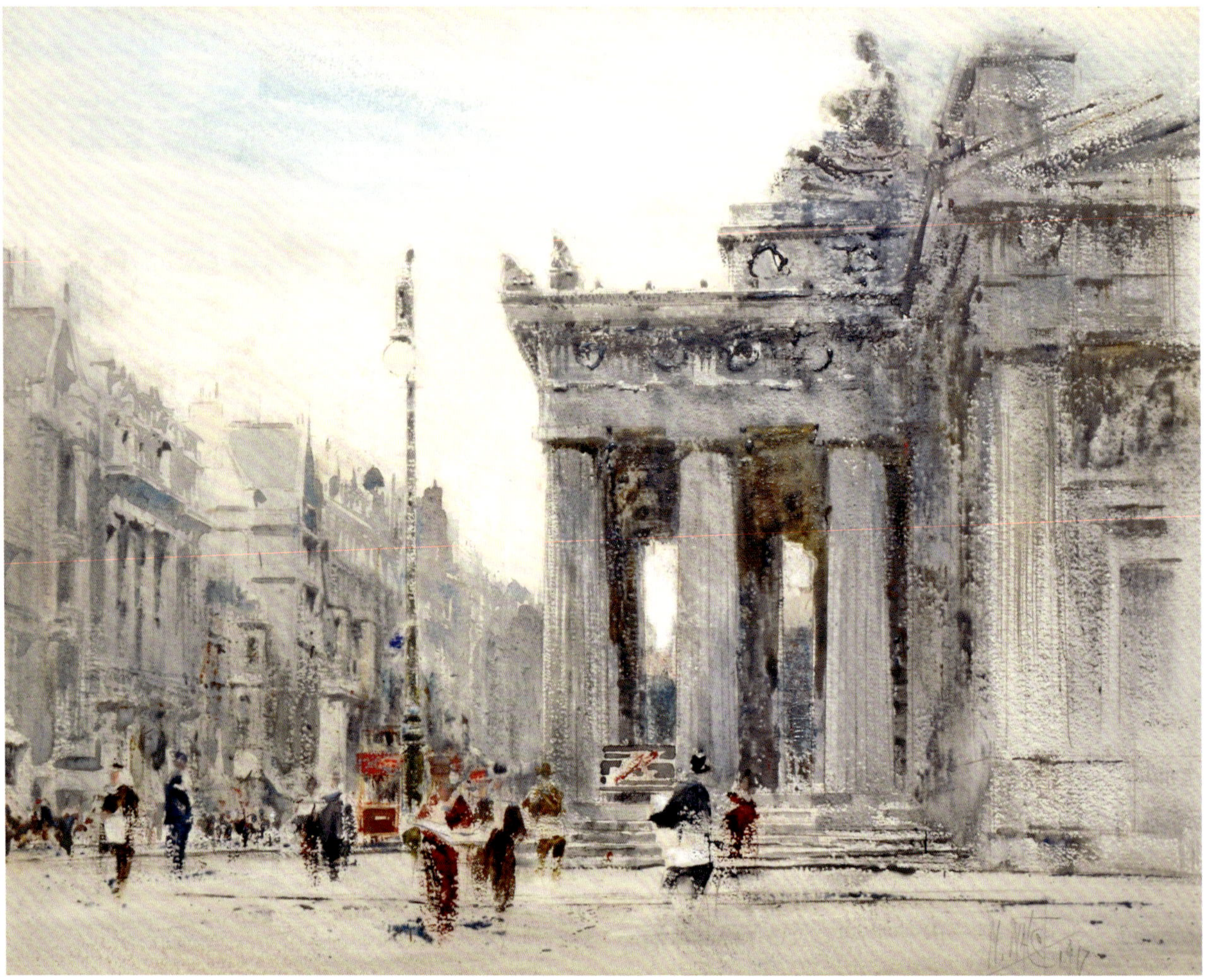

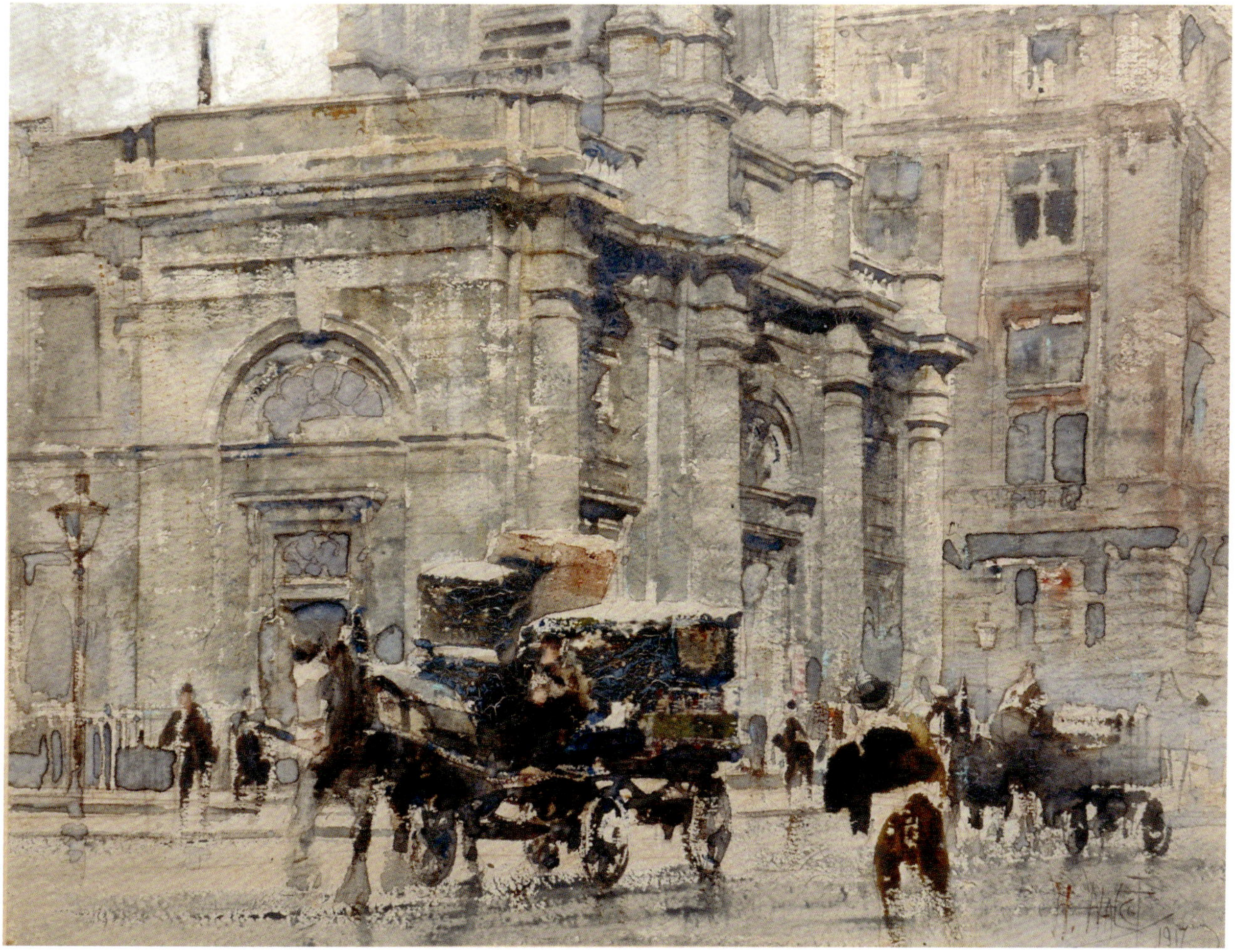

78 St George's Church, Buchanan Street, Glasgow
Signed and dated 1917
Watercolour with pencil, bodycolour and gum arabic on tinted paper
9 ¾ x 11 ¾ inches
Provenance: Aitken Dott, Edinburgh

77 RSA Galleries, Princes Street, Edinburgh (opposite)
Signed and dated 1917
Watercolour with pencil and bodycolour
10 ½ x 13 inches
Provenance: Doig, Wilson and Wheatley, Edinburgh
This watercolour relates to the etching, Royal Scottish Academy [76]

ROSE BARTON

Rose Maynard Barton, RWS ASWA (1856-1929)

Even by her contemporaries, Rose Barton was appreciated as the equal of Hebert Menzies Marshall in her work as an urban topographer.

For a biography of Rose Barton, please refer to *Chris Beetles Summer Show*, 2008, page 7.

Further reading

Rose Barton RWS (1856-1929), London: Christie's, 1987

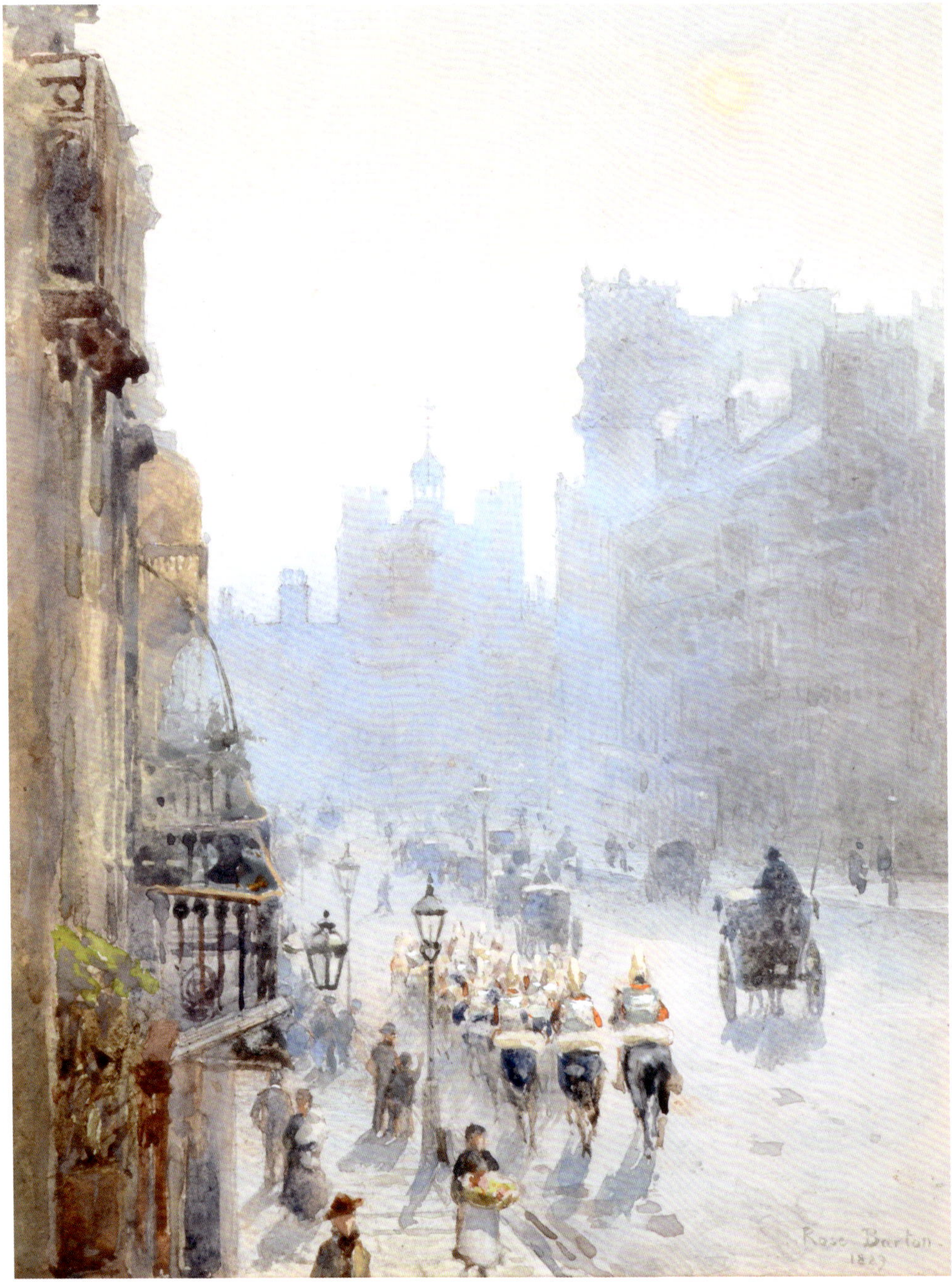

79 **A View of St James's**
Signed and dated 1889
Signed and inscribed 'No 3 – St James £10.10.0' and '15a Cromwell Place' on label on reverse of frame
Watercolour with bodycolour and pencil
9 ¾ x 7 ¼ inches

'I must not pass over the subject of the London omnibus. What an institution it is for people who, like myself, cannot afford the luxury of a barouche, or a victoria, and certainly not a motor car! As Mr Gladstone put it, where can one see London and London life so well as "from the top of a 'bus"? An omnibus is such a place, too, in which to study character, and very often anatomy, for it seems to be the vehicle par excellence for the two extremes of "fat and lean kine." Carlyle was wont to use the humble 'bus, generally wearing his broad-brimmed white hat. On one occasion, when he got out at his destination, one of the "insides" said to the conductor, "Queer hat that old gentleman wears!" "Ah! p'r'aps it is a queer 'at; but, lor', what would you give for such an 'ead as is inside it?"

(Rose Barton, *Familiar London*, London: Adam and Charles Black, 1904, page 197)

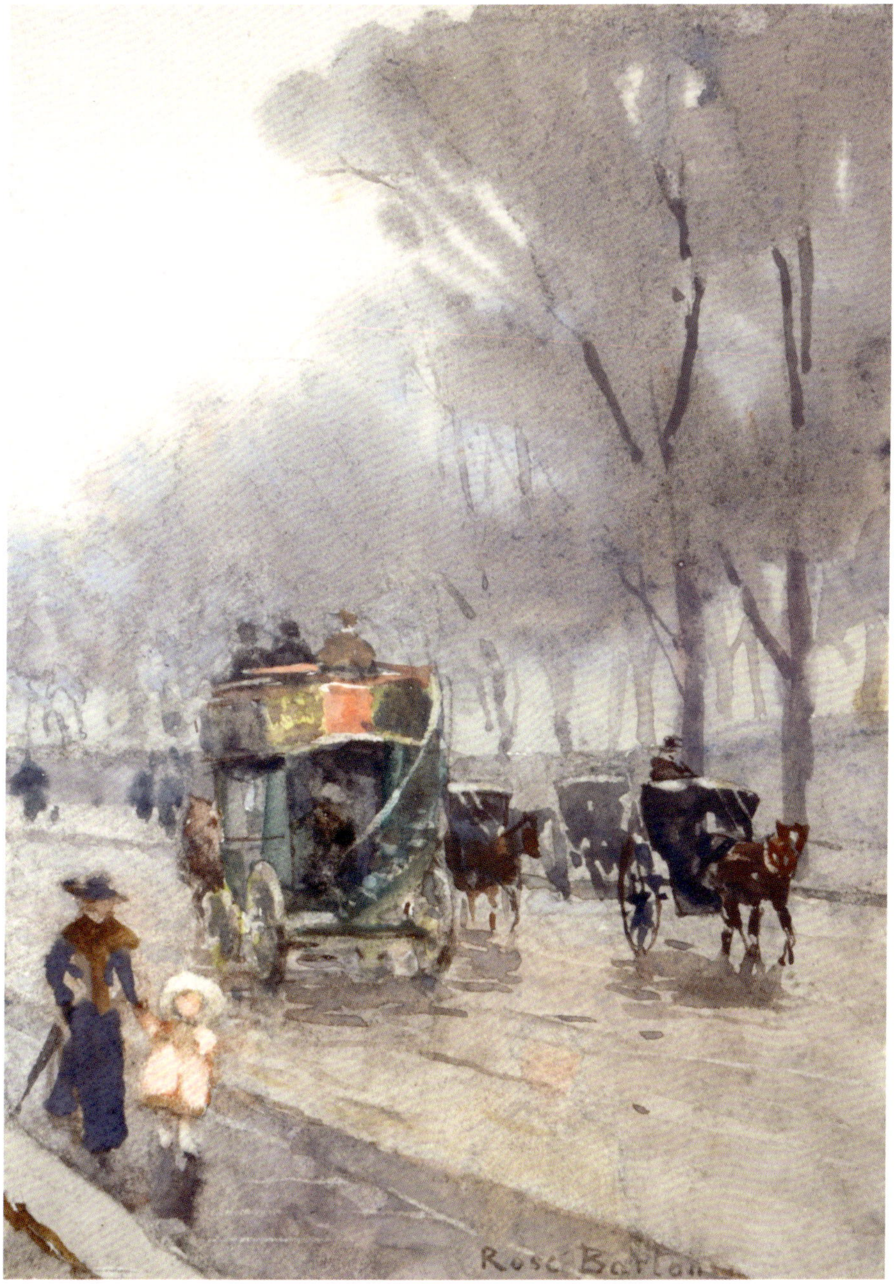

80 **Park Lane with Omnibus**
Signed
Signed on reverse of original backboard
Watercolour
6 ½ x 4 ½ inches

MILDRED ANNE BUTLER

Mildred Anne Butler, ARWS SWA UAA (1858-1941)

The Irish watercolourist, Mildred Anne Butler, worked with a lightness of touch in order to portray scenes of nature and domesticity, which were often based both on life at her home in County Kilkenny and on her travels.

Mildred Anne Butler was born on 11 January 1858 at Kilmurry, a Georgian house near Thomastown, County Kilkenny, Ireland. She was the youngest daughter of Captain Henry Butler and, through him, the great-granddaughter of Edmund Butler, 11th Viscount Mountgarret.

Butler probably gained her interest in painting from her father, who was an amateur artist. However, she left Ireland in order to undertake formal artistic training. She seems to have studied in London at Westminster School of Art in the early 1880s, before travelling on the Continent in 1885, to visit France, Switzerland and Italy. On her return to London, she studied under Paul Naftel alongside, or on the recommendation of her friend, Rose Barton.

From the late 1880s, Butler sent works from her home at Kilmurry to exhibitions in London, including those at the Society of Women Artists (1887-1935, for much of which she was a member), the Dudley Gallery (from 1888), the Royal Academy (1889-1902), the Royal Society of Painters in Water-Colours and the New Gallery. She also exhibited in Ireland at the Watercolour Society of Ireland and the Belfast Art Society (becoming an honorary member of the latter in 1904).

Through the 1890s, Butler continued to develop as an artist. She spent a term in the London studio of the animal painter, Frank Calderon, and the summers of 1894 and 1895, studying

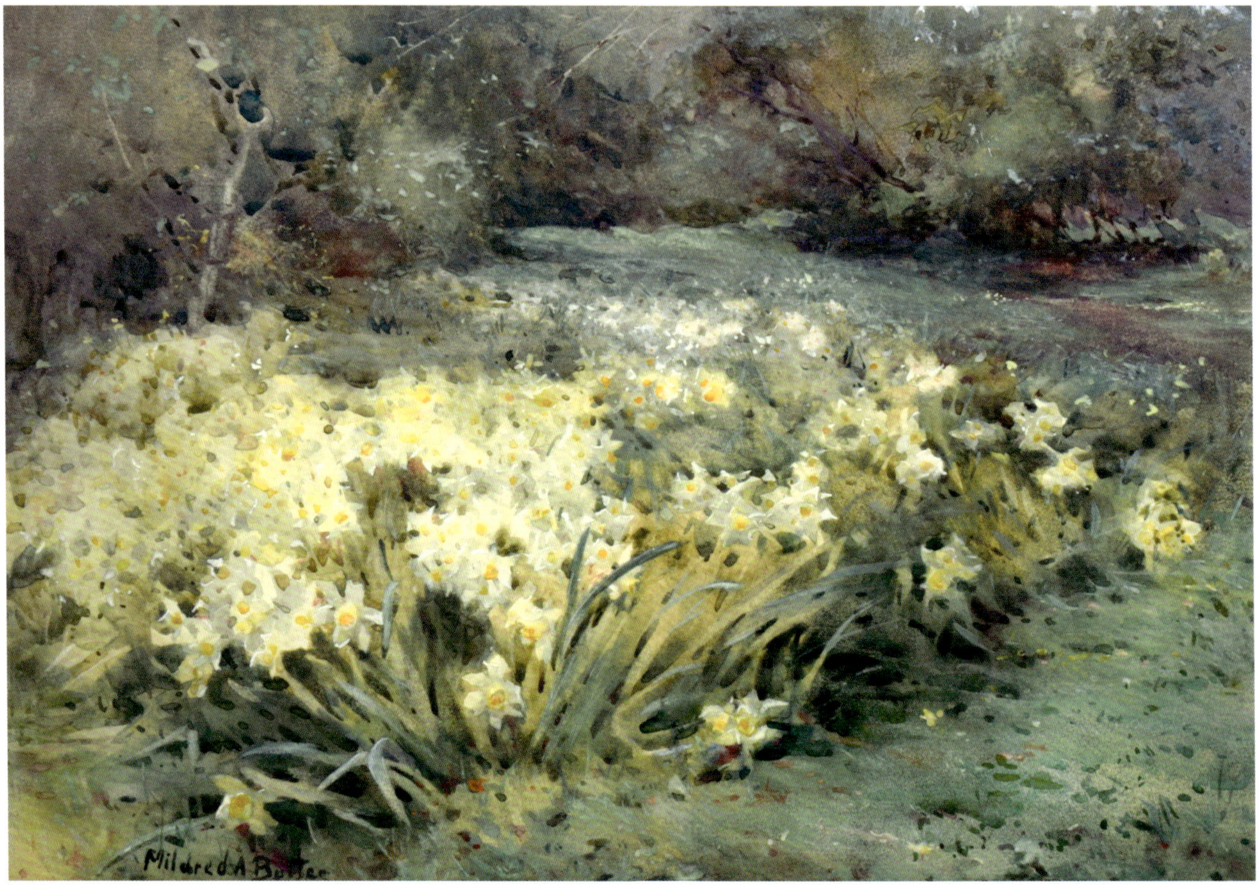

81 **Profusion**
Signed
Watercolour with bodycolour
10 ½ x 14 ½ inches

in Newlyn, Cornwall, under Limerick-born Norman Garstin and Dublin-born Stanhope Forbes, in the company of her friend, May Guinness. Calderon influenced her subject matter, and the French-inspired Newlyn School her style.

Her confident use of watercolour led Butler to be elected an associate of the Royal Society of Painters in Water-Colours in 1896, though full membership would be achieved only in 1937. Also in 1896, she scored a particular success with *Morning Bath*, showing doves at a pool, which she exhibited at the Royal Academy, and which was then bought by the trustees of the Chantrey Bequest for presentation to the Tate. She was the first woman to be honoured in this way. Other patrons included Queen Mary and Grand Duke of Hesse.

After the turn of the century, Butler continued to travel to find subject matter for her painting. From 1905, she made regular trips to Aix-les-Bains, the spa town in southeast France.

Holding a joint show with Percy French at the New Dudley Gallery in 1907, she continued to exhibit until the 1930s, and was one of the first nine academicians to be elected to the Belfast Art Society, when it was renamed the Ulster Academy of Arts in 1930. She stopped painting as the result of arthritis.

Butler spent some time late in life in Wellington, New Zealand, but returned to Ireland, and died at home at Kilmurry on 11 October 1941.

Her work is represented in the collections of Ulster Museum (Belfast); and the National Gallery of Ireland (Dublin).

Further reading

Anne Crookshank, *Mildred Anne Butler. 1858-1941*, Dublin: Town House, 1992

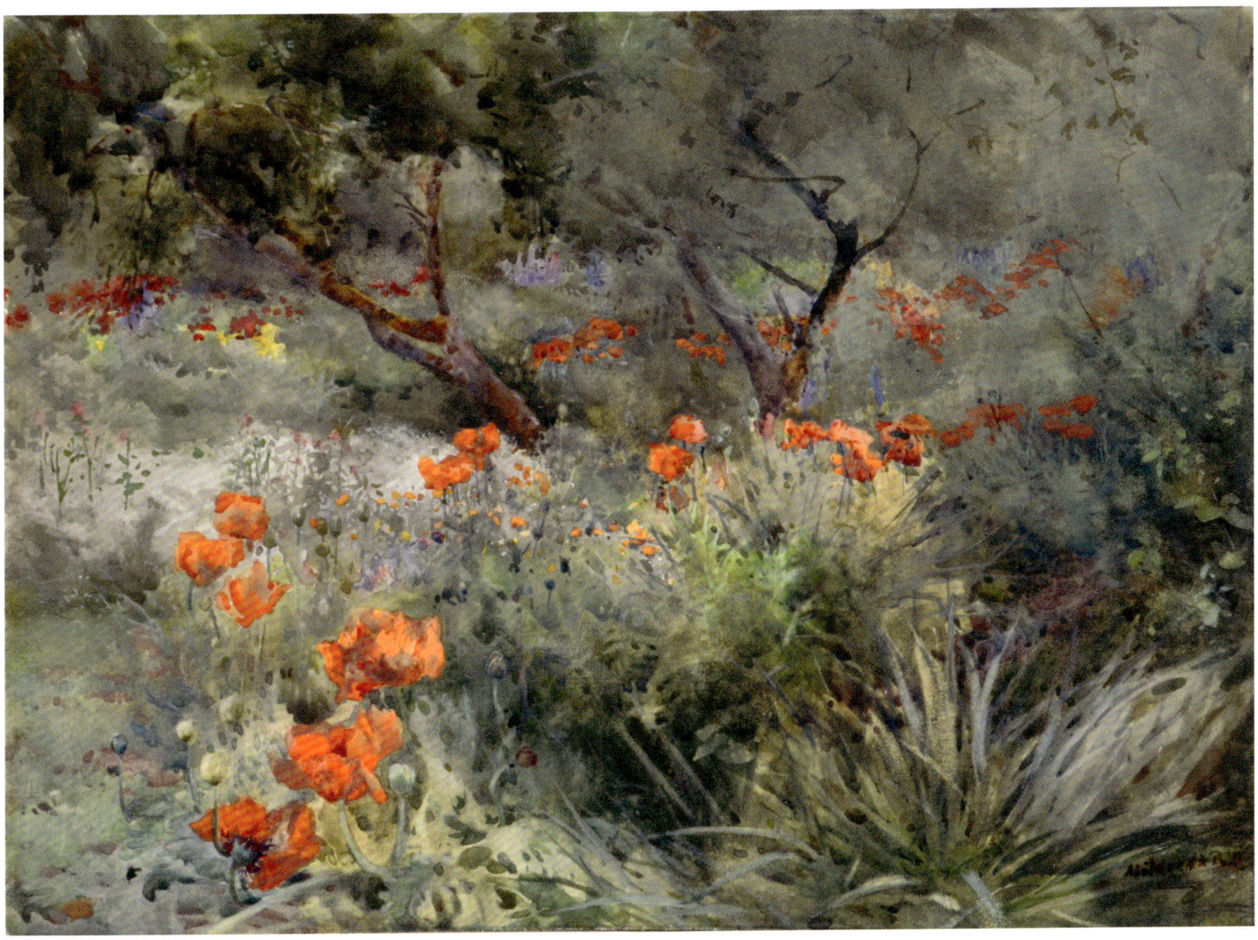

82 **Oriental Poppies**
Signed
Watercolour with bodycolour
10 ½ x 14 ½ inches

BENJAMIN WALTER SPIERS

Benjamin Walter Spiers (1845-1894)

Benjamin Walter Spiers packed every corner of his still life watercolours with objects that test a skill for mimetic detail and reveal an antiquarian turn of mind. Some of his compositions actually show the interiors of his favourite antique shops in Wardour Street, in London's Soho, while one of his largest pieces may even depict a room in his own Bayswater home. Certainly the frequency with which he reused objects suggests that he owned them or could access them quickly and regularly.

Spiers painted in contrary to the type of still life recently established by William Henry Hunt, commended by Ruskin, in which nature is represented modestly, and in miniature, by a bird's nest, a mossy bank and a few nuts, fruits or flowers. He may stand as the leading Victorian exponent of another, much more established, still-life tradition for displaying accumulated man-made possessions with almost *trompe l'oeil* accuracy. However, his cluttered collections of battered, mismatched objects often seem to undermine the usual intention of such displays to confirm the wealth of conspicuous consumers. They concentrate not on monetary worth, but on associative value, a quality perhaps best conveyed by books.

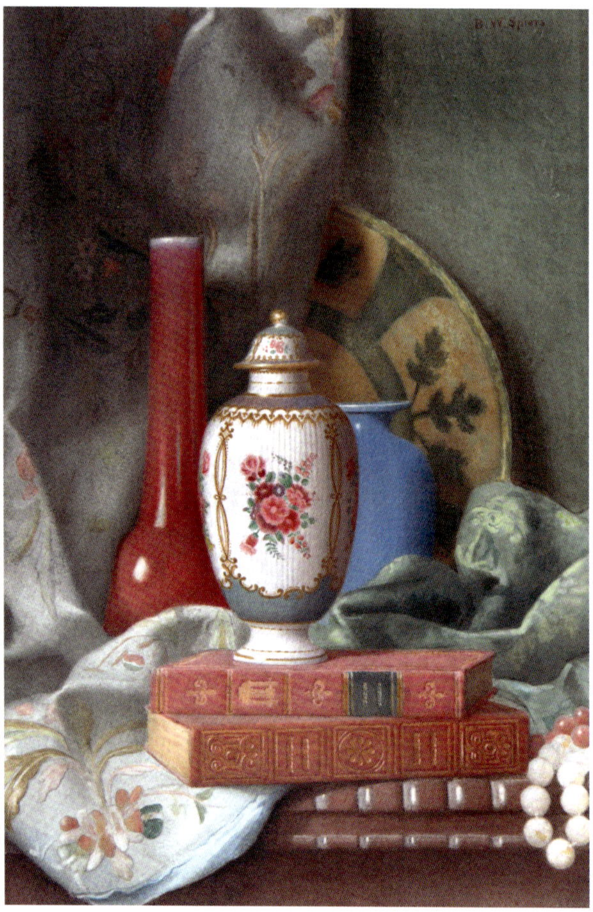

Little is known of Spiers' life or circle. He was born in 1845, the son of Benjamin Spiers and Amy Blake, who had married two years earlier, in 1843. His two sisters – Amy Mary (born 1847) and Emily Jane (1849-1874) – were both born in Marylebone. In 1863, the family seems to have been living at 29 Hereford Road North, Bayswater (now the northern section of Hereford Road).

It has been suggested that the family was related to the Oxford Spiers, a family that included Richard Phené Spiers, architect and artist, and his brother, Walter Lewis Spiers, architect and curator of Sir John Soane's Museum.

No information has yet emerged of Spiers' education or professional training. By 1871, he was living at 70 Hereford Road, Bayswater, with his mother and sisters. Of his two sisters, it is known that Emily died during a visit to Chelmsford, in the autumn of 1874, just before her brother made his artistic breakthrough.

Between 1875 and 1893, Spiers exhibited a total of 75 watercolours at the Royal Academy, the Royal Institute of Painters in Water Colours and the Royal Society of British Artists.

Spiers continued to live at 70 Hereford Road until 1890 (and with his mother until at least 1881). He then moved to 'Longwood', 12 Acol Road, West Hampstead, dying there four years later on 28 June 1894 'after a long and painful illness' (as recorded in *London Standard* for Saturday, 30 June 1894).

Further reading

Christopher Wood, 'Knicknacks and Silly Old Books', *Country Life*, 10 June 1993, pages 124-125

83 **Collector's Choice**
Signed
Watercolour
13 ½ x 9 inches

85 **Literature and Art** (opposite)
Signed and dated 1881
Signed and inscribed with title and '70 Hereford Road, Bayswater' on reverse
Watercolour and bodycolour with pencil, 11 x 14 ½ inches

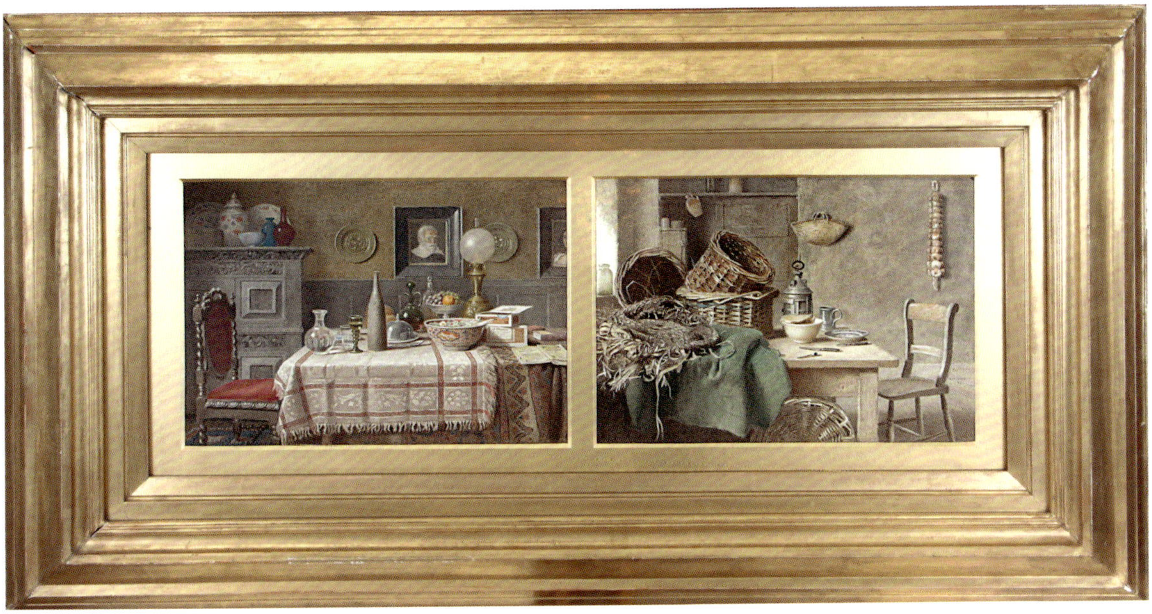

84 **High Life and Low Life**
Signed and inscribed with title on labels on backboard
Watercolour
Two images each measuring 8 ¾ x 12 ¼ inches
Exhibited: Royal Academy of Arts, 1887, nos 1217 and 1218

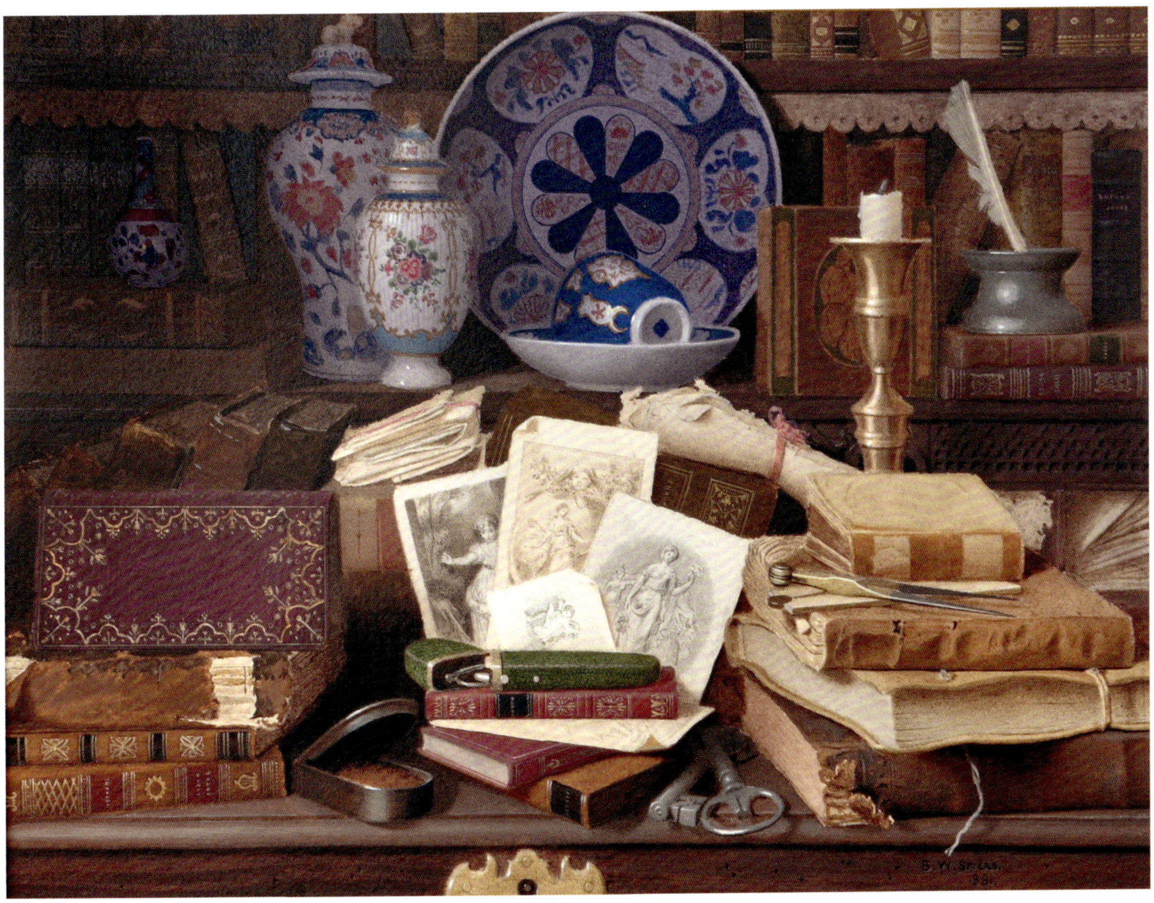

GEORGE FREDERICK NICHOLLS

George Frederick Nicholls (circa 1857-1939)

Specialising in landscapes, gardens and hunting scenes, George Frederick Nicholls sustained a Victorian tradition of watercolour painting well into the twentieth century. He received support from specialist dealers and the publisher, A & C Black, which developed the genre of the 'Colour Plate Book'.

George Frederick Nicholls was born in Staines, Middlesex, the son of George Nicholls and Mary Drewett, and was possibly the twin of Mary Elizabeth Nicholls. Nothing is known of his development before 1879, when he married Lucy Fitzgerald Best Tarleton in Tranmere, Birkenhead, Cheshire. Together they would have at least two sons and four daughters, their first child, Frances, being born in 1880. By 1886, they were living at 12 Seymour Street, Higher Tranmere. By 1899, they had moved to 15 Highfield South, Rock Ferry.

Beginning to contribute to exhibitions at the Walker Art Gallery, Liverpool, from 1885, Nicholls soon established himself as a painter of rural England, and especially of the Cotswolds. In 1905, he commissioned the Arts and Crafts architect, C R Ashbee, to design a studio-house at Chipping Campden, Gloucestershire. However, this was never built, and he lived instead in Hampton, near Evesham, Worcestershire, until 1912. During this period, he confirmed his artistic identity by exhibiting 70 watercolours of the Cotswolds at the New Dudley Gallery, in London in 1907, and producing *The Cotswolds*, a book with a text by F R G Duckworth, which was published by A & C Black in 1908. Another solo show, of 'Water-colours of English By-ways', was held at the New Dudley Gallery in 1910. The combination of exhibition and publication set the pattern for the remainder of his career.

Moving to 106 Abingdon Road, Oxford in 1912, Nicholls held an exhibition of watercolours of Gloucestershire and Wiltshire at Walker's Galleries, in London, in the same year. Further solo shows soon followed: 'Water-colour Drawings of Cotswolds and Avon, Hunting Scenes in the South Oxfordshire, Old Berks, and Cotswolds Country', at Messrs Ryman's Gallery, in Oxford, in 1913, and one of drawings of Wiltshire, Worcestershire and Gloucestershire at Walker's Galleries, in 1914. He widened his geographical sweep, in 1915, when he produced *Cornwall*, with a text by G E Mitton, and further broadened his range, in 1916, by illustrating an edition of Thomas Gray's *An Elegy Written in a Country Churchyard*. These were issued by his regular publisher, A & C Black.

From 1914, Nicholls lived in Oxford High Street. However, he spent part of the First World War in London at 43 South Hill Park Gardens, Hampstead, and his wife seems to have died in the capital in 1917. Moving out of Oxford in the early 1920s, he settled to the east of the city at 'Hill Haven', a house in the village of Horspath. Publishing *Gloucestershire*, with a text by J D Newth, in 1927, he continued to paint and exhibit into the late 1930s. His work appeared in exhibitions of the Royal Academy, the Royal Institute of Painters in Water Colours and the Royal Cambrian Academy, among other institutions.

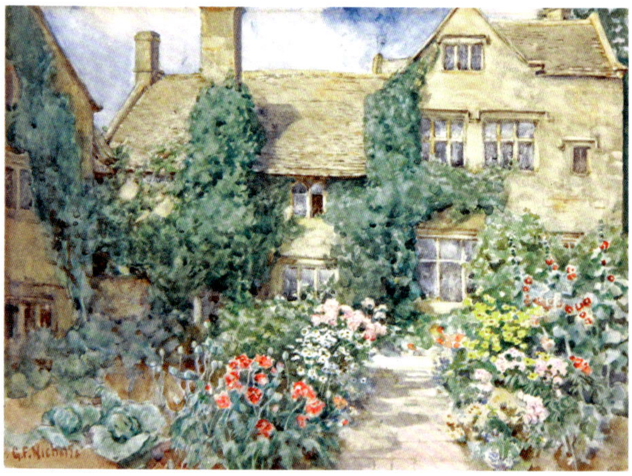

87 **A Cotswold Mansion**
Signed
Watercolour
10 ¼ x 14 ¼ inches

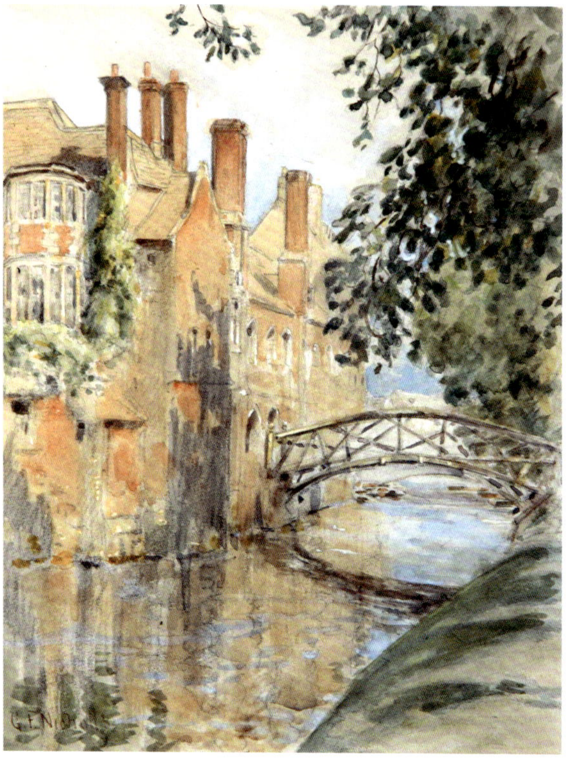

86 **The Mathematical Bridge, Cambridge**
Signed
Watercolour with pencil
12 ½ x 19 ¾ inches

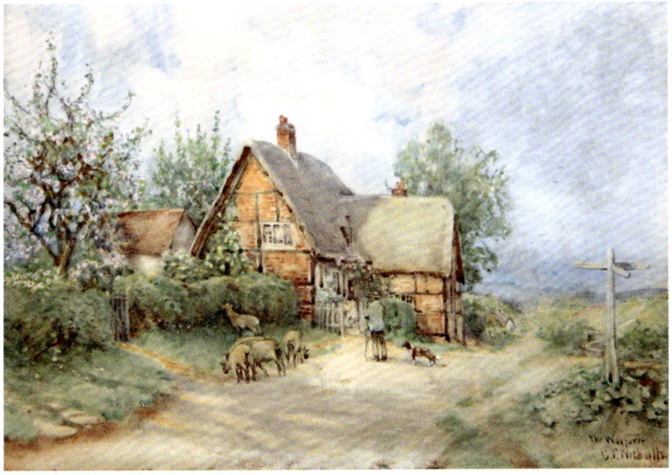

88 **The Wayfarer**
Signed and inscribed with title
Watercolour and bodycolour
14 x 21 inches

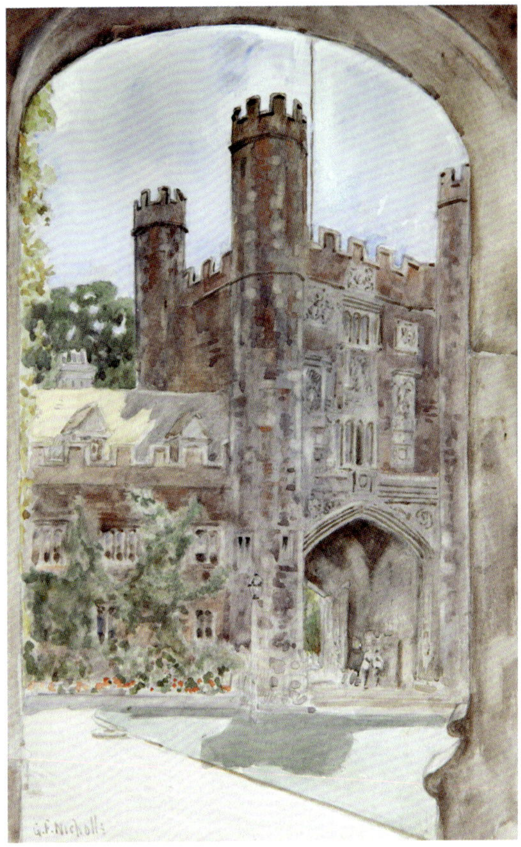

89 **Gateway from Chapel Doorway, Trinity, Cambridge**
Signed
Signed, inscribed with title and 'Hill Haven, Horspath, Oxon' on reverse
Watercolour and pencil on board
14 ¾ x 9 ¼ inches

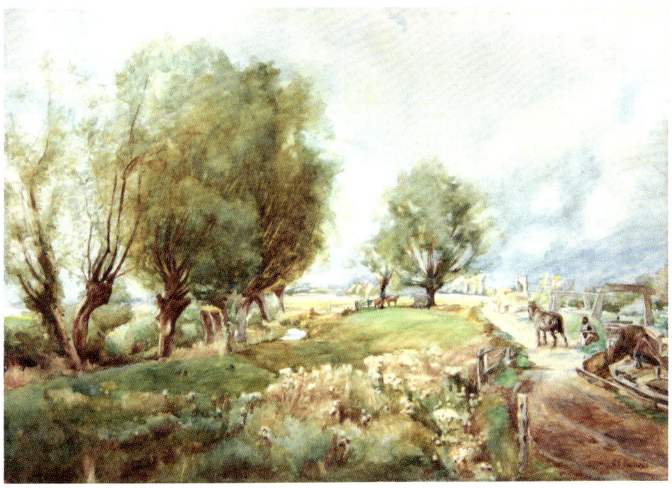

90 **The Lock**
Signed
Watercolour and bodycolour on board
14 ¼ x 21 inches

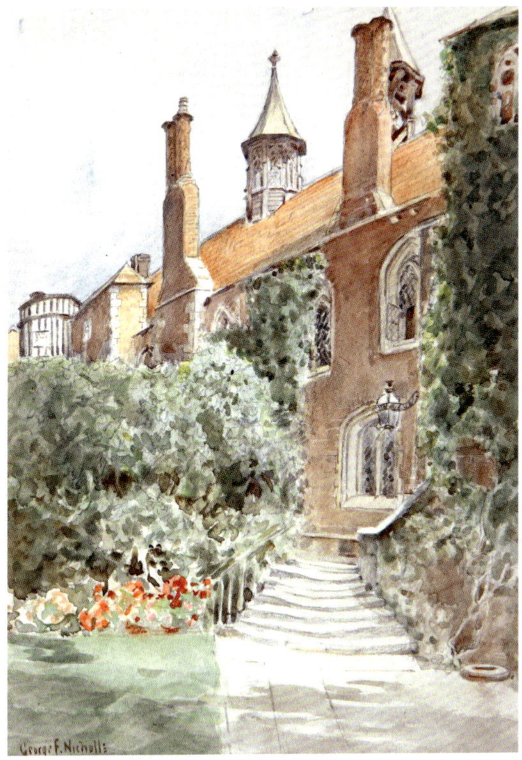

91 **A Country Manor**
Signed
Watercolour and pencil on board
14 ¾ x 10 ½ inches

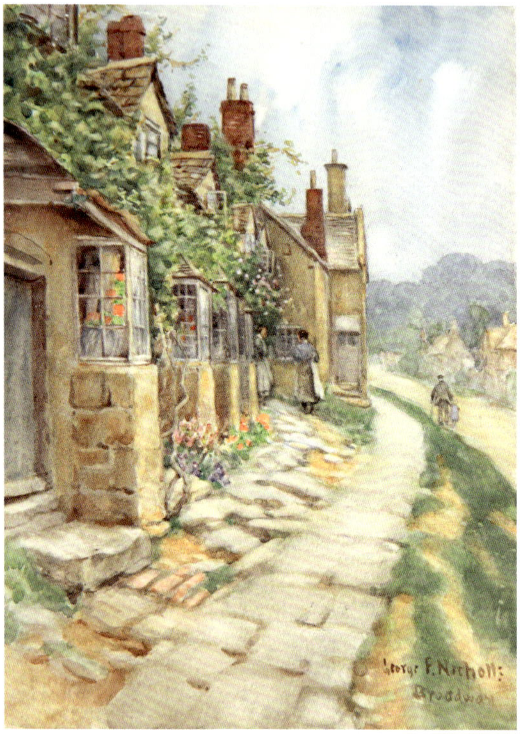

92 Broadway
Signed and inscribed with title
Watercolour
12 ¾ x 9 ¼ inches

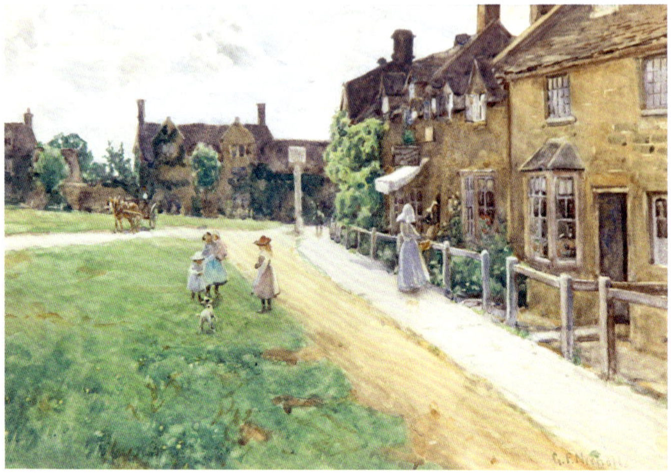

93 Village Green
Signed
Watercolour
8 ½ x 12 ½ inches

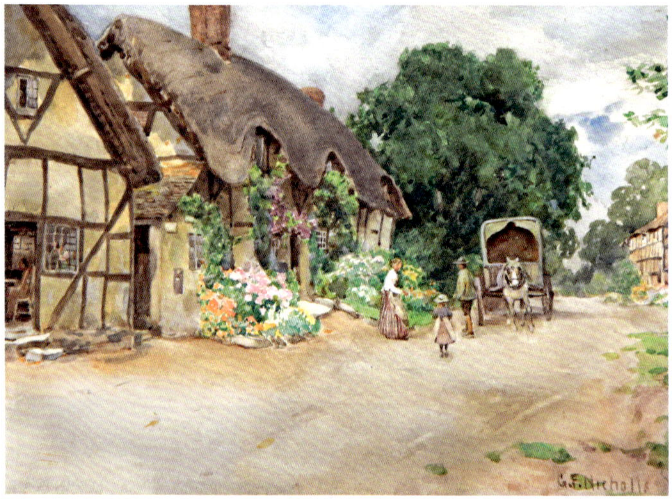

94 Cropthorne, Worcestershire
Signed
Inscribed with title on reverse
Watercolour
9 x 12 ½ inches
Provenance: The Brook Street Art Gallery

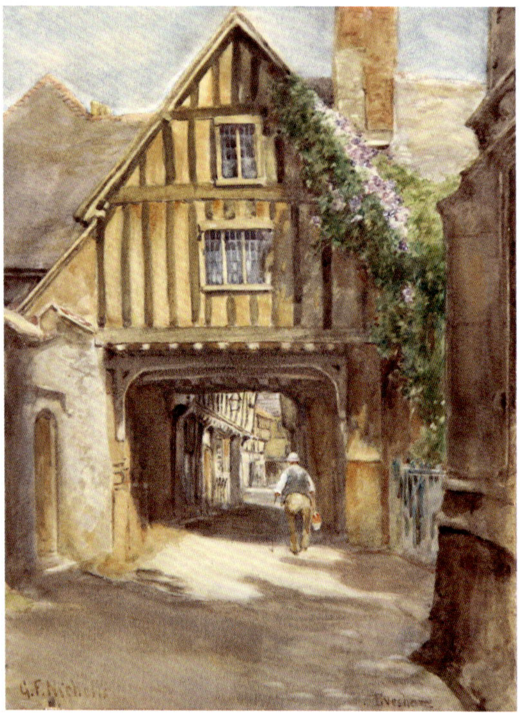

95 Evesham
Signed and inscribed with title
Watercolour
12 ½ x 9 ¼ inches

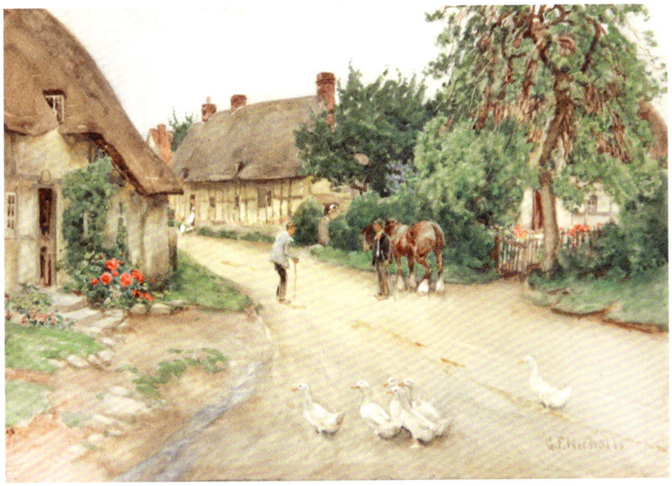

96 A Country Lane
Signed
Watercolour on board
9 ½ x 14 ¼ inches

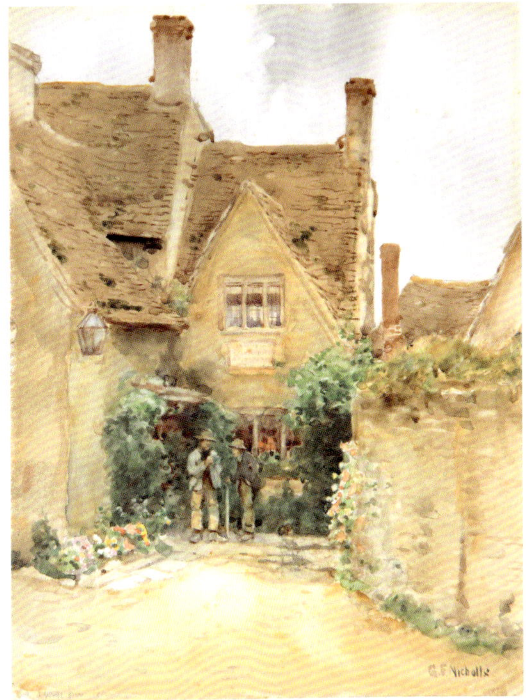

98 Old George Inn, South Cerney, Gloucestershire
Signed and inscribed 'Old George Inn, Cerney'
Inscribed with title on reverse
Watercolour on board
11 ¾ x 8 ¾ inches

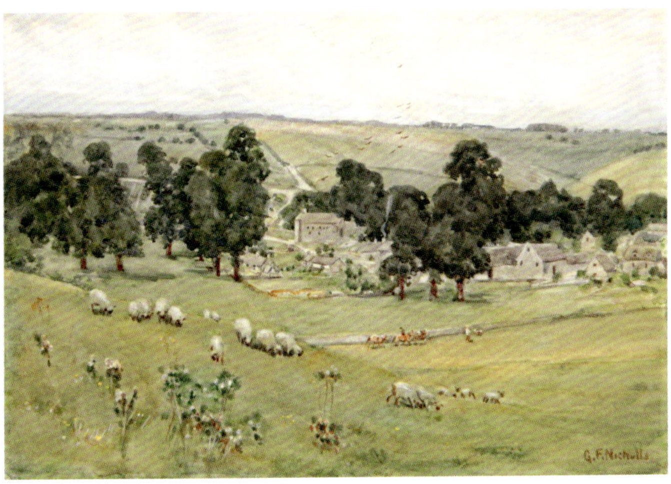

97 A Rural Hamlet
Signed
Watercolour
9 ½ x 14 ¼ inches

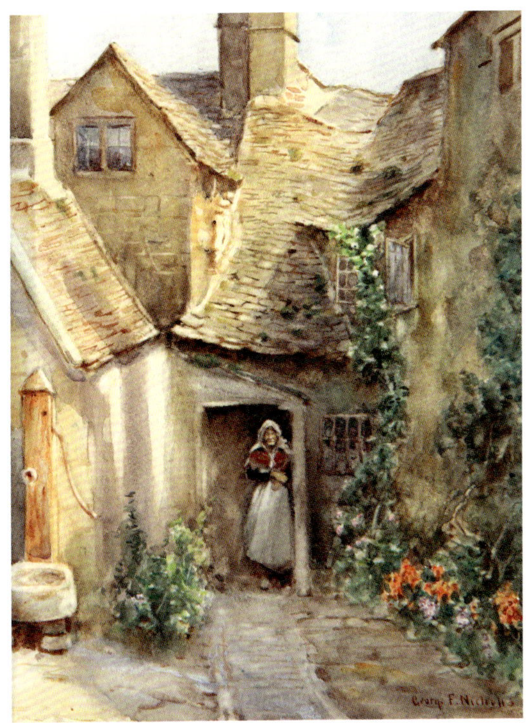

99 Old Houses, Chipping Campden, Gloucestershire
Signed
Watercolour
12 ¼ x 9 inches

EDWARD STEEL HARPER

Edward Steel Harper (1878-1951)

The work of the Birmingham artist, Edward Steel Harper, possesses a distinctive quality that combines late Pre-Raphaelitism with something more modern.

For a biography of Edward Steel Harper, please refer to *Chris Beetles Summer Show*, 2008, page 16.

His work is represented in numerous public collections, including Birmingham Museums & Art Gallery.

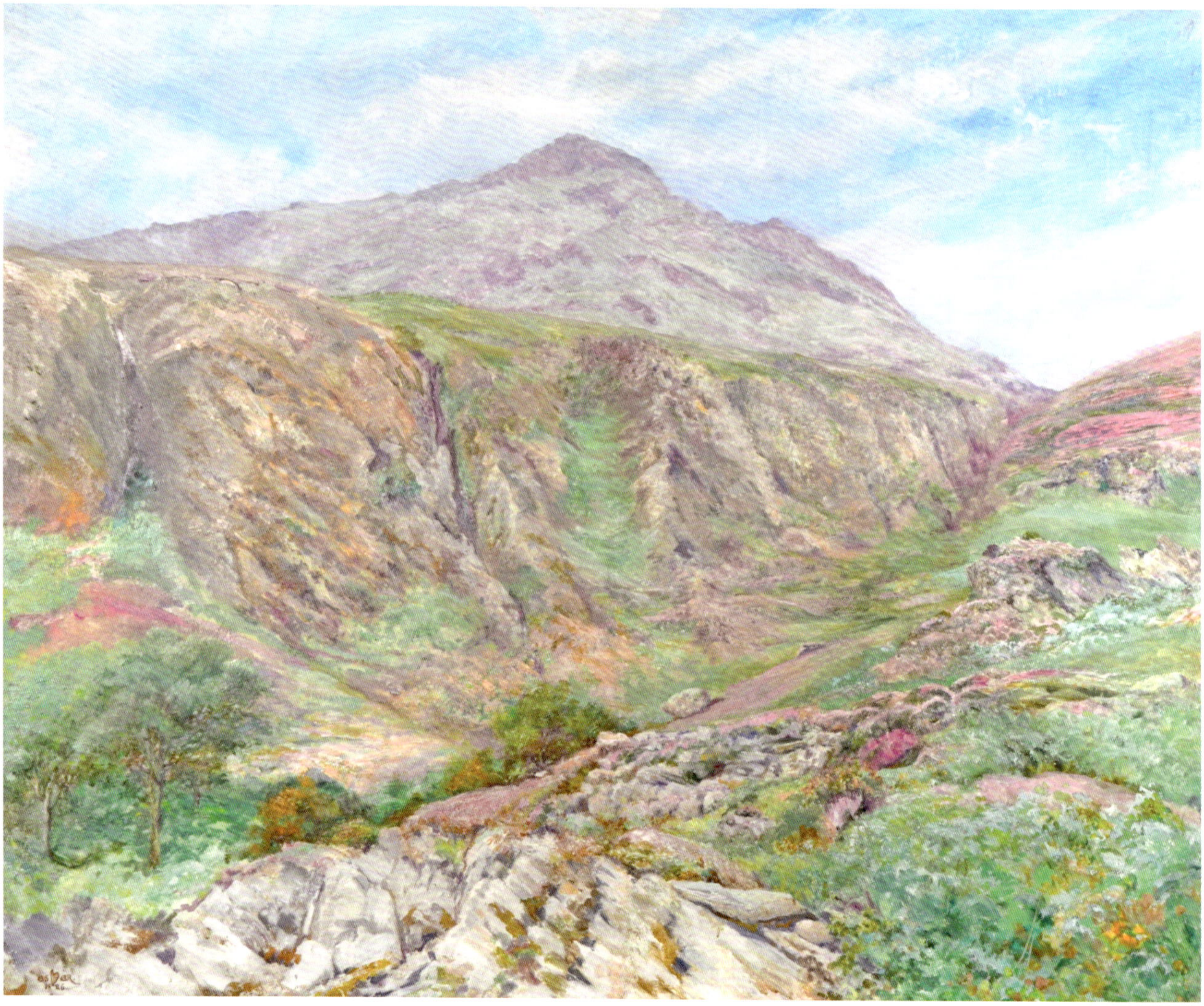

100 **Welsh Landscape**
Signed with monogram and dated 1926
Oil on canvas
28 x 36 inches
Provenance: Sir Granville and Lady Bantock

Welsh Landscape
This work was once in the collection of the composer, Sir Granville Bantock, who was a close friend of Edward Steel Harper, and owned a number of his landscapes.

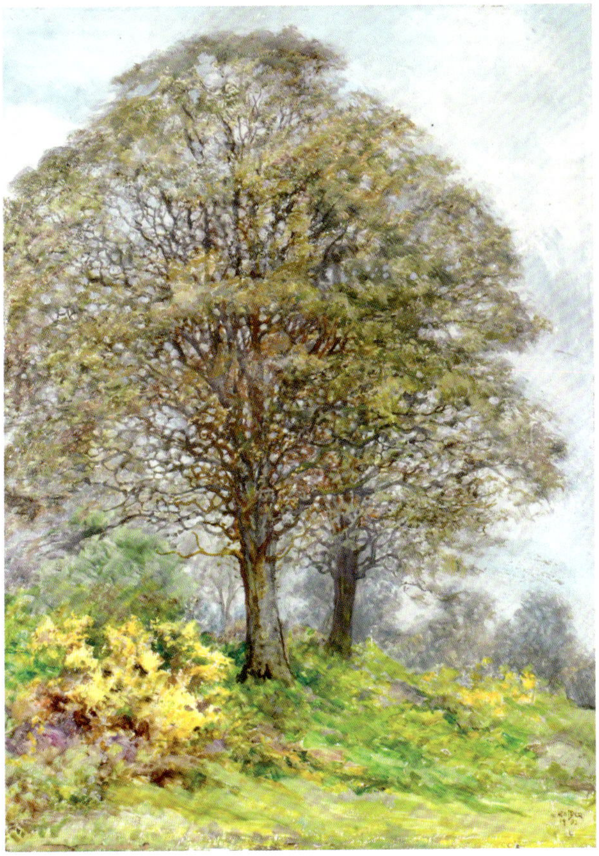

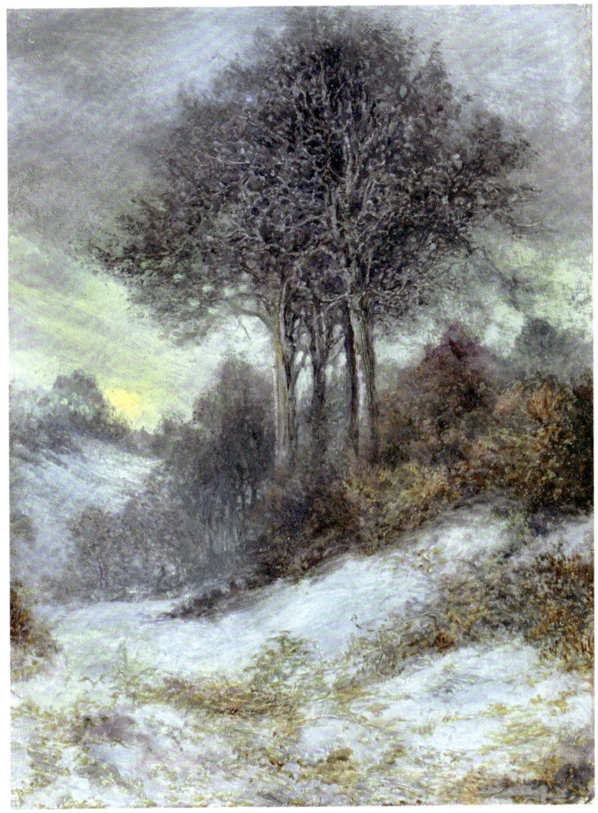

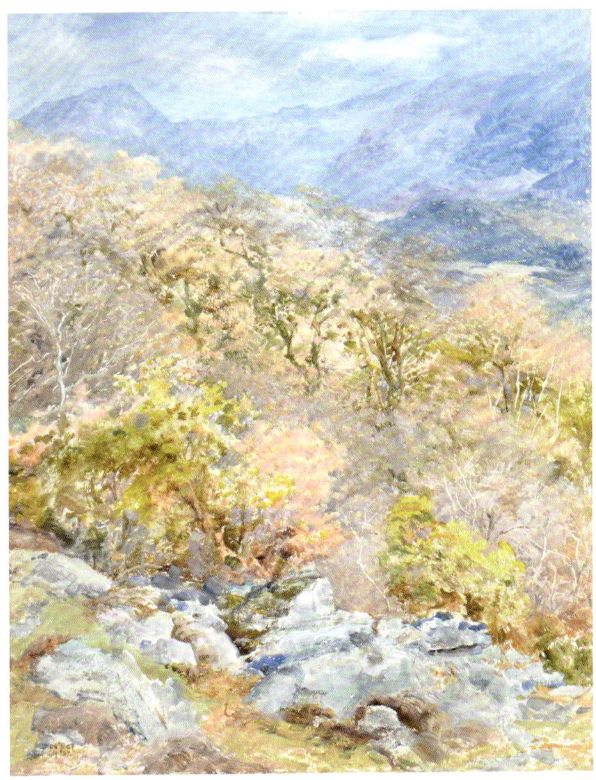

101 Trees at the Edge of the Wood
Signed with monogram and dated 1932
Oil on canvas laid down on board
16 x 12 inches

102 Winter Landscape
Oil on canvas
15 ¼ x 11 ½ inches

103 The Valley
Signed and dated 1937
Oil on canvas
16 x 12 inches

EDMUND BLAMPIED

Edmund Blampied, RBA RE (1886-1966)

Edmund Blampied is one of the most significant artists to have hailed from the Channel Islands. Greatly versatile, he worked as a painter, illustrator, and occasional sculptor, though is best remembered as a printmaker and, especially, an etcher. Having been born on a farm, he produced some particularly evocative etchings of agricultural and peasant subjects. Their fluidity of line, strong sense of humanity and Gallic humour suggest a kinship with Daumier and Gavarni.

Edmund Blampied was born on a farm in the Parish of St Martin, Jersey, on 30 March 1886, the youngest of four sons of John and Elizabeth Blampied. His father died five days before he was born, and his mother brought up the family, working as a dressmaker and shopkeeper in the Parish of Trinity. His first tongue was the Norman language of Jèrriais.

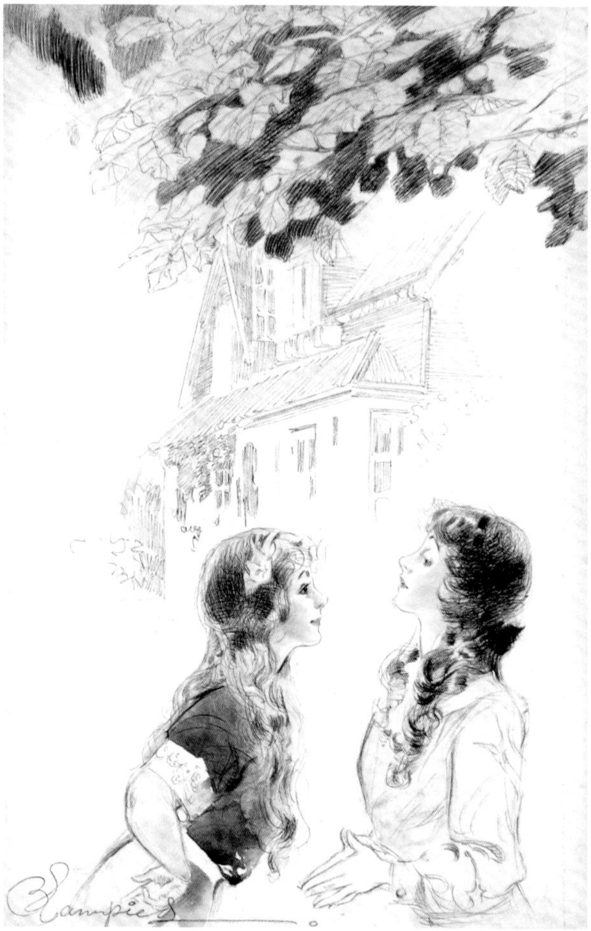

Blampied left school at the age of 14, and went to work in an architect's office in St Helier, the capital of Jersey. A year later, he exhibited some drawings at an agricultural show, and these came to the notice of Marie Josephine Klintz, who ran a private art school in the town. As a result, she gave him his first formal lessons in art. His caricatures of local politicians attracted the attention of the businessman, Saumarez James Nicolle, who offered to sponsor his art studies in England.

In January 1903, the 16-year-old Blampied left Jersey for England, and enrolled at Lambeth School of Art, in London, studying there under Philip Connard and the Principal, Thomas McKeggie. McKeggie chose him to work part-time on the staff of the *Daily Chronicle*, and his first illustrations appeared in its pages on 13 January 1905. In the September, he transferred to the LCC School of Photo-Engraving and Lithography at Bolt Court, where he studied under Walter Seymour and through him perfected the art of etching. While there, he made a number of friends, including Salomon van Abbe, whose sister, Marianne, he would marry in 1914. In 1911, he established his own studio, and worked there, mainly as a magazine illustrator, into the early years of the First World War.

Following the introduction of conscription in Britain in 1916, Blampied returned to Jersey. Though classified as not fully fit for active service in 1917, he took up guard duties in the Royal Jersey Militia, and remained on the island until 1919, when he resumed his professional life in London.

Though Blampied had been producing etchings from as early as 1909, he only now began to establish himself as a printmaker. In 1920, he became an associate of the Royal Society of Painter-Etchers and Engravers, with full membership following just a year later. Also in 1920, he held a solo show of etchings and drypoints in London at the Leicester Galleries. His first American exhibition took place at Kennedy and Company, New York, in 1922. Many other joint and solo exhibitions followed.

Experimenting with lithography from 1920, Blampied joined the Senefelder Club of lithographic artists in 1923. He took classes in the medium from Archibald Hartrick, a founder member of the Senefelder, at the Central School of Arts and Crafts in

104 **'Two little girls were coming home from school, when one commenced to tease the other'**
Signed
Stamped '3 Apr 1913' below mount
Pen and ink with pencil
10 x 6 inches

1925, but was already sufficiently expert by that date to win a Gold Medal for lithography at the Paris International Exhibition.

During the 1920s and 30s, Blampied worked extensively as an illustrator, contributing to numerous magazines, especially *The Bystander* and *The Illustrated London News*, and illustrating a number of books, including an edition of Robert Louis Stevenson's *Travels with a Donkey in the Cevennes* (1931). His illustrations of children's books such as the 1939 edition of J M Barrie's *Peter and Wendy*, published by Hodder and Stoughton, were met with particular acclaim.

Between the wars, Blampied and his wife often travelled to France, and regularly wintered on the Riviera. In 1926, they sold their house in South London, and spent five months in southern France and Tunisia, Blampied producing a number of North African drawings and etchings.

Though he became a member of the Royal Society of British Artists in 1938, Blampied decided to return to Jersey just before the outbreak of the Second World War and stayed there, with his wife, during the German Occupation, despite the fact that she was Jewish. While he found little work as an illustrator, he received some commissions from the State of Jersey to design bank notes and postage stamps. Continuing to live on Jersey beyond the end of the war, he worked mostly in oil and watercolour during his final years. A large exhibition of his work was mounted at the John Nelson Bergstrom Art Center and Museum, Neenah, Wisconsin, in July 1954. A retrospective took place at the Societe Jersiaise, Jersey Museum, a decade later. He died on Jersey on 26 August 1966.

His work is represented in numerous public collections, including The Fitzwilliam Museum (Cambridge); Jersey Museum (St Helier); and Boston Public Library and the Cleveland Museum of Art (Ohio).

Further reading

Jean Arnold and John Appleby, *A Catalogue Raisonné of Etchings, Drypoints and Lithographs of Edmund Blampied*, St Ouen: John Appleby Publishing, 1996; Andrew Hall, *Edmund Blampied. An Illustrated Life*, Jersey Heritage Trust, 2010

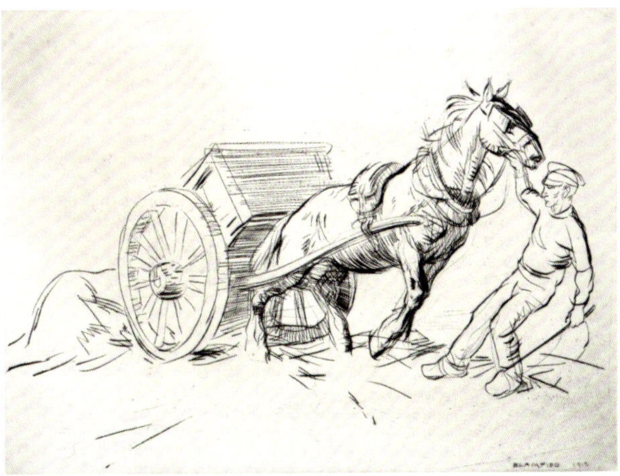

105 Work in the Fields
Signed
Inscribed with title below mount
Drypoint
8 ½ x 11 inches
1913, edition of 65
Campbell Dodgson 21, E Allhusen 9, Arnold & Appleby 31
Literature: E L Allhusen, 'The Etchings of Edmund Blampied', *Print Collectors' Quarterly*, vol 13, no 1, February 1926; Campbell Dodgson, *A Complete Catalogue of Etchings and Dry-Points of Edmund Blampied*, London: Halton & Truscott Smith, 1926; Jean Arnold & John Appleby, *A Catalogue Raisonné of Etchings Drypoints & Lithographs of Edmund Blampied*, Jersey: John Appleby Publishing, 1996

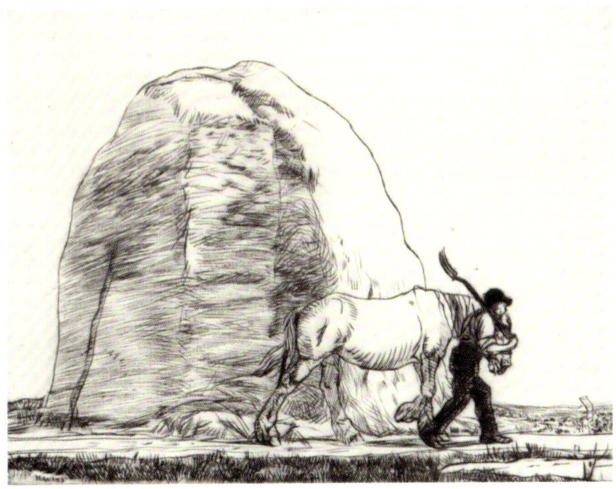

106 The Haystack
Signed
Inscribed with title on reverse
Drypoint
5 x 6 ½ inches
1913, edition of 29
Campbell Dodgson 20, E Allhusen 7, Arnold & Appleby 19
Literature: E L Allhusen, 'The Etchings of Edmund Blampied', *Print Collectors' Quarterly*, vol 13, no 1, February 1926; Campbell Dodgson, *A Complete Catalogue of Etchings and Dry-Points of Edmund Blampied*, London: Halton & Truscott Smith, 1926; Jean Arnold & John Appleby, *A Catalogue Raisonné of Etchings Drypoints & Lithographs of Edmund Blampied*, Jersey: John Appleby Publishing, 1996

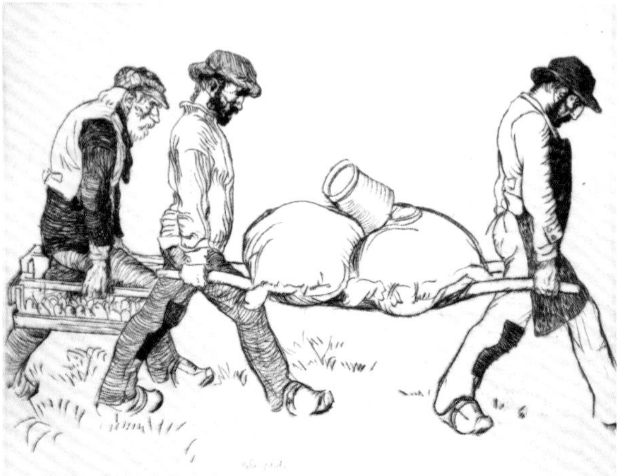

107 Potato Planters
Signed
Inscribed with title below mount
Drypoint
9 ¾ x 13 inches
1920, edition of 100
Campbell Dodgson 44, E Allhusen 26, Arnold & Appleby 63
Literature: E L Allhusen, 'The Etchings of Edmund Blampied', *Print Collectors' Quarterly*, vol 13, no 1, February 1926; Campbell Dodgson, *A Complete Catalogue of Etchings and Dry-Points of Edmund Blampied*, London: Halton & Truscott Smith, 1926; Jean Arnold & John Appleby, *A Catalogue Raisonné of Etchings Drypoints & Lithographs of Edmund Blampied*, Jersey: John Appleby Publishing, 1996

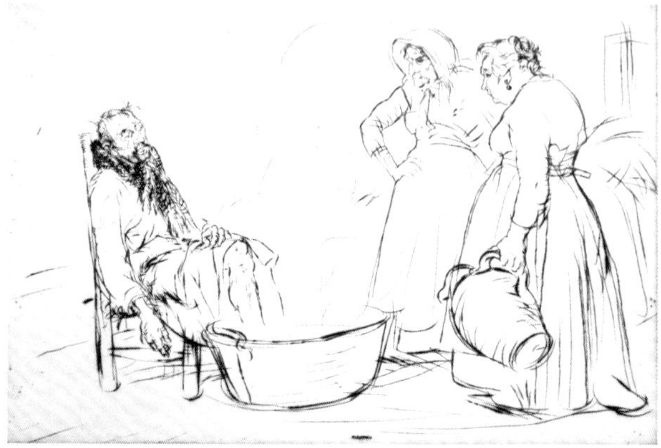

108 The Sick Man
Signed in pencil
Drypoint
7 ¾ x 11 ½ inches
1921, edition of 100
Campbell Dodgson 65, E Allhusen 42, Arnold & Appleby 79
Literature: E L Allhusen, 'The Etchings of Edmund Blampied', *Print Collectors' Quarterly*, vol 13, no 1, February 1926; Campbell Dodgson, *A Complete Catalogue of Etchings and Dry-Points of Edmund Blampied*, London: Halton & Truscott Smith, 1926; Malcolm Salaman, *Modern Masters of Etching*, vol 10, Edmund Blampied', London: The Studio, 1926, plate iv; Jean Arnold & John Appleby, *A Catalogue Raisonné of Etchings Drypoints & Lithographs of Edmund Blampied*, Jersey: John Appleby Publishing, 1996

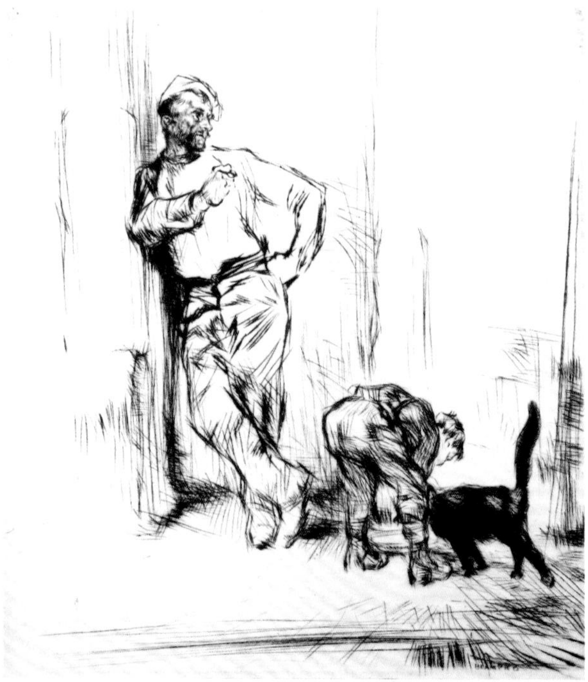

109 Fisherman's Pet
Signed in pencil
Drypoint
10 x 9 ¼ inches
1923, edition of 100
Campbell Dodgson 82, E Allhusen 57, Arnold & Appleby 87
Exhibited: Royal Hibernian Academy of Arts, 1929
Literature: *Fine Prints of the Year 1925*; Malcolm Salaman, *Modern Masters of Etching*, vol 10, Edmund Blampied, London: The Studio, 1926, plate vii

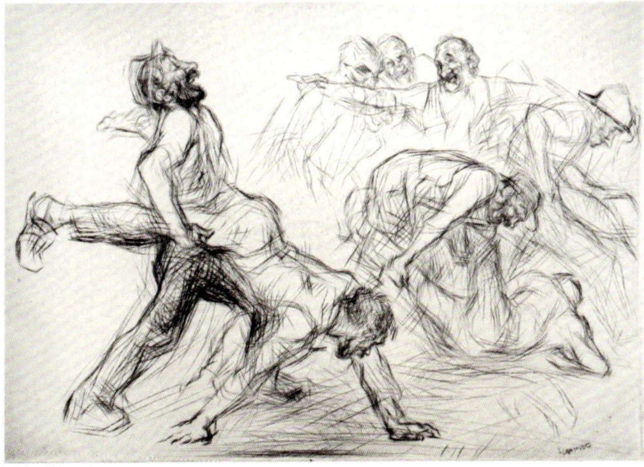

110 A Wheelbarrow Race
Signed and numbered 50/100
Inscribed with title below mount
Drypoint
8 ¾ x 12 inches
1925-26, edition of 100
Arnold & Appleby 114
Literature: *Fine Prints of the Year 1926*

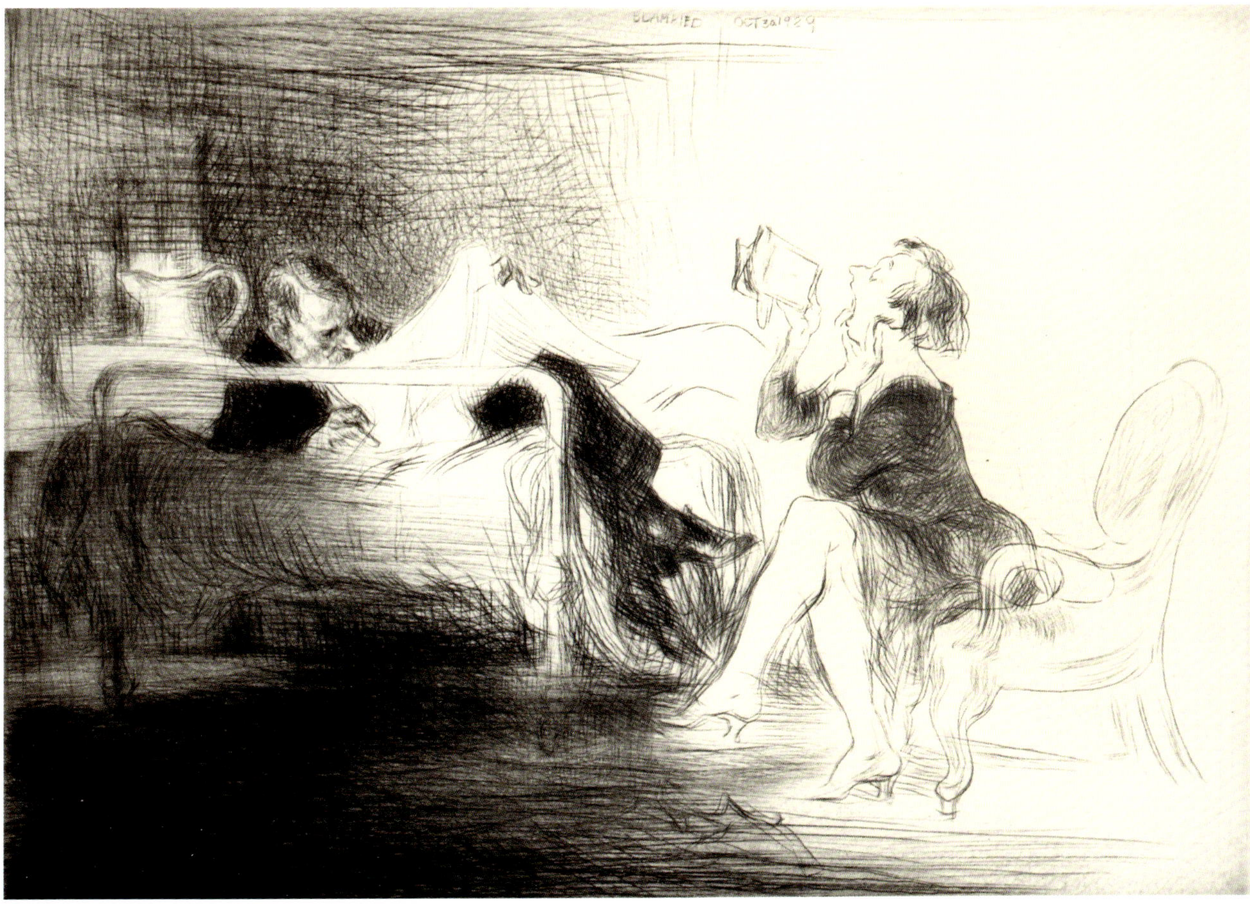

111 En Pension
Signed and numbered 24/100
Signed and dated Oct 30 1929 within the plate
Drypoint
8 ½ x 12 inches
1929-30, edition of 100
Arnold & Appleby 142

Literature: *Fine Prints of the Year 1930*; Kenneth M Guichard, *British Etchers 1850-1940*, London: Robin Garton, 1981, page 26; Jean Arnold & John Appleby, *A Catalogue Raisonné of Etchings Drypoints & Lithographs of Edmund Blampied*, Jersey: John Appleby Publishing, 1996

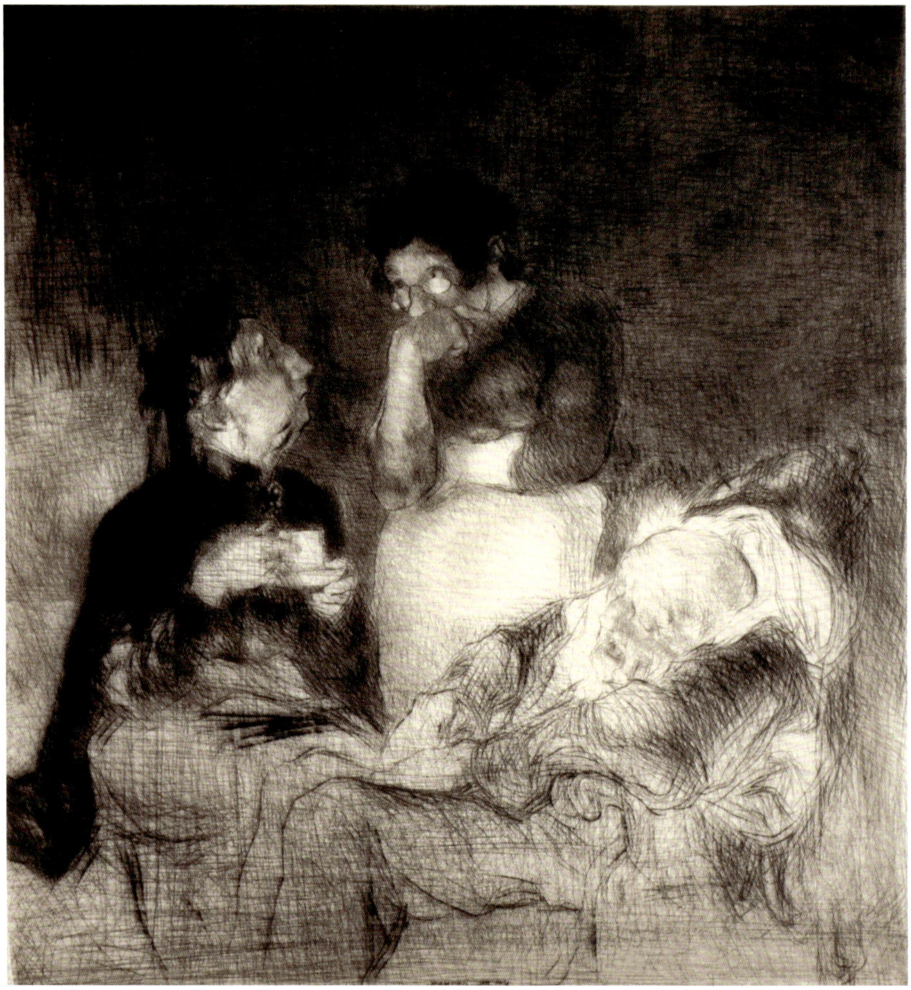

112 The Centenarian
Signed and numbered 70/100
Inscribed with title below mount
Drypoint
10 ½ x 10 ¼ inches
1930-31, edition of 100
Arnold & Appleby 144
Literature: *Fine Prints of the Year 1931*, vol 9, plate viii

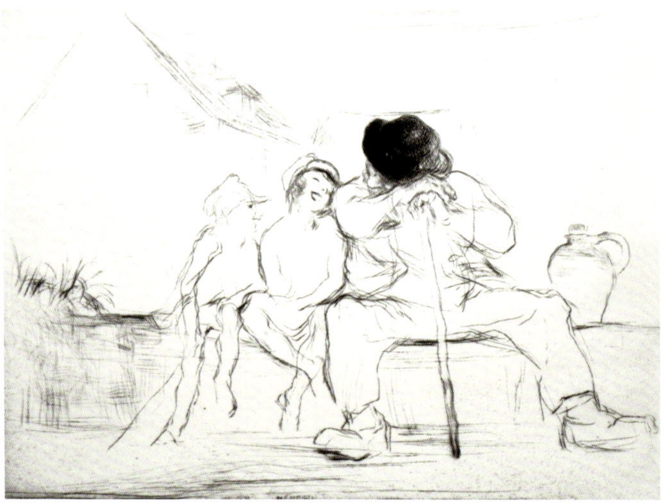

113 Fairy Tales
Signed and numbered 51/100
Signed and dated 1931 within the plate
Drypoint
8 x 10 ¾ inches
1931, edition of 100
Arnold & Appleby 154
Literature: *Fine Prints of the Year 1931*

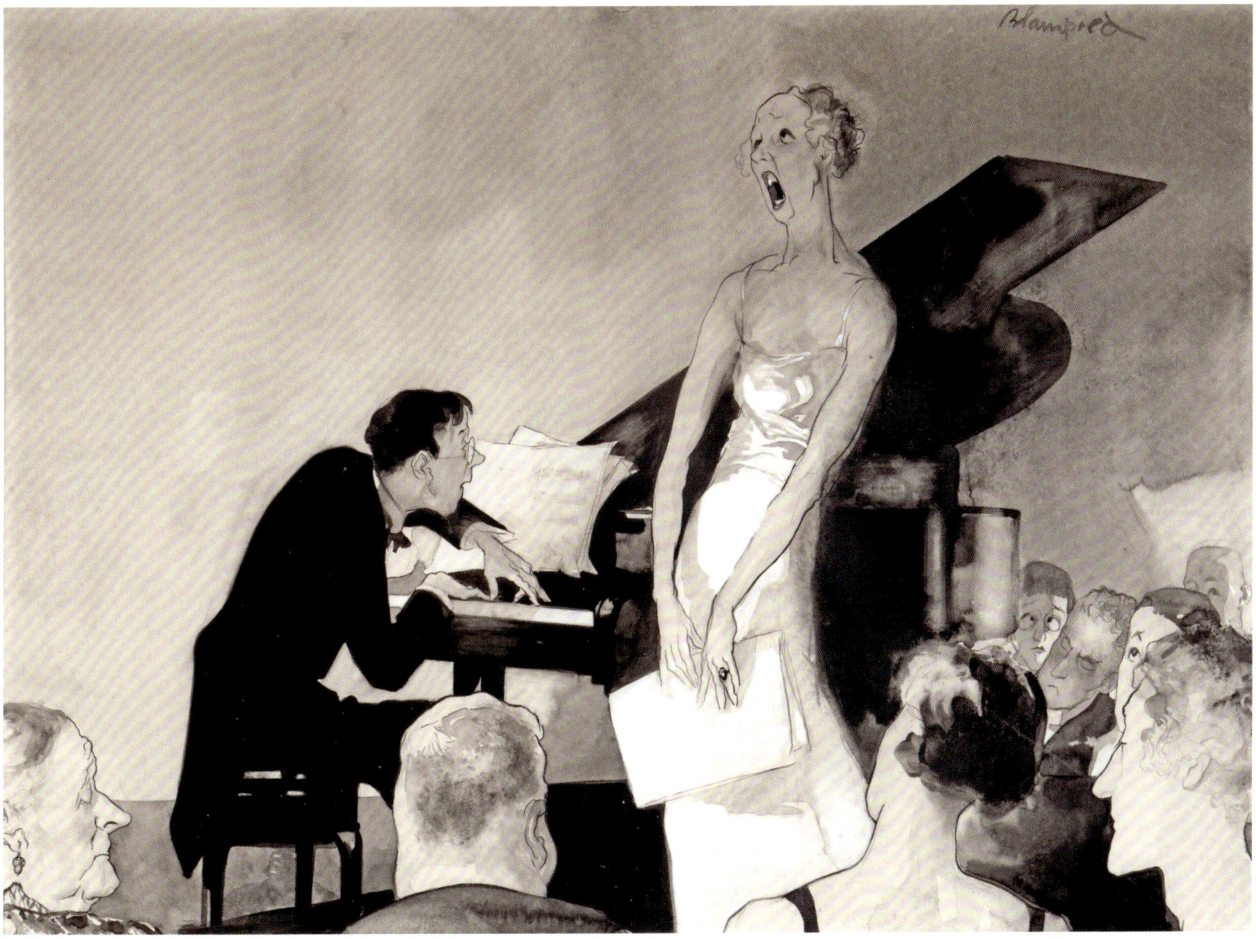

114 Charity Concert
Signed
Pen ink and bodycolour
14 ¾ x 21 ¼ inches
Illustrated: *The Illustrated London News*, 1933, page 441

KEITH GRANT

Keith Frederick Grant (born 1930)

One of the greatest living British landscape painters, Keith Grant has travelled extensively, and has confronted the elements in order to produce extraordinary, resonant images of nature, especially in the north. Recently, he has preferred to recollect his experiences in the tranquility of his studio in Norway, and work imaginatively to produce an exciting series of what he calls 'autobiographical' paintings.

Representing Keith since 2009, the Chris Beetles Gallery held the highly successful solo show, 'Elements of the Earth', in 2010, and is busy preparing a major monograph on the artist for publication in the near future.

For a biography of Keith Grant, please refer to *Chris Beetles Summer Show*, 2008, page 44-45.

On pages 74-85 all quotes are entries taken from Keith Grant's diaries written between 19 December 2013 and 8 April 2014.

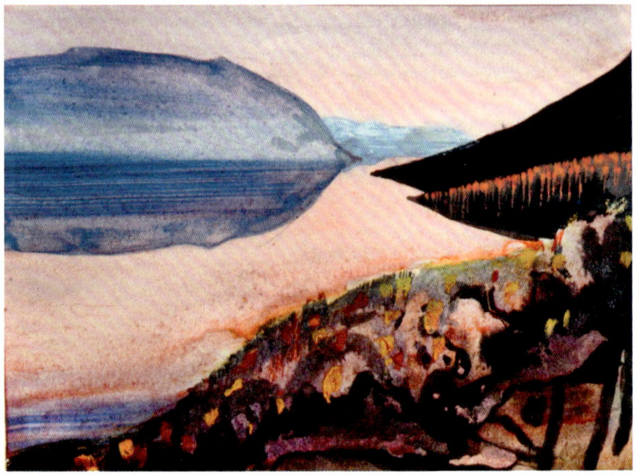

115 **Norwegian Sunset**
Watercolour, bodycolour and ink
5 x 6 ½ inches
Exhibited: Roland, Browse & Delbanco, as 'Sunset, North Norway'

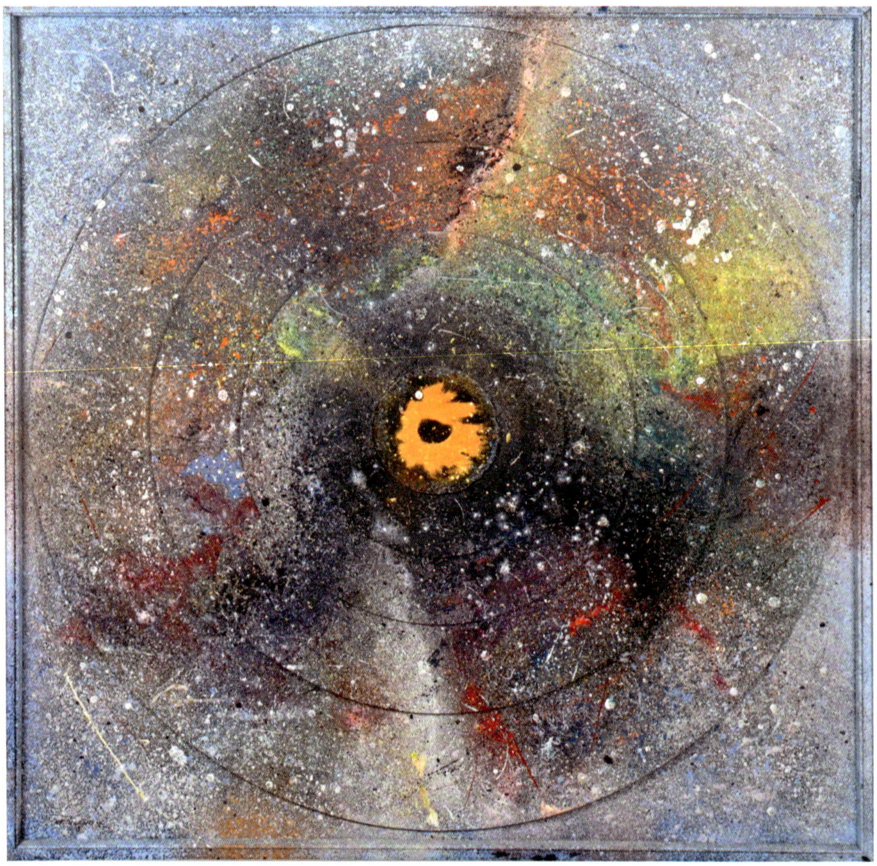

116 **Creation of the Elements II**
Signed and indistinctly dated [1994]
Signed and inscribed with title on reverse
Acrylic on convex relief board
41 ¼ x 41 ¼ inches
Exhibited: 'Landscapes of Exploration', A T Kearney, 2000

119 **Nest** (opposite)
Signed and dated 8/12
Signed, inscribed with title and dated 'Aug/Sept 2012' on stretcher
Oil on canvas
39 ½ x 47 ½ inches

117 **The Beacon**
Signed
Inscribed with title on reverse
Oil on canvas
26 x 32 inches

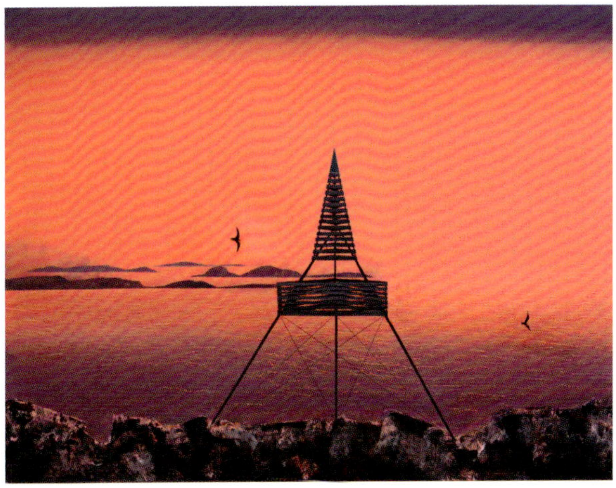

118 **Sea Beacon circled by two Birds II**
Signed and dated 9/11
Signed, dated Oct 2011 and inscribed with title on reverse
35 ¾ x 47 ½ inches

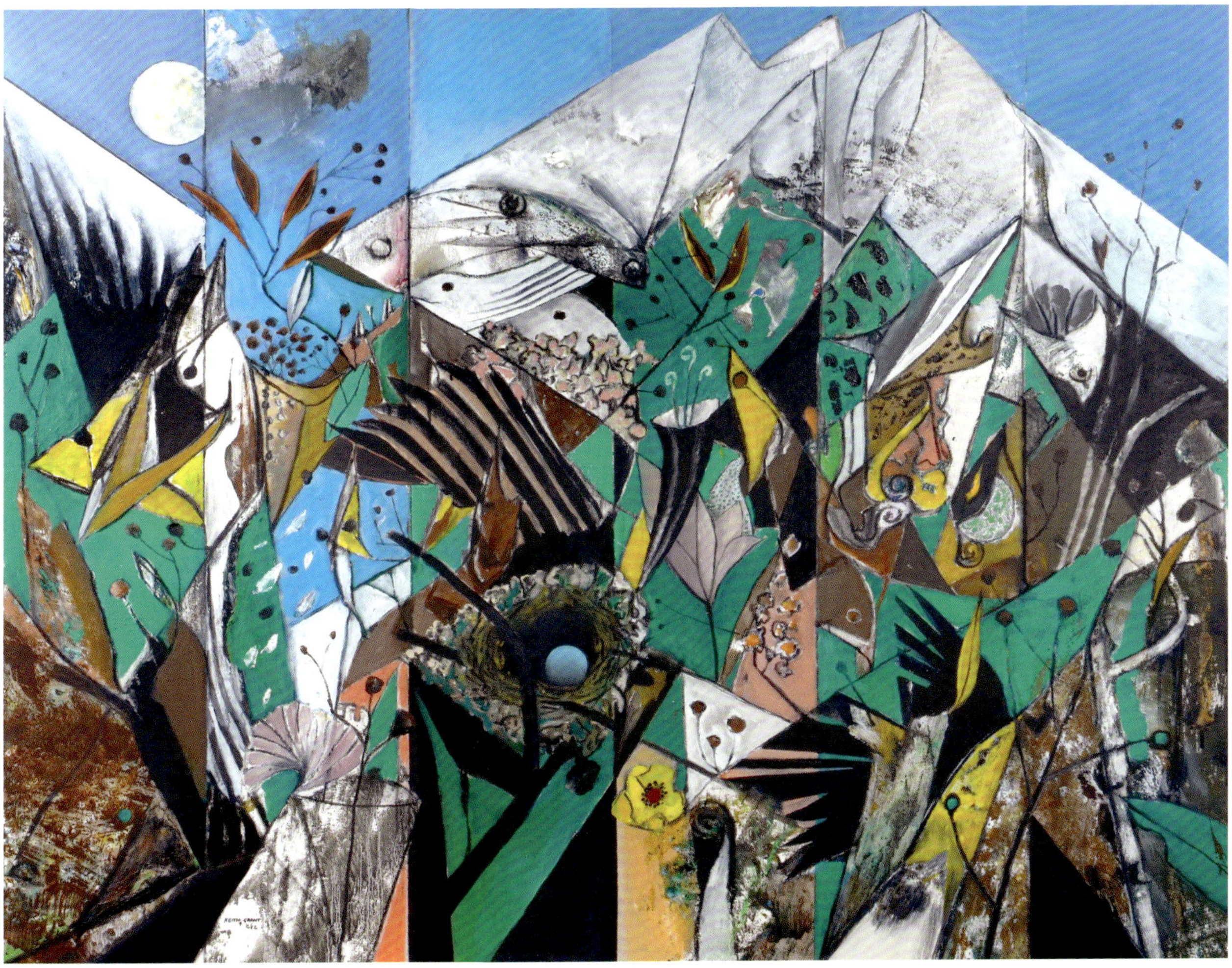

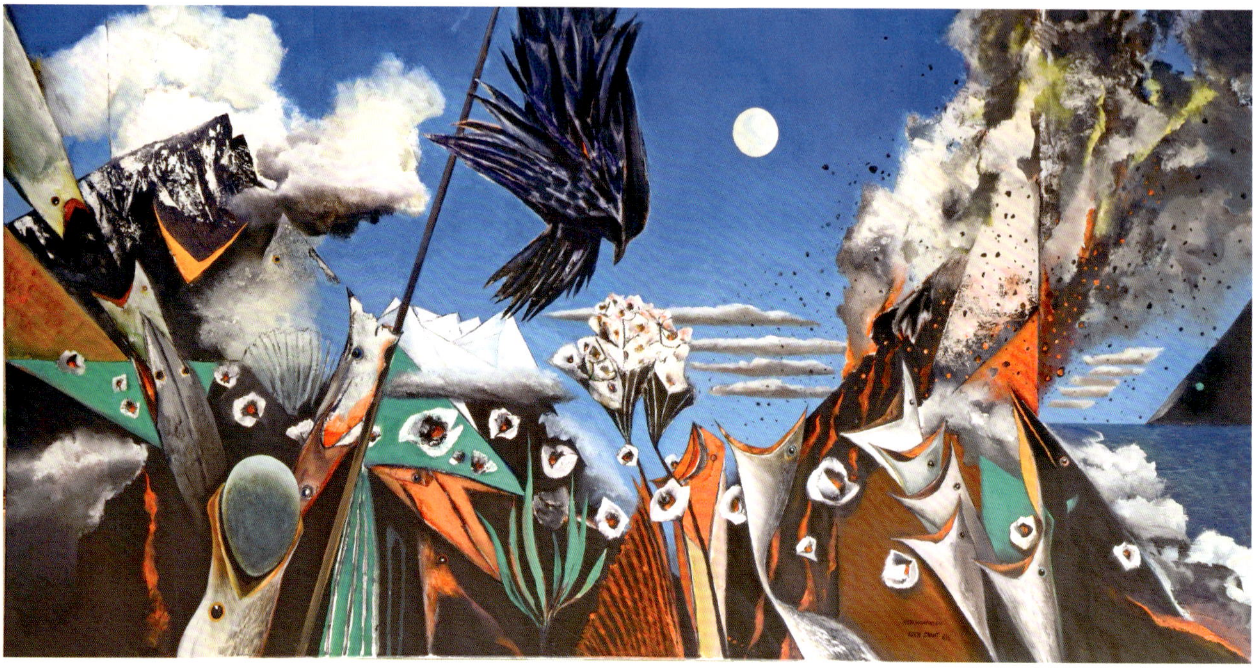

120 Metamorphosis
Signed, inscribed with title and dated 6/12
Signed, inscribed with title and dated 'June 2012' on stretcher
Oil on canvas
39 ½ x 79 inches

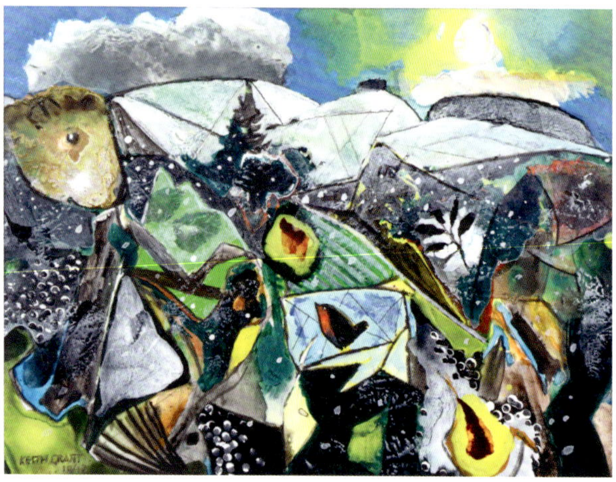

121 Snow comes to England
Signed and dated 10/13
Signed and inscribed with title, 'New English Series XIV' and dated 'Oct 2013' on reverse
Acrylic with ink
7 ¼ x 9 ¾ inches

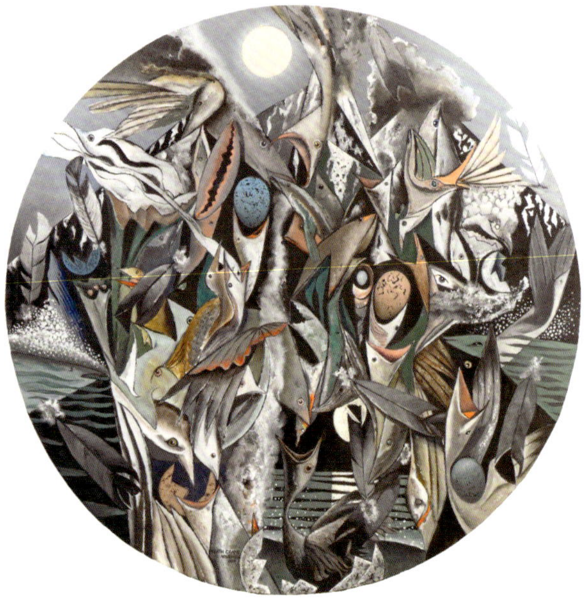

122 Tondo (frontispiece)
The winged hours of the Seabirds
Signed and dated 'November 2013'
Signed, inscribed with title and dated 'Nov 2013' on reverse
Oil on board
55 ¼ inches diameter

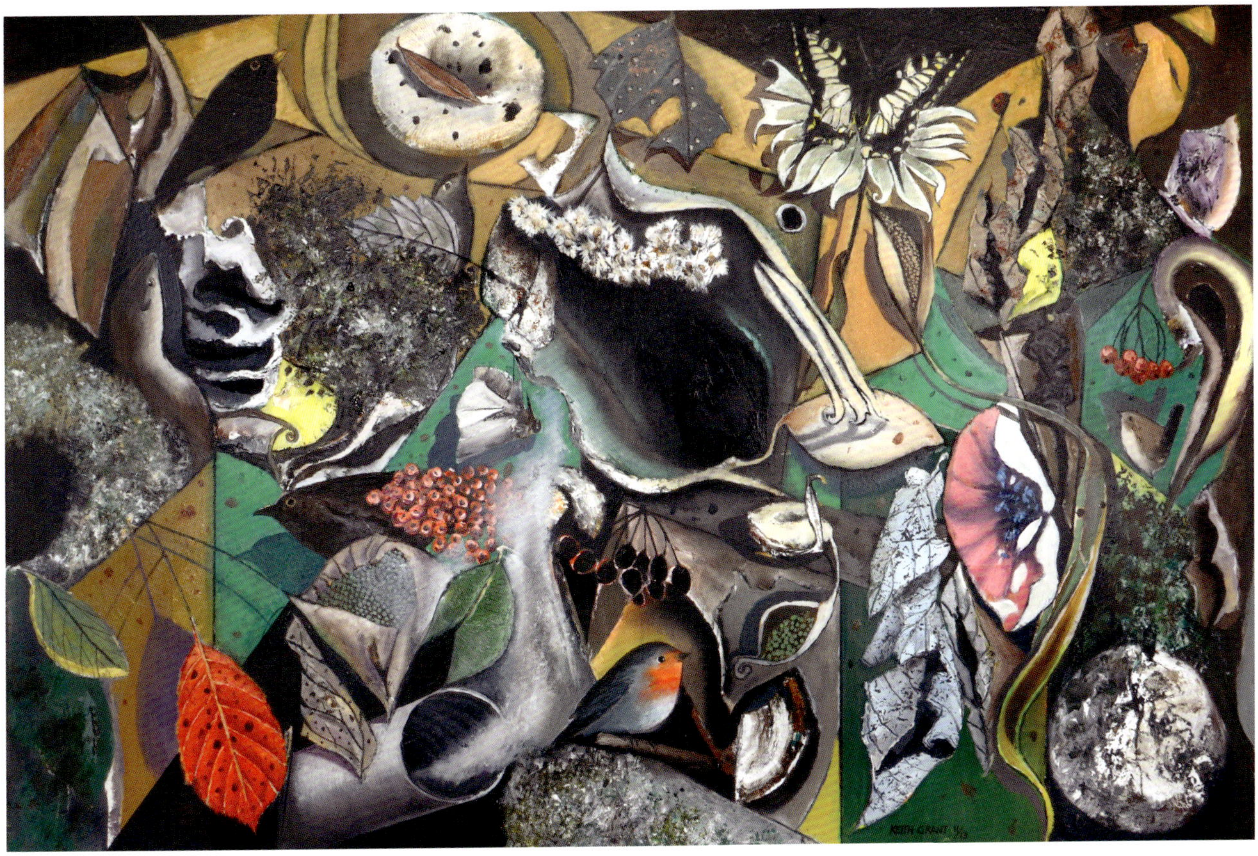

123 **Finale**
Signed and dated 11/13
Signed, inscribed with title and dated 11/12 2013 on reverse
Oil on canvas
31 ½ x 47 ½ inches

'The painting 'Finale' is more pervadingly species-specific than 'Confusion of Moonlight' [131] *but alludes to the same threat of the pollution of the natural environment (symbolized by the fumes from the pipe-like vent). I make no excuse for the sombre prediction of this work but have to admit that visually decay and corruption can be subjectively beautiful and represents that other side of life from which most of us turn away.'*

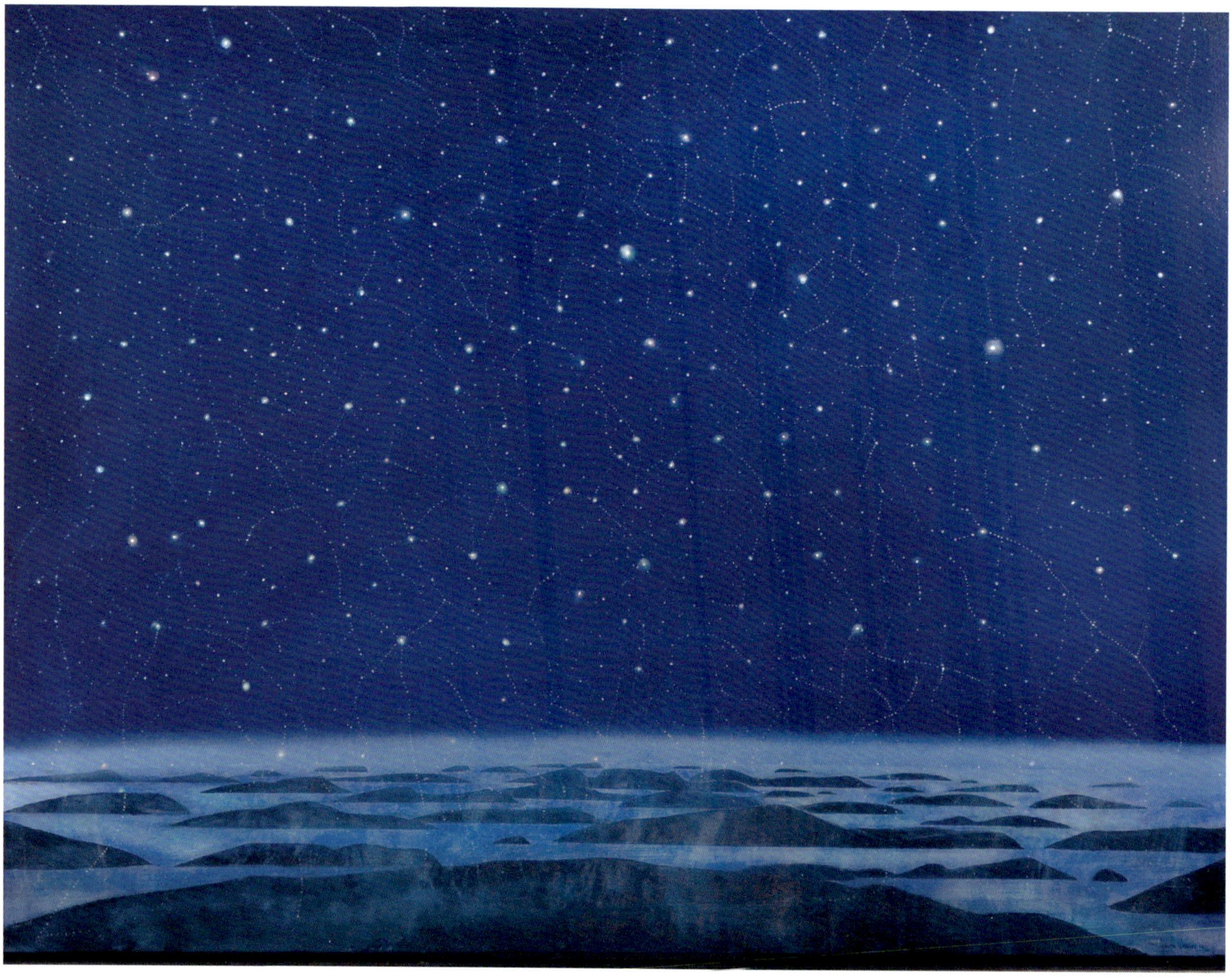

124 Arcticum Stellis
Signed and dated 12/13
Signed, inscribed with title and 'Considerably altered 16, 17, 18 June 2012'
and 'Dec 2013' on stretcher
Oil on canvas, 47 ¼ x 59 inches

'I have totally repainted "Proscenium Articus" which becomes "Articum Stellis", only the depiction of the islands reminds me of the former work. I have begun the work-intensive process of painting hundreds of stars one by one. But as this tapestry of the night develops I hope it will provide the observer through focused looking, luminous patterns; the structure of the night sky. Already in some areas pinpoints of light are forming "strings of pearls" linking the stars writing their signatures on the night.'

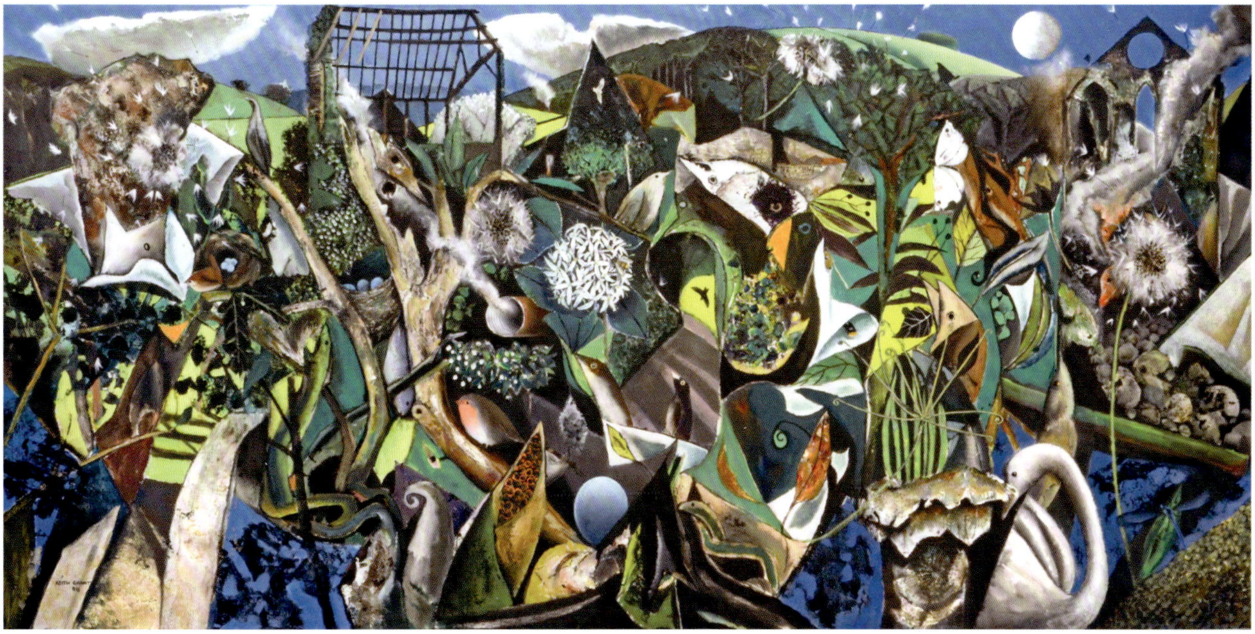

125 Return
Signed and dated 8/13
Oil on canvas
39 ½ x 78 ½ inches

126 Moonlight
Signed and dated 21.1.14
Signed, inscribed with title and dated 'Jan: 2014' on reverse
Oil on canvas laid down on board, 24 ½ x 45 ½ inches

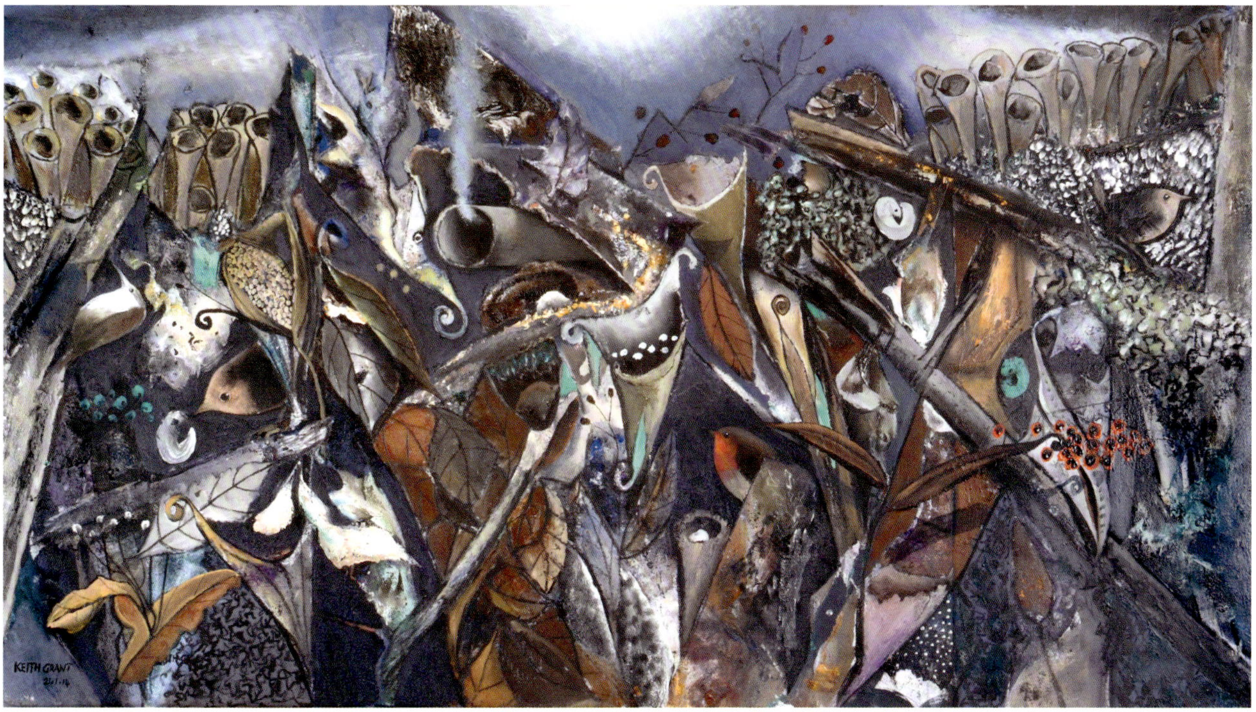

'"Return" is a combination of the inspiration I derived from revisiting places in Shropshire I experienced as a student in the late 50s with my recent explorations of the forests near my home in Norway. The painting 'Moonlight' has developed into a more general "metaphysical" portrait of the night. Mentors for the mood of this work might be Blake, Palmer, Nash and Braque but only as fleeting ghosts.'

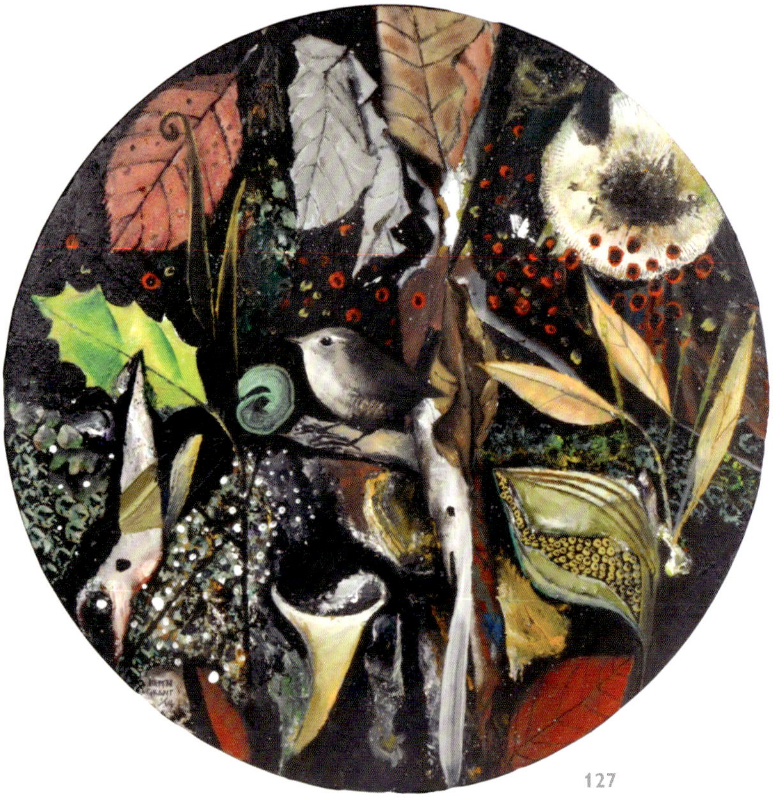

127

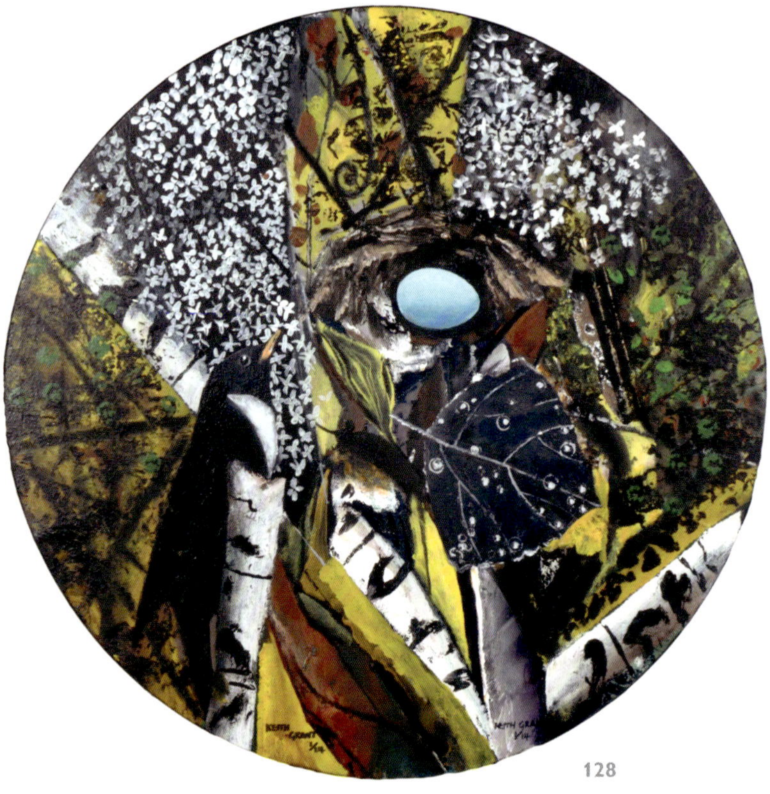

128

'This new series … perhaps will mark an end or at least a change in the style of subsequent oil paintings of mine dealing with the "forest theme". I would like the paint to take place of the imagery of actuality and allude to rather than describe the elements, which comprise my compositions … I have noticed how fortuitously oil paint can express the natural textures and appearance of the humblest forest entity but cannot analyse how it comes about. Obviously I see similarities of shape, form, colour and the tactile reality of things as stored in my visual memory but I also feel these "retentive" realities sensuously coming into virtual being with little conscious effort from me.

Forest Quartet No 1
Allusive shape gives rise to non-specific reality

Forest Quartet No 2
The egg in its fragile perfection of form contrasts with every other feature in the forest

Forest Quartet No 3
One passable likeness of a species permits multiple abstractions

Forest Quartet No 4
Separate shapes harmonise purposefully'

127 **Forest Quartet No 1**
Signed and dated 1/14
Signed, inscribed with title and dated 1/2014 on backboard
Oil with charcoal and oil pastel on canvas
19 ¾ inches diameter

128 **Forest Quartet No 2**
Signed and twice dated 1/14
Signed, inscribed with title and dated 1/2014 on backboard
Oil with charcoal and oil pastel on canvas
19 ¾ inches diameter

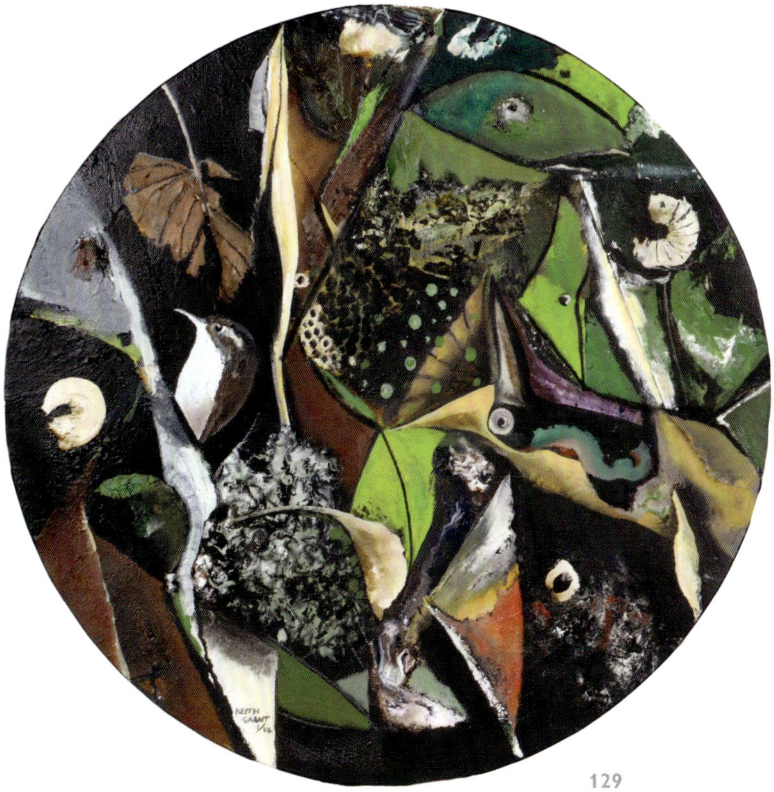

129

129 **Forest Quartet No 3**
Signed and dated 1/14
Signed, inscribed with title and dated 1/2014 on backboard
Oil with charcoal and oil pastel on canvas
19 ¾ inches diameter

130 **Forest Quartet No 4**
Signed and dated 1/14
Signed, inscribed with title and dated 1/2014 on backboard
Oil with charcoal and oil pastel on canvas
19 ¾ inches diameter

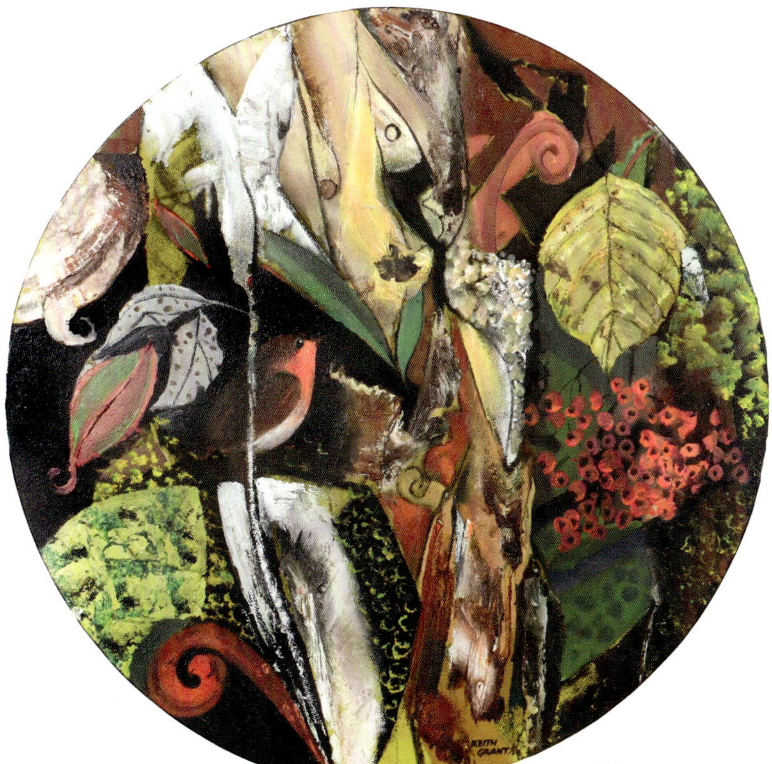

130

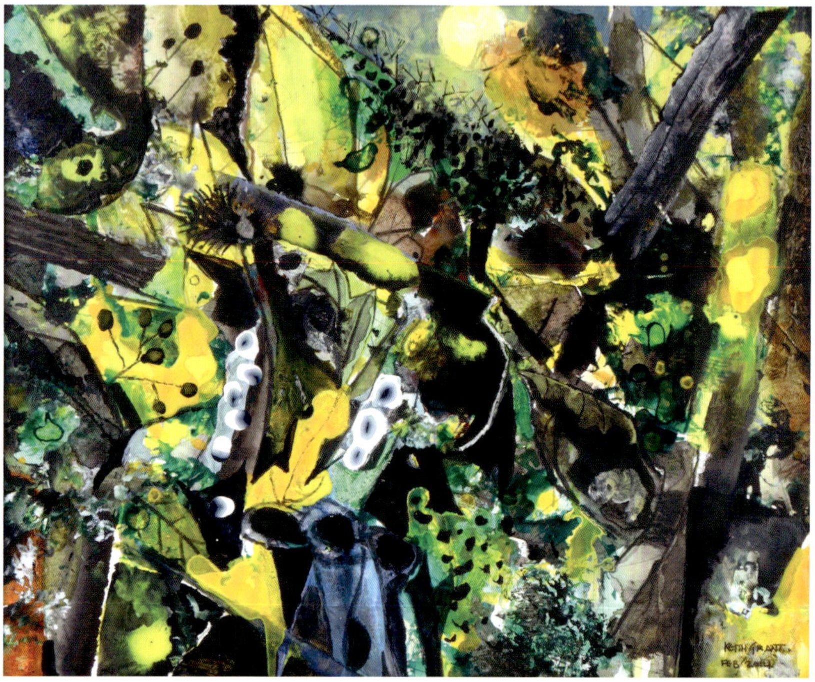

131 A Confusion of Moonlight
Signed and dated 'Feb/2014'
Signed, inscribed with title and 'I love it when you write of painting a meaning which transcends subject. That and the mysterious reality of minuteness and the physical properties of paint – I'm sure that's the way your work lies, in further investigation of these qualities ... Andrew Lambirth in a letter to KG dated 23.1.2014', and dated 'Feb/2 2014' on reverse
Acrylic with oil pastel and wax pencil
12 x 14 inches

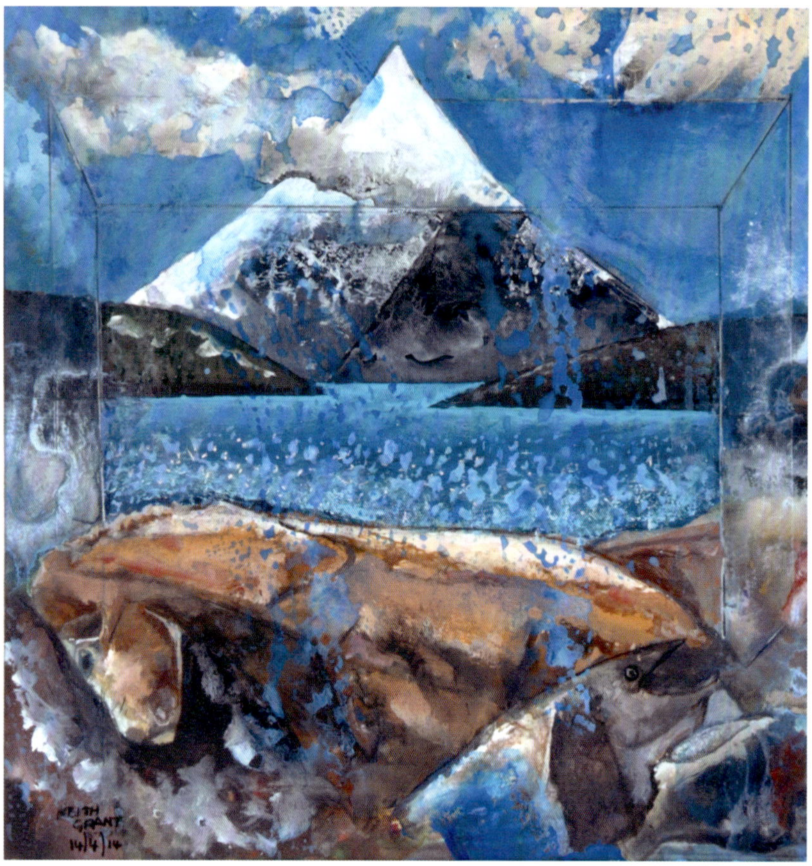

132 Rock Horse in the North
Signed and dated 14/4/14
Signed, inscribed with title and dated 13.4.2014 on reverse
Acrylic with mixed media
10 x 10 inches

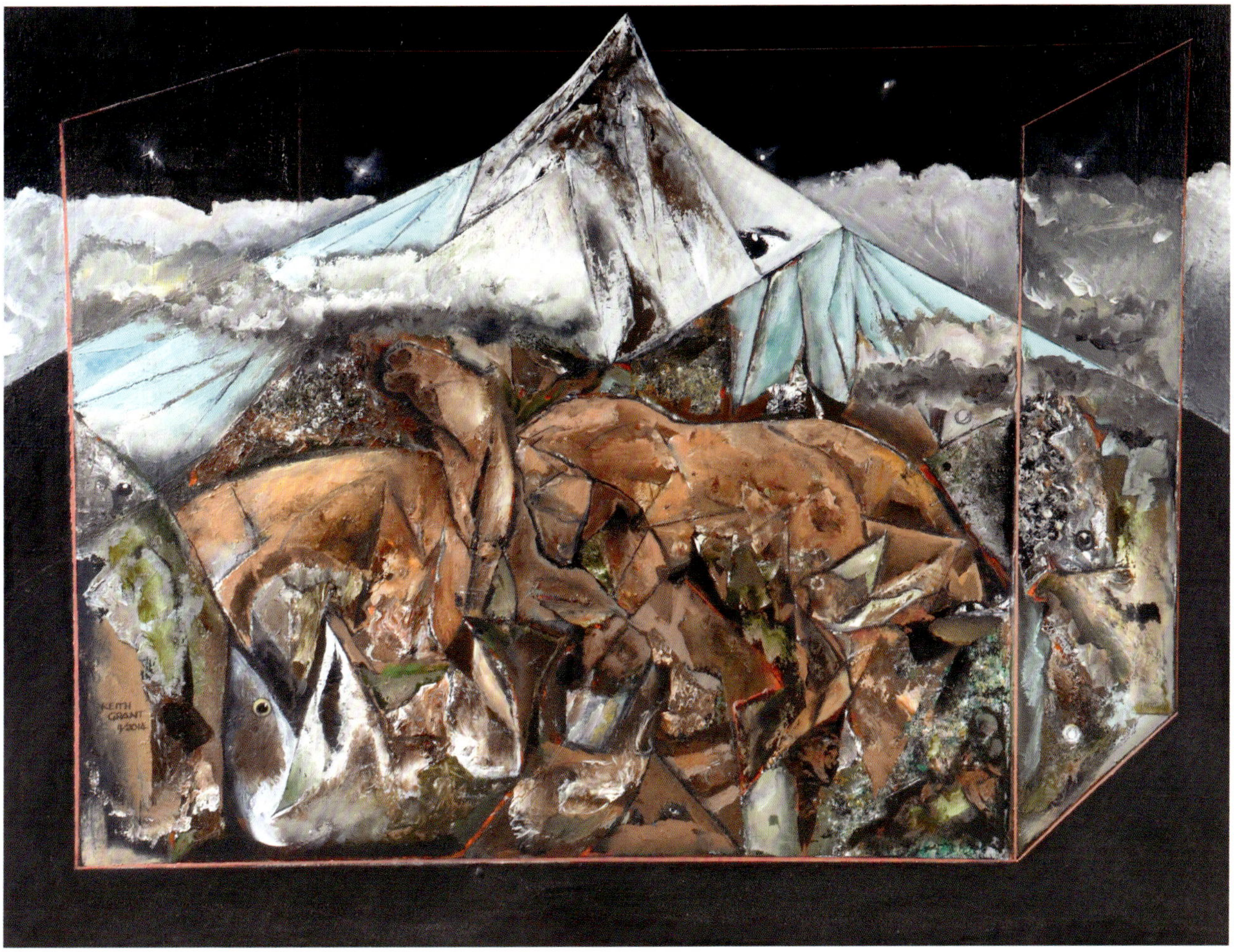

133 Rock Horses
Signed and dated 4/2014
Signed, inscribed 'Rock Horses, Vesteralen' and dated 4/14
and 'April 2014' on stretcher on reverse
Oil on canvas
32 x 43 inches

'The composition has engaged all my faculties … over the past ten days or so. I have been involved in the intensest struggle to invest the subject with a surrealistic interpretation ... The materiality used goes beyond any recent work of mine and in fact harks back to the 60s and early seventies. The structure of the work pretends to a spatial box containing all the elements used, except where the peak breaks through the invisible, transparent ceiling. The idea came from my observing natural rock formations, which disconcertingly resembled a bas-relief of a horse.'

'… completed the composition which for over two weeks has bound me to its realization by a process of heavier and heavier layers of paint. But I have achieved density, a measurable depth and yet a transparency of a kind I have not succeeded in creating before.'

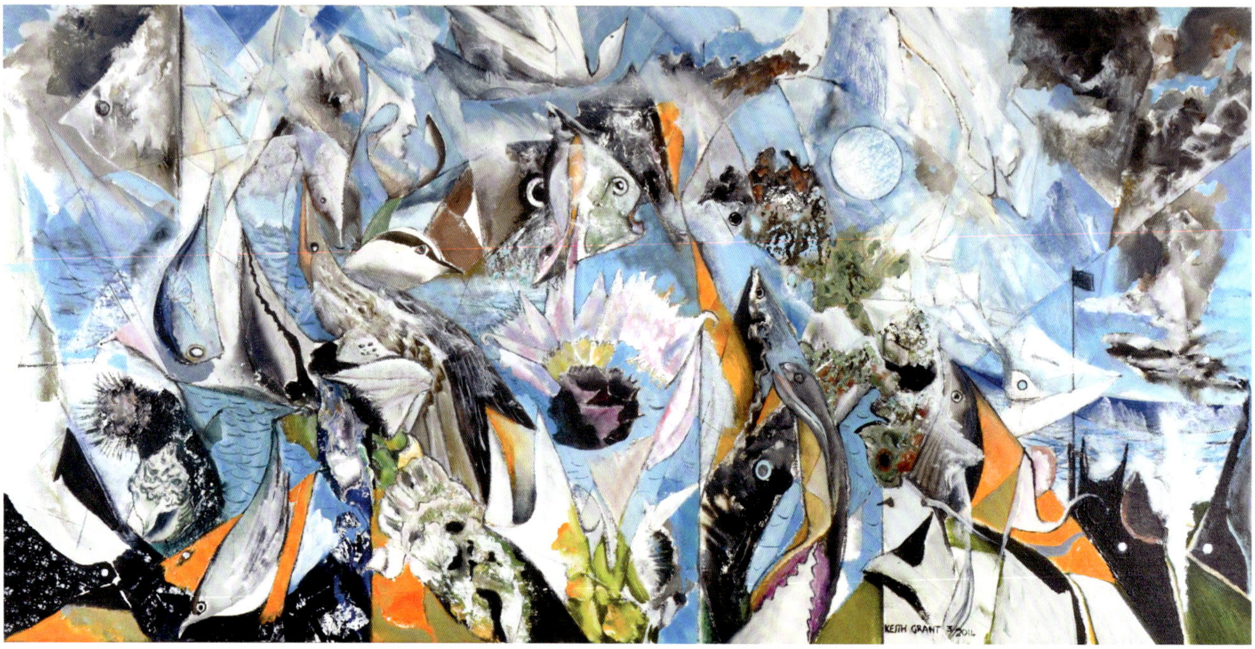

134 **Maritime Polar, North**
signed and dated 3/2014
Signed, inscribed 'Maritime North' and dated 3/2014 on stretcher on reverse
Oil on canvas
24 x 47 ½ inches

135 **Before the Hurricane**
Signed
Signed, inscribed 'Approaching storm-force'
and dated 3/2014 on stretcher on reverse
Oil on canvas
28 ¾ x 36 ¼ inches

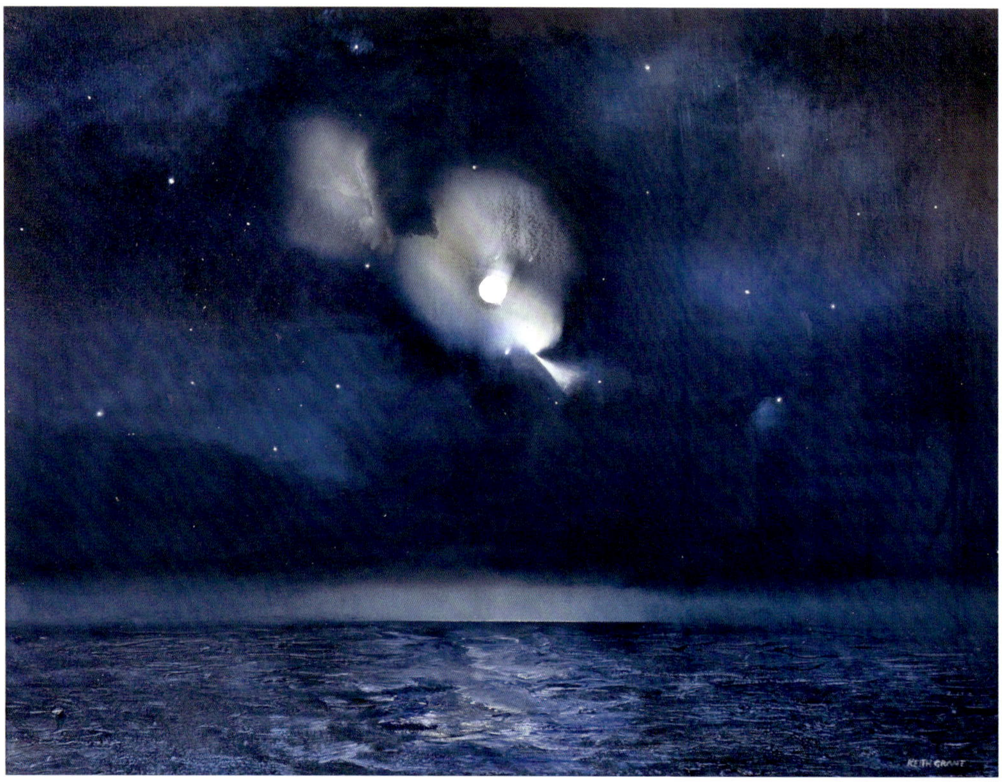

136 The Awakening Forest
Signed and dated 4/2014
Signed, inscribed 'The Waking Forest'
and dated 16/4/2014
on reverse
Acrylic and watercolour
8 x 15 inches

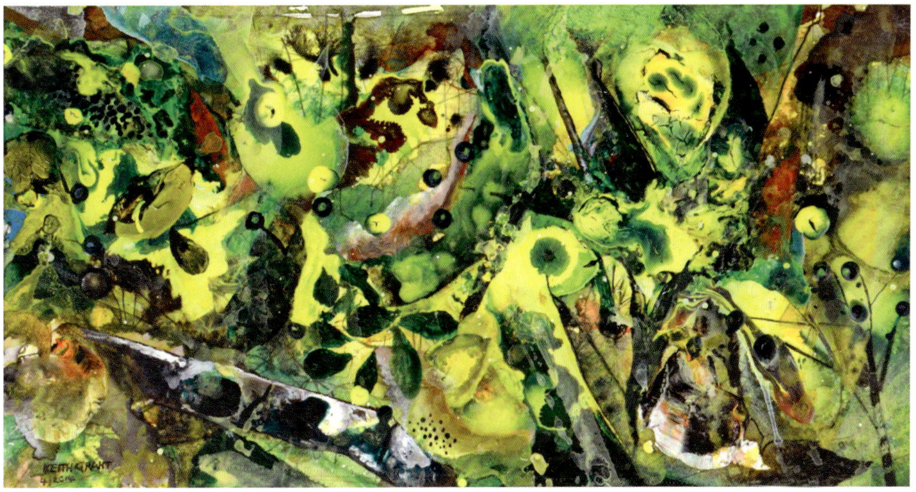

'This evening I began another small painting the scale of which is in no way comparable to the amount of work I envisage before I am able to resolve the whelter of detail, which the forest at present displays after the havoc created by last weeks fierce winds. Strangely, there is for me an intense inspirational return from viewing natural destruction, especially in the forests, it is as if the raw side of nature usually clothed in benign greens, ochres, umbers and blacks is revealed; an open suppurating wound from which exploded trunks, splinters of wood sap and water prodigiously issues. This small work has no reference to birds or animals contrary to almost all my previous forest works.'

137 The Moon through plate-glass windows
Signed and dated 14
Signed, inscribed with title and 'Three experimental studies of the Northern Night No II', and dated 27/4/2014 on reverse
Acrylic, pen ink, silver ink and varnish on board
6 ¼ x 11 ¾ inches

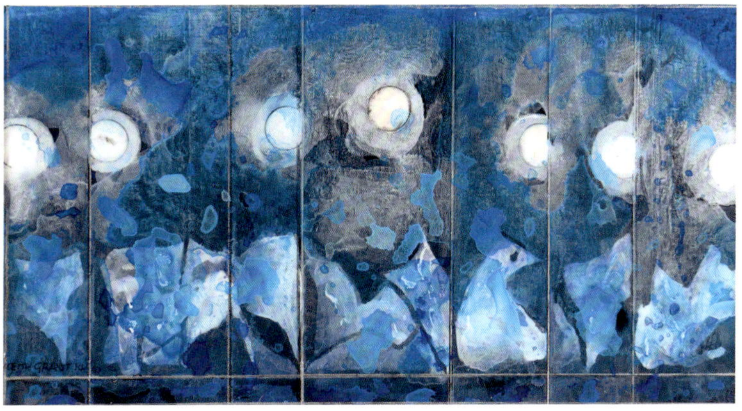

138 The Moon and the Mountain
Signed and dated /14
Signed, inscribed with title, 'Night Window I' and 'Three experimental studies of the Northern Night I', and dated 24/4/2014 on reverse
Acrylic, pen ink, silver ink
and varnish on board
7 ¼ x 13 ¾ inches

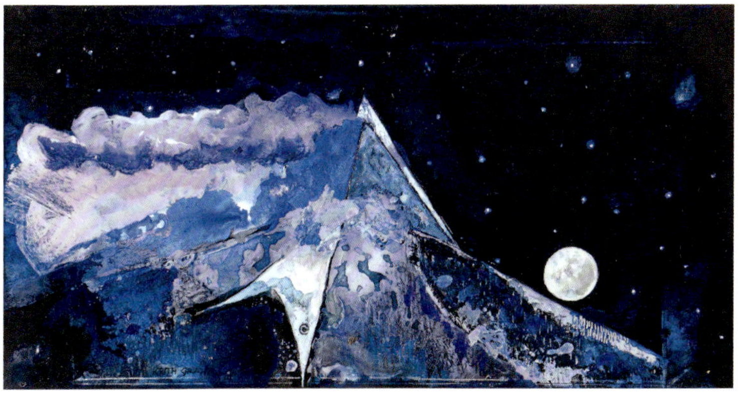

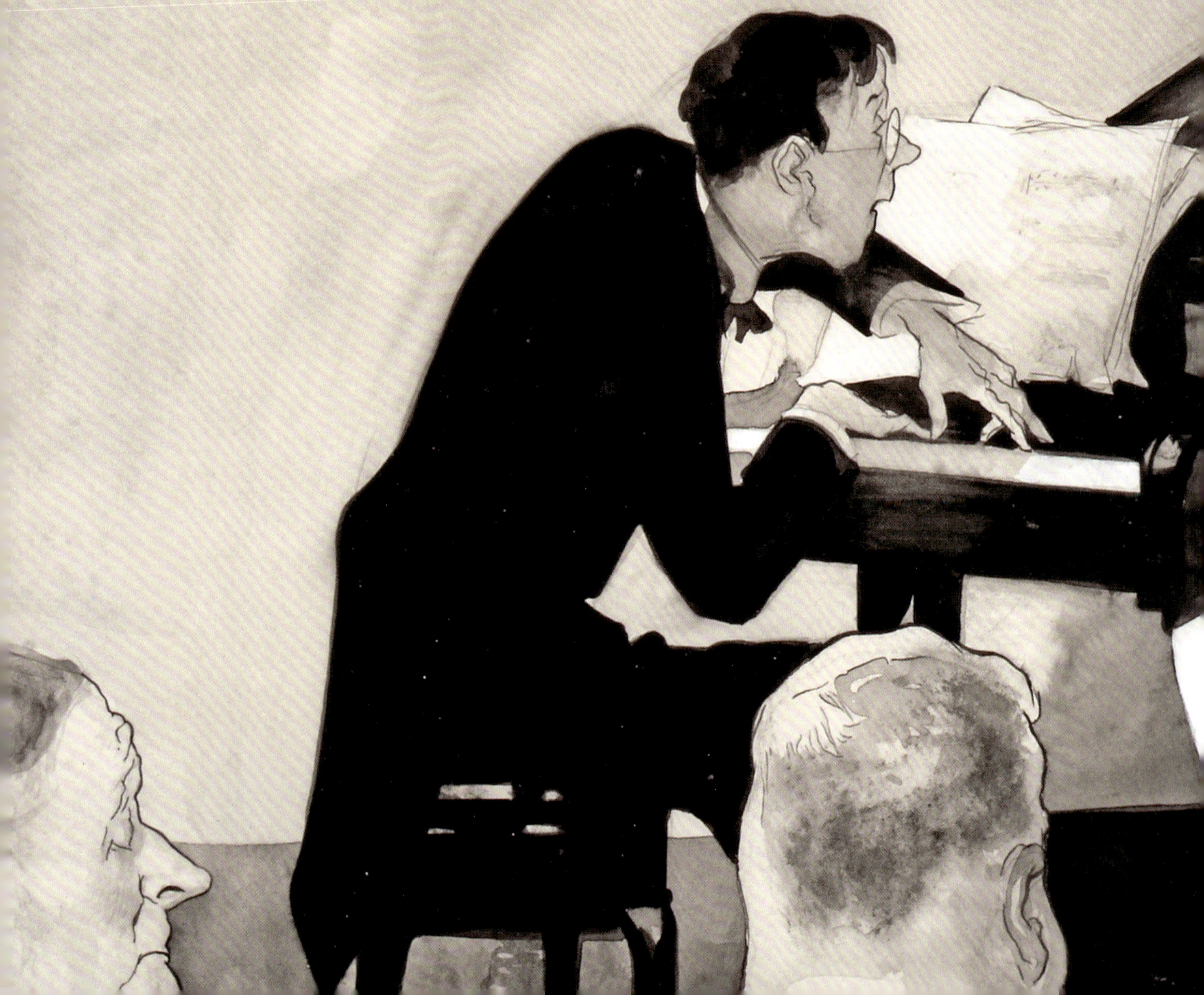